WARRIORS
OF THE DARK
AGES

WARRIORS OF THE DARK AGES

JENNIFER LAING

Cover illustration: Barbarian fighting a Roman legionary. Stone relief from Rome 84 x 88 cm MA 412 Location: Louvre, Departement des Antiquites Grecques/Romaines, Paris, France. (Photo © Erich Lessing / Bridgeman Images)

First published 1999
This paperback edition first published 2025

The History Press
97 St George's Place, Cheltenham,
Gloucestershire, GL50 3QB
www.thehistorypress.co.uk

© Jennifer Laing, 1999, 2025

The right of Jennifer Laing to be identified as the Author of this work has been asserted in accordance with the Copyright, Designs and Patents Act 1988.

All rights reserved. No part of this book may be reprinted or reproduced or utilised in any form or by any electronic, mechanical or other means, now known or hereafter invented, including photocopying and recording, or in any information storage or retrieval system, without the permission in writing from the Publishers.

British Library Cataloguing in Publication Data.
A catalogue record for this book is available from the British Library.

ISBN 978 1 83705 107 6

Typesetting and origination by The History Press
Printed and bound in Great Britain by TJ Books, Padstow, Cornwall

The History Press proudly supports

Trees for LYfe

www.treesforlife.org.uk

EU Authorised Representative: Easy Access System Europe
Mustamäe tee 50, 10621 Tallinn, Estonia
gpst.request@easproject.com

Contents

	Introduction	7
1	The Visigoths	15
2	The Huns	40
3	The Ostrogoths	60
4	The Vandals	69
5	The Franks	83
6	The Saxons, Danes, Frisians and Angles	94
7	The Panoply of War and Ostentatious Display	135
8	Warfare and Society	142
9	Ways of Looking at the Period	166
10	Primary and Secondary Sources	171
	Notes	177
	Bibliography	197
	Index	206

Dis Manibus, and AJF and HCR, who turned twenty and sixteen during the writing, and Lloyd, without whom the archaeological sections would not have been written at all.

Introduction

The Vandals, Huns and, less widely perhaps, Goths have remained by-words for mindless violence and destruction since they and other barbarians breached the Roman frontiers in the fourth and fifth centuries AD. Yet many such warring groups have given their names to settled and peaceful places such as France (Franks), Burgundy (Burgundians), Andalucia (Vandals), Jutland (Jutes), Saxony (Saxons), Frisia (Frisians) and England (Angles). The languages they spoke form the basis of languages now spoken widely throughout the world, of which English is the most widespread.

This book examines the events which led to the barbarians' reputations for 'mindless' violence or destruction. It considers, in passing, the extent to which these people are remembered by posterity as the result of excessively hostile criticism by the rich, educated and powerful elements in society whose lifestyle was threatened by people they had themselves attempted to exclude by force. Often, events were moved through the interaction of individuals with considerable talent and all-too-human failings. A few men (of whom Alaric the Goth and Attila the Hun are outstanding) had exceptional organisational and military ability as well as personal charisma. Their Roman opponents, generals such as Aëtius, Constantius and Belisarius, were no less formidable. The gradual transformation of the Roman Empire of Augustus in the first century AD into modern Europe owes much to the exploits of these people. They were excluded by physical barriers which were policed by the Romans, from nearly all the attractive, fertile and mineral-rich areas and, by extension, from normal interaction through trade and intermarriage. The harsh environment of the Steppes where many Huns congregated fostered the skills of formidable fighters.

It was a period in which the energy and enthusiasms of youth often prevailed over the wisdom and caution of age. Indeed, youth and the quest for booty were in many ways the driving forces in the period. Since training started in childhood, many of the warriors who fought the Roman Empire were probably not out of their teens. Theodoric the Great was eighteen when, without his father's knowledge, he led a 6,000-strong force on a successful plundering expedition. Age was not, however, a bar to an experienced commander: Ermaneric, the early warrior-king died at a great age (reputedly 110).

Opportunities for major personal gain abounded, though misery was rife. The emperors in Italy and Constantinople rarely died of old age and some of them reigned only for a matter of months. They could gain power through *coups d'état*: some were unwillingly elevated by the armies in particular areas. At the start of AD 410, there were no fewer than six emperors, of whom only two had gained the title through legitimate means (Honorius in Ravenna, Theodosius II in Constantinople and the usurpers Attalus, Constantine, Constans and Maximus). Men of barbarian origin never prospered in bids for the highest office, though a few totally controlled the emperors. The teenage Emperor Valentinian II bravely handed letters of dismissal to his Frankish advisor Arbogastes, who contemptuously destroyed them in public and went unchallenged.

The leaders of barbarian warrior groups were equally under the control of their followers. Raiding, to gain booty and personal prestige, was a way of life and no self-respecting warrior would accept any peace treaty for long unless there was demonstrable benefit to him. In addition, few of the warriors seem to have considered that, once they had gained entry, living in another culture required huge personal commitment. Raiding the neighbours and carrying off their women and cauldrons was only workable if the neighbours would and could counter-attack to recirculate the booty. The system totally foundered in a settled state which depended on cooperation and local security. By and large, the Burgundians, the Franks, the Alamanni and (eventually) the Visigoths and Ostrogoths prospered because both Romans and barbarians were prepared to compromise. Until that happened many lives were lost in battle. For reasons of space, time and readability, the catalogues of destruction – whether caused by Romans or barbarians – have largely been omitted, but it should not be forgotten that for every word in this book there were probably ten deaths in combat or from related causes. City after city was looted and fields were laid waste. Disease set in. People starved to death. Bones were left exposed where men had fallen. People in possession of huge amounts of booty but no financial acumen meant prices rose. Extortion and bribery were commonplace.

It is notoriously difficult to establish 'the truth' even if a group of reliable eye-witnesses are expertly questioned immediately after an event. The later

Introduction

fourth-century historian Ammianus Marcellinus reflects this in relating a particular battle between Goths and Romans, in 376: 'I ask my readers ... not to demand a completely accurate account of events or the exact number of dead, because there was no way of finding out.'

The subject matter of this book is particularly open to speculation – it has been calculated to be (as it were) correct to the first two or three decimal places because there is such a wealth of uncertainty in the material. A fairly simple picture has been achieved at the inevitable expense of much data, many worthy characters and intricate academic debates. Over fifty Theodorics flourished in the period, of whom readers will doubtless be pleased to know only two feature prominently in these pages, but possibly less delighted to learn that they are both called Theodoric I. (One was a Visigoth, the other an Ostrogoth.) The text also mentions two men called Leo I (one a Pope, the other an emperor) and two Saints Augustine. Two of Attila's secretaries were called Constantius. It has been claimed that the man known for centuries as Odoacer was in fact two men of the same name. The Empress Galla Placidia (daughter, sister, wife and mother of emperors) was buried in the Monastery of St Nazarius, Ravenna, not in the well-known tourist attraction known as the Tomb of Galla Placidia.

The lists of tribal names is almost hypnotic. Some seem to have been repeated entirely for their exotic, romantic allure and still roll poetically off the tongue. Jordanes, for example, mentions but does not describe the Grannii, Augandzi, Eunixi, Taetel, Rugi, Arochi and Ranii, and elsewhere the Ahelmil, Finnaithae, Fervir and Gauthigoth – 'a bold race of men'.[1] Names were liable to change over time as new groups were formed. It is possible that some units were extended families or clans. Some may have been political entities, others were named after regions. The minor group of the Peukini (also known as the Bastarni), for example, were named after the island of Peuke which lay in the Danube. Geographical areas changed names in antiquity as well as in modern times and some scholars favour ancient Greek terminology over more recent.

The barbarians have often been categorised by the languages they spoke or the basic repertoire of material goods they used. Both methods can be misleading, so in general linguistic terminology has here been avoided where possible (see Chapter 9).

SUMMARY AND BACKGROUND

Gaul was subdued by Julius Caesar in the first century BC and the Romans continued to push northwards. Serious problems arose in the late summer of AD 9 when three of the Empire's twenty-eight legions, under Publius Quinctilius Varus, were massacred in the Teutoburg Forest. Varus committed suicide, and the victorious barbarian leader, Arminius of the Cherusci, moved effortlessly into the pages of history, and later into heroic legend as Herman ('the German').

The Emperor Augustus reluctantly decided not to attempt any further Roman expansion in the area. After this time the frontier in northern Europe was marked by the Rhine and Danube rivers, controlled from towns and fortresses. There were turf-and-timber road posts, later replaced in stone, with watch towers such as that at Valkenburg. One of the most easily fordable places on the Rhine was defended at Novae, the headquarters of the First Legion. Bridges, such as that linking Mainz (Mogontiacum) and Mainz-Castell (Castellum), were defended and Roman boats patrolled the water, just as the Roman Fleet patrolled the English Channel and east coast.

As soon as Augustus fixed the Empire's northern frontier, settlement of barbarians south of it began. Submissions were received from the Ubii and Sicambri who were given lands on the left bank of the Rhine. The Emperor Tiberius (AD 14–37) took 40,000 Germani to the same area. Some Batavians fled from their own people and distinguished themselves in Roman cavalry units. Such pacts continued intermittently through the centuries and the barbarians were expected to provide military assistance when required. The Empire's frontiers were pushed forwards in the first and second centuries through the efforts of a few military-minded emperors. Especially from 224 onwards, military threat came from the Persians, so that relations with the north European tribes were often affected when Roman troops were deployed to the East. Lands beyond the Rhine/Danube frontier became buffers between the Empire and the non-Romanised tribes beyond; a similar situation prevailed in Britain and North Africa. Annual payments to such tribes were often negotiated on the understanding they would protect the Empire from their neighbours. As time went on, this deteriorated into bribes to avoid attack by the buffer areas themselves.

Economic, social and climatic as well as cultural and military factors forced change upon the Roman Empire and the barbarian world alike. In the early fourth century the imperial capital was moved from Rome to Constantinople by the Emperor Constantine, who also adopted Christianity instead of the Roman pantheon headed by Jupiter, Juno and Minerva. Both these moves had very far-reaching effects. Some of the barbarian groups were converted, but some of those favoured a heresy, Arianism. The new beliefs could be bargaining points in negotiations for land or payments. By the late fourth century the Empire had been divided into East and West, with the two emperors not always in agreement with each other. Both sides of the Empire were forced to deal with the non-Romanised warrior groups. The Eastern Empire survived as the Byzantine Empire while the Western was transformed by the barbarian migrations that are the subject of this book.

The most lasting changes started during the 370s when the Huns overran the Alans and the two then put pressure on the Goths. Most of the tribes that later became known as the Ostrogoths were conquered, but many tribes who later formed the Visigoths were formally allowed to cross the Danube in 376. They beat the Roman forces at Adrianople in 378, sacked Rome in 410 under Alaric, and were officially settled in Aquitania Secunda (part of Gaul) in 418 until finally moving into Spain. In 395 the Huns crossed the frozen Danube and until Attila's death in 453 were important catalysts on the European political scene, particularly through their special relationship with the western general, Aëtius. After Attila's death in 453 they disintegrated as a recognisable unit. The Rhine/Danube frontier was effectively destroyed in 405 and 406, when huge numbers of barbarians forced their way across. The Vandals, Alans and Sueves established themselves in Spain in 409 and twenty years later moved to North Africa where they remained important until the reconquest of the area by the Byzantine general Belisarius in 533. Different groups of Franks were settled by treaty within the Empire from the third century onwards and many Franks rose to positions of high command by the mid-fourth century. Under Clovis, the Franks effected the conquest of most of South and Central Gaul in 481 and eventually developed into the Merovingian and Carolingian dynasties.

The last Roman Emperor in the West (himself a puppet usurper) was the young Romulus Augustulus, who was deposed in 476 by the barbarian ruler Odoacer (who may have been half-Hunnic). He in turn was removed from power in Italy by Theodoric the Great of the Ostrogoths at the invitation of the Eastern Emperor Zeno. The Burgundians established a kingdom south of the Rhine between 411 and 414 and were later formally settled in Savoy. Two groups of Alans were settled in Gaul.

In the early sixth century the Roman world (by then the Byzantine) took by conquest both Italy and North Africa. Britain, Spain and Gaul were never recovered, but were left to develop the multi-cultural societies which eventually formed modern Europe.

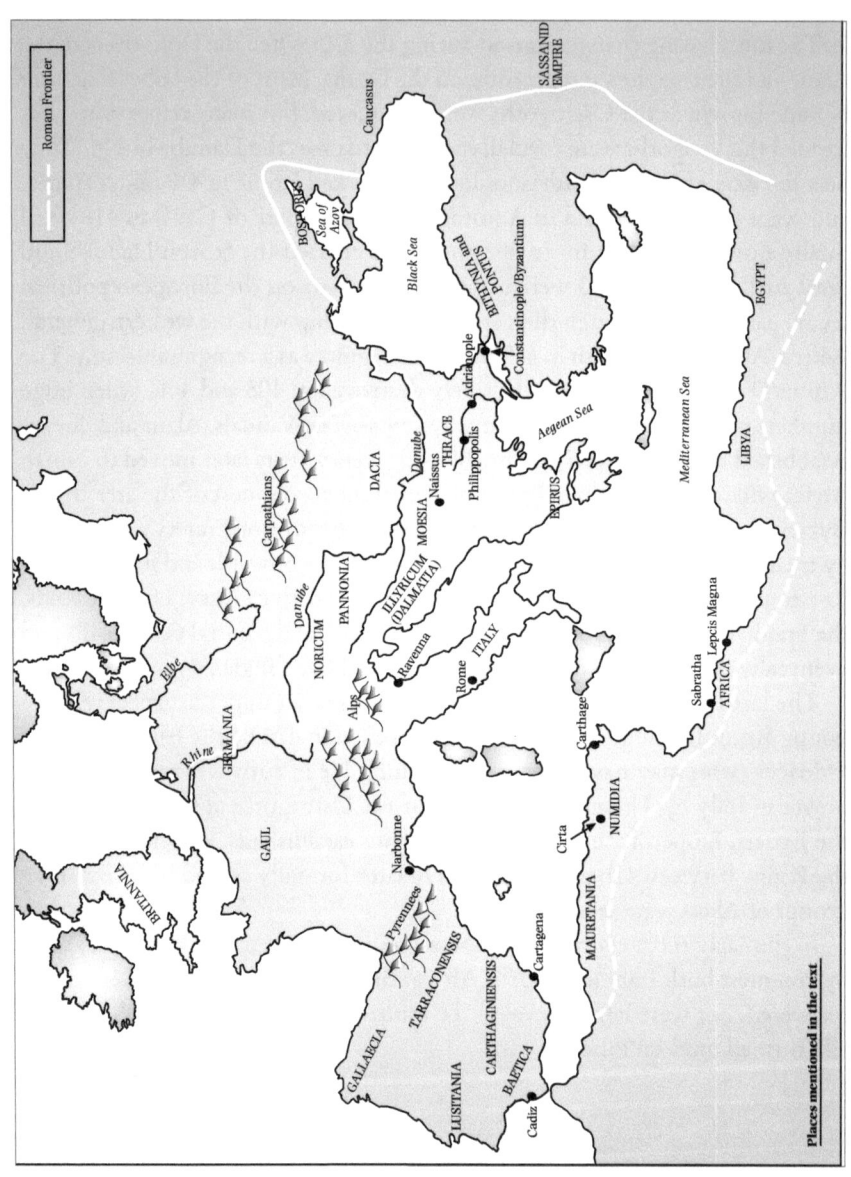

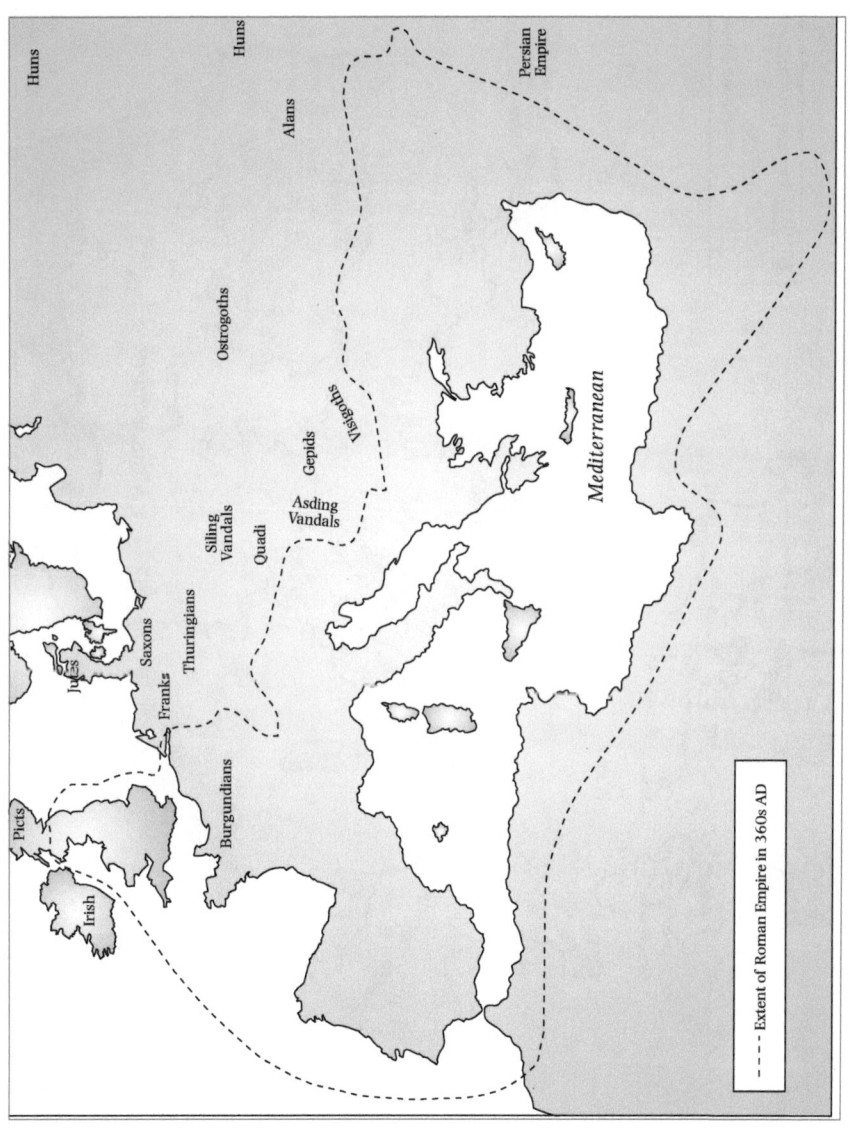

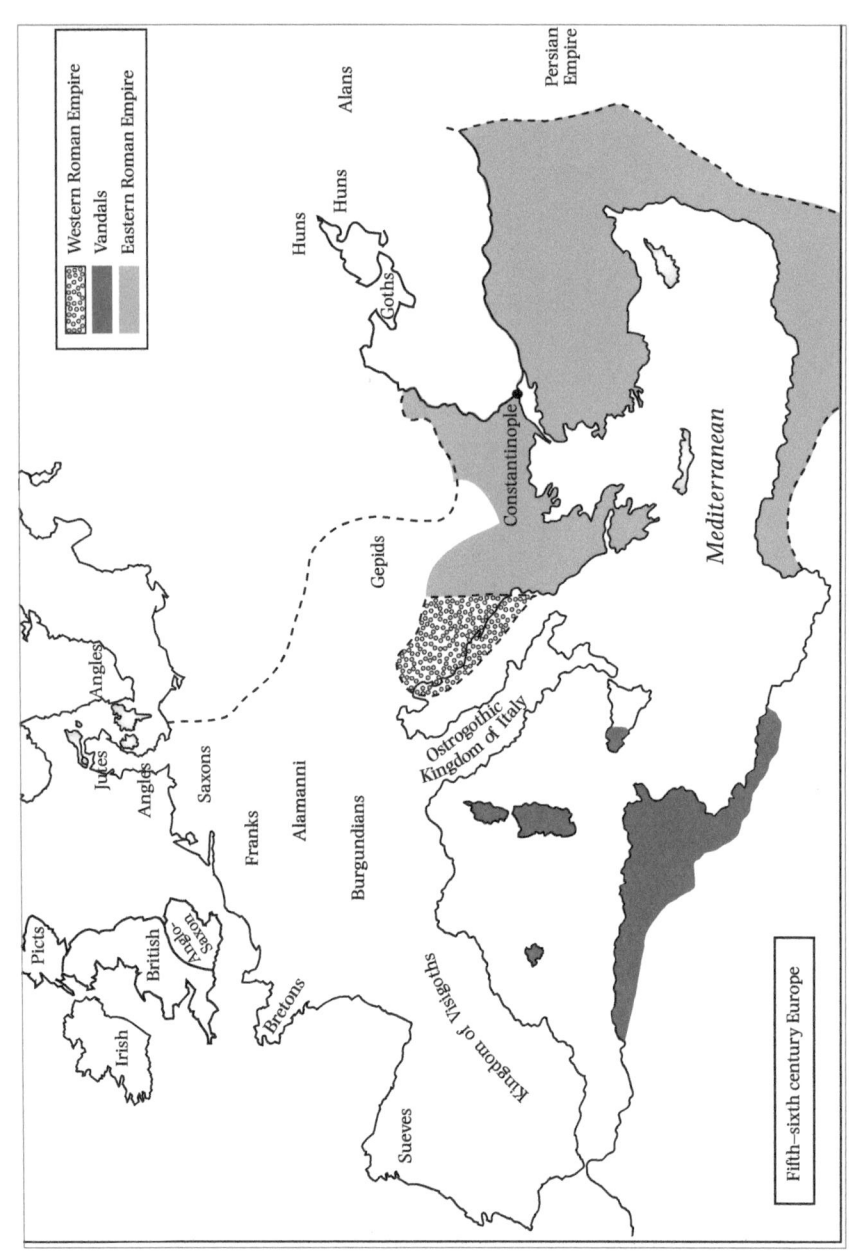

Chapter 1

The Visigoths

At first he wanted to obliterate the Roman name and to make the entire Empire that of the Goths alone and to name it ... Gothia.[1]

Orosius (an early fifth-century theologian and Church historian) referring to the Gothic leader Athaulf.

The term Goth (or Gothic) is now most widely used to describe a particularly florid script, and an 'over-the-top' style of both novel and architecture.[2] Occasionally, it is a fashion concept. At the time the term Goth covered a mixture of different barbarian peoples, grouped together for convenience by historians and for military purposes in times of need.[3] Two main groups emerged in the later fourth and early fifth centuries: Visigoths (in the West) and Ostrogoths (in the East). The terms correspond roughly to the tribal groupings over which the Tervingi and Greutungi, respectively, seem to have been dominant. Their story is here divided into four parts: their first appearance on the Roman frontiers until AD 376 when they crossed the Rhine; the career of Alaric; the career of his successor, Athaulf; and the aftermath in which they settled into a non-warrior-based society.

The tribal history was recorded by the mid-sixth-century Goth, Jordanes, writing from a base in Constantinople. He drew upon traditional Gothic history,[4] which was preserved, at least partly, through song.[5] He thought that the Goths originally migrated from Scandinavia.[6] By the period covered in this book they were firmly established north of the Black Sea.[7] Jordanes says the migration was unified, but archaeology points to a series of separate movements under the leadership of different chiefs – true warrior bands.[8] These apparently conflicting statements fit the other historical sources which show that the Goths were organised under chiefs (*reiks*) who, in times of crisis, chose two or three temporary leaders, occasionally only one – the *thiudans* or judge.[9] Such a method allowed the specialist fighting skills of various groups to be fully exploited; for example, those from open plains tended to be expert horsemen.

GOTHIC ATTACKS ON THE ROMAN EMPIRE[10]

In AD 238 Goths penetrated Roman territory and plundered Histria at the head of the Adriatic. Eventually, annual payment was arranged in return for Gothic service in the army. In 248 the Emperor Philip the Arab (244–9) decided (after a series of victories in the area) to discontinue the annual payments to the Goths. It may be that the festivities that year, held to celebrate the thousand years since the foundation of Rome, led to complacency. Philip used 'Thessalonian persuasion' (i.e., giving him 'Hobson's choice') on an efficient commander named Decius and sent him to the Danube frontier.[11] This man was then proclaimed emperor by the legions and in 249 marched to Italy where Philip was killed in battle at Verona. As a result, the north-east frontier was left undefended at the very time when the Goths were dissatisfied. In 250 a Gothic leader, Cniva, crossed the Danube with supporters who included some Carpi, Bastarni, Taifali and Asding Vandals. The Gothic forces divided into three groups which worked together, aided by the fact that Decius, the new emperor, was preoccupied with some of the Carpi in Dacia. Decius pursued Cniva without success and the Goths managed to besiege Philippopolis in Thrace.[12]

THE SIEGE OF PHILIPPOPOLIS

Cniva's followers used primitive scaling towers which the defending force had to smash with boulders. When Decius was unable to come to their relief, the Roman troops preferred fraternisation to fighting, but lacked a credibly authoritative mediator. A feature of negotiation between Romans and barbarians through the centuries was the importance placed by both sides upon the high status of the negotiators. People of lowly birth were likely to be rejected forthwith. On this occasion the troops in Philippopolis hailed a new emperor from among their number. They had miscalculated: once inside the gates, the Goths killed or took captive the inhabitants, regardless of rank, and the short-term emperor disappeared from history.

The Goths delayed returning home with their booty and prisoners. They familiarised themselves with the land in Thrace, which remained on their list of requests for over a century. In midsummer 251 they met the Roman forces at Abrittus (near Razgrad in modern Bulgaria). Cniva lured his opponents into a marshy area and encircled them. In the resultant slaughter both Decius and his son, also Decius, were killed. The battered remnant of the Roman forces rallied under the future emperor,[13] who allowed the Goths to leave (with their booty) and arranged for payments to be made to them.

ROMAN AND GOTHIC WARFARE TECHNIQUES

The siege of Philippopolis demonstrates how Gothic tactics were never designed to cope with walled towns or sieges. Like almost all the non-Celtic barbarian groups, the Goths lived in scattered, undefended, wooden villages.[14] Their warfare was conducted through small-scale raiding parties. Strongly defended towns often had substantial food and water supplies, whereas besiegers were obliged to live off the land. The Tervingian troops were generally unmounted warriors but they were known to call upon their neighbours, the Taifali, the Alans and the Greutungi, to provide cavalry. Obtaining fodder would have been a constant problem and must have been a factor behind the widespread 'devastations' that accompanied every barbarian campaign.

In contrast, the Roman army at its best was highly disciplined and well supplied. The Roman infantry, for example, typically formed a 'tortoise'; the first line held their shields in front of them, while the men behind held theirs over the heads of the men in front. Their right (sword) arms were thus free but protected. The whole advanced like a giant threshing machine, though in the event of wholesale slaughter, the formation would be broken up by the need to step over the dead and dying. The Roman repertoire included such refinements as the *tolleno* – a beam set upright on town walls, with an attached crosspiece (similar to a modern crane), to the longer end of which was fixed a spike. Swinging on a pivot, the spike could sweep assailants to the top of the wall. Since only the legions used *ballistae* (catapults),[15] which hurled stone balls of up to 175 pounds in weight, the barbarians often stood some chance against lesser troops or ordinary citizens.

As time went on, however, both discipline and the 'straight line' Roman approach often foundered and Gothic siege techniques improved (though they never rivalled the Huns in this). Sometimes barbarians acquired the information by employing captured Roman technicians. The Goths learned to armour their scaling towers. At Thessalonika, in 269, the Goths used reservoirs of water to stop the flames spreading when the defenders soaked wicker fireballs in olive oil to bomb the towers.[16] In 248 the Goths piled stones against the walls to create a ramp at Marcianopolis, but were unsuccessful. In contrast, at Masada in AD 66 the same technique had been used successfully by the Romans, with chilling ruthlessness, against the Jews – but the Romans had possessed the resources to spend many months on the project. Violent measures were often unnecessary, however, since the quickest way to take a town was usually through treachery.

The empire changed its military policies around this time in recognition of the fact that its vast territories could not be defended by a single command. In 253 Publius Gallienus was made co-emperor (with his father Valerian). A highly experienced commander, he introduced a heavy dependence upon cavalry and began the tradition of putting military operations under the command of equestrian officers rather than senators. This policy had a dramatic personal effect since he was murdered in 268 by his cavalry commander, Claudius II.[17]

THE GOTHS AS INEPT SEAFARERS

Despite the change in imperial military policy, Goths and others attacked the empire in 253 and 254. In 255 'Scythians' (a general term which could include Goths, Huns and many other eastern barbarians) hijacked the fleet of a Roman client kingdom in the Crimea but were so disorganised that they sent it away when they had reached their destination and only managed the return journey by chance. The outcome was two years of widespread destruction in Bithynia and Propontis (the Black Sea), for many groups were involved.

In 268 Goths sailed from the mouth of the Dniester in alliance with the Heruli who voyaged from bases in the Sea of Azov.[18] They reached the Aegean in a reputed 6,000 boats with 320,000 men (according to one source) and 2,000 ships (according to another).[19] It seems that unseaworthy craft and Gothic inexperience, added to a strong current, led to collisions and losses. Using Dalmatian horsemen, Gallienus left over 3,000 Heruli dead. Naulobatus, the defeated leader of the Heruli, was subsequently recruited into the Roman army. This episode illustrates clearly how the warrior's ideal of fighting for the best chief – who by definition was the one who provided the opportunity for the best booty – was beginning to evolve into a mercenary's agreement in which loyalty to the chief was replaced by devotion to the fattest purse. From the Roman point of view it made sense to employ rather than fight a warrior.

GOTHIC RELATIONS WITH ROME

From this time on Gothic/Roman relations were mixed. Some Goths perished with the Emperor Valerian when he was defeated by the Persian King Shapur I, in 260, to die in humiliating captivity. Conversely, a large number of migrant Goths were resoundingly defeated near the town of Naissus in 269 by Claudius II. This emperor died of the plague in 270, to be succeeded in 271 by his cavalry commander, Aurelian. The new emperor (titled 'Gothicus Maximus') killed 5,000 Goths with their king,[20] a defeat that was important not only for the high mortality rate, but also because it effectively destroyed united Gothic effort.[21] By the late third century the Tervingi and the Greutungi, with their respective allies, were increasingly separate entities.

Despite his military successes Aurelian adopted a cautious approach, and the part of the Roman province of Dacia which lay north of the Danube (roughly modern Romania) was abandoned. It became known as Gothia as Goths gradually moved into the area. There they undoubtedly absorbed many elements of Roman life, a factor which undoubtedly coloured their later relationship with the Roman world.[22]

The part of Dacia that the Romans retained was defended by a series of forts and border towns such as Marcianopolis and Naissus, linked by roads. Behind lay fortified cities, such as Philippopolis, Serdica and Adrianople. The area prospered, coincidentally making it increasingly attractive to plunderers such as the Huns.

CHRISTIANITY AND BARBARIAN WARFARE[23]

There was general quiet on the Gothic front until the civil war in which the victor was Constantine the Great (Goths having fought on both sides). The new emperor made many changes, one of which was to adopt Christianity as the official state religion in 313. Within a generation, many Goths were converted by Bishop Ulfilas (who was said to be the descendant of Cappadocian prisoners captured by the Goths over a century before). Having been sent to Constantinople in an embassy,[24] he was consecrated in 341 during a short period when orthodox Catholic Christianity was ousted by Arianism.[25] This belief denied the divinity of Christ (He was seen *not* to be 'of the same substance' as the Spirit and the Father). The importance of the Catholic belief that the three elements of the Christian Godhead were 'of the same substance' set it aside from any pagan religion. Christianity allowed for only one God, but the three elements only too easily appeared to pagans as another three godlings to be added good-naturedly to their existing pantheon. The Arian view was therefore easier for barbarian pagans to adapt to their own use. All factions found Christianity a useful focus for, or excuse for, armed disputes.[26]

Like many barbarian warrior-based peoples for whom death was a very real everyday expectation, the Goths were very superstitious. Since they would not discuss religion, little is known about their beliefs, though by the mid-fourth century the Romans were able to identify a Gothic 'Mars' to whom they dedicated first booty (and, on occasion, sacrificial victims).[27] Gothic religion included ancestor worship: Tanausis, king of the Goths, is specifically mentioned as being posthumously worshipped.[28] The Goths habitually went into battle shouting the praises of their ancestors.[29] This was the equivalent of the impressive battle shout (the 'barritus') used by the Romans, and was said to have derived from the trumpeting of an elephant. (It began in a low tone which gradually increased to a roar.)[30]

Notably, the Goths passed on the Christian faith to others (in particular the Vandals), and willingness to convert became an important bargaining point for the warrior groups. To gain entry into the empire, they were capable of cynically dressing their priests and priestesses as bishops or monks.[31] All they had to do, said the late fourth-century writer Eunapius, contemptuously, was 'drag along grey cloaks and tunics', and swear oaths which meant nothing to them.[32]

Bishop Ulfilas invented the Gothic alphabet (not to be confused with the much later Gothic script) and translated the Bible into Gothic. Only fragments of his version now survive (the *Codex Argenteus*), written in gold and silver on purple/red parchment. These fragments incorporate the sole surviving Gothic words relating to warfare. Arguably by design, or merely by accident of survival, the most warlike parts, such as the *Book of Kings*, are missing.

Gothic Armour

Ulfilas' Bible uses the word *sarwa* for armament. Other terms included *brunjo* (coat of mail), *skildus* (shield), *hilms* (helmet) and *meki* (sword). The subdivision of the army (*harjis*) was the horde (*hansa*), both probably of variable size.

Eunapius amuses his audience at the expense of the 3,000 warriors sent by the Goths to fulfil their federate obligations. He says their coats of mail made them look like wasps. From this ancient joke we can deduce that the armour was close-fitting at the waist and/or had wide shoulders.

Athanaric – A Pagan Warrior Leader

From 350 onwards the Romans were preoccupied by usurpers while the Huns put pressure on the barbarians in northern Europe. Not surprisingly there were barbarian attacks on all the frontiers. In 364, shortly after becoming emperor, Valentinian I gave his militaristic younger brother Valens the Eastern Empire, and himself retained power in the West.[33] An Arian Christian, Valens was required to repulse threats from Persia as well as from the Danube tribes. He took seriously possible threats from the Goths and ordered the commander of Dacia to restore the frontier watch towers or build new ones. In the winter of 366/7, Valens crossed the Danube at Daphne on a bridge of boats, but little was gained in a number of skirmishes. In 368 the Danube was too flooded to allow any crossing, but in 369 another bridge of boats was made at Noviodunum and after several long marches Valens found Athanaric, the Gothic *thiudans*, ready for pitched battle.[34] The outcome was that both sides opted for peace, but Athanaric was hampered in his negotiations by an oath he had made to his father never to set foot on Roman soil. This complex military and political situation was resolved in September 369, when the protagonists were rowed into the middle of the Danube to negotiate peace afloat.[35]

Valens restricted the places on the frontier where the Visigoths could legally trade.[36] Athanaric was free to persecute Gothic Christians: between 367 and 378 there are reports of twenty-six Gothic martyrs. It is possible to see the persecutions as an outlet for frustrated warrior band instincts which were curtailed both by the treaty with the Romans and by the insuperable strength of the Huns.[37]

The Threat of the Huns

By 375 the Huns had overrun the Alans, neighbours of the Greutungi, many of whom gradually moved towards the borderlands of the Tervingi. Aware of the increasing dangers from both the Huns and the Greutungi, Athanaric led a strong army to the western bank of the Dniester where he prepared for battle. Giving the Greutungi stockade a wide berth, he sent a reconnaissance force some 20 miles ahead.[38] Things did not go as he expected. Temporarily ignoring both the Greutungi forces and the Tervingian scouts, the Huns took advantage of the clear moonlight to ride along the river to a suitable crossing-point and launch an attack. Athanaric's forces managed to withdraw without meaningful losses, but he was sufficiently worried to order high protective walls to be built from the Danube to the banks of the River Gerasus (the Pruth).[39] Of the many possible archaeological sites, an earth-built linear dyke with a ditch on the south side between Brahasesti and Stoicani (a distance of 85 kilometres) has been interpreted as Athanaric's.[40] Also highly plausible is the suggestion that the Tervingi refortified the former Roman frontier line of Dacia.[41] A second unexpected Hunnic attack left Athanaric's forces relatively unscathed because the Huns were hampered by the weight of their booty.[42]

Although these two incidents were minor, the threat from the Huns was not and Athanaric had no solution. The majority of the Tervingian warriors deserted him and rallied under two new *thiudans*, Fritigern and Alaviv. Athanaric took the remnant of his followers into the inaccessible mountains and forests of the Carpathians. He had no choice, suggests Ammianus Marcellinus: since he had compelled Valens to meet mid-stream, he could not appeal to Constantinople for help.[43] He worked out his undoubted frustrations on the local Sarmatians.[44]

Refugees at the Danube Frontier

The situation was critical for the Tervingi who followed Fritigern and Alaviv since the terrible reputation of the Huns was growing.[45] Throughout 375 and 376, Tervingi and others began to leave their homes and flee to the south. By late 376 Roman sources state that the numbers gathering on the northern banks of the Danube totalled 200,000. Opinions vary over the extent of exaggeration involved here.[46] Ammianus Marcellinus merely adapted a quotation from Virgil, likening the refugees to the grains of sand which were swept over the Libyan plain by the wind god Zephyrus.[47] The fugitives were not solely warriors in search of booty but entire communities, desperately dragging along their movable belongings. Fritigern and Alaviv negotiated for permission to cross the river, but the emperor was 1,000 kilometres away in Antioch and the round-trip for the ambassadors must have caused delay.

Probably because Valens was short of manpower for his eastern campaigns, he activated a policy of *receptio* on behalf of the Tervingi. This required the barbarians to surrender arms (but not their personal belongings) in return for food and legal status. They were then expected to give military service, and acceptance of Christianity was probably part of the terms.

Finally the motley crowd of barbarians were given promises of land for cultivation in Thrace. The commander in Thrace, Lupercinus, was brought in to supervise the crossing. The bargain made at the river banks proved overwhelming to the Romans owing to the sheer numbers of people involved. The ferrying system was hampered by high water and corruption. Boats, rafts and hollowed-out tree trunks were employed day and night.[48] People drowned in attempts to swim across. The refugees were illegally deprived of all their possessions, so they set foot on Roman soil totally destitute, with their families split up. The orders were that those who were too young to fight were to be distributed throughout the empire as hostages. The plan went awry owing to the greed of Romans hoping to replenish their farms with workers and their houses with domestic servants, as well as to gratify more personal desires. One, it was said, was smitten by a pretty boy. Another was attracted to a beautiful wife. They were all overwhelmed by the valuable gifts they were offered, such as linen shirts and coverlets with fringes.[49]

There was general disorder because the refugees had not been fed and Lupercinus attempted to move them on quickly. In the chaos at the Danube, it is known that some Greutungi seized Roman patrol boats which were lying unused and reached the opposite bank. After this, they pitched camp 'at a long distance' from Fritigern.[50] The refugees resorted to bartering; the going rate was one Goth (destined for slavery) for one dog (for food).[51] Jordanes quotes a loaf of bread or ten pounds of meat.[52] This emotive story must be viewed in context – the largest commercial commodity the Goths possessed from at least the time of the Emperor Julian (360–3) was slaves. What would have been shocking was that the Goths were selling their nearest and dearest, including the sons of chieftains, as opposed to their neighbours taken in tribal raids. Jordanes is clear that (despite the disgraceful prices, even for the frontier where bargains were always to be found), it was better (for his ancestors) to be sold and 'mercifully fed' than to die free.[53]

Despite their plight, the Goths were sure of their legal position: the terms of *receptio* had not been met. Lupercinus invited Fritigern and Alaviv to dinner at Marcianopolis. A huge crowd of Goths fruitlessly begged to be allowed into the town to obtain food, and predictably fighting broke out. Ammianus Marcellinus graphically describes the scene at the dinner table. The sleepy and half-drunken Lupercinus, evidently aware of what was happening outside the walls (which was being obscured by 'noisy entertainments'), ordered Fritigern's attendants to be killed.[54] Fritigern saved himself and his supporters by offering to negotiate, and escaped on horseback. Jordanes suggests that the incident gave the Goths an excuse to do what they most wanted: to fight, not starve.[55] They engaged recklessly and enthusiastically in a battle with the Romans, during which 'mad and bloody strife' much of the army and many of its tribunes died. The barbarians then split up and rampaged across the countryside.[56]

The Battle by the Willows (Ad Silices)

The complex situation led to Valens having to come to Lupercinus' aid. Under the overall command of a Frankish general, Richomeres, the Romans eventually met the Goths in combat at Ad Silices ('By the Willows').[57] The Goths had placed their wagons in the traditional circle and were relaxing with their booty. A Gothic wagon-ring was not necessarily a hastily arranged affair. The late fourth-century court poet Claudian describes one in which the Goths dug a double moat, placing stakes along the top 'two deep'. The wagons covered in ox-hide were placed around 'like a wall'.[58]

At Ad Silices the Romans decided to wait until the Goths moved and then attack them from the rear with pikes. The Goths heard of this (possibly from deserters) and stayed put, eventually summoning their scattered bands. Once the forces were ready, after a short armistice, they spent the night with food and drink but no sleep. Next day both sides sounded their trumpets and the Goths attempted to reach high ground in order to sweep down on the Romans. The Romans stood fast and gave their usual war-cry. The barbarians responded by yelling out their ancestors' feats. There were a number of skirmishes from a distance with javelins and other missiles, followed by hand-to-hand combat. A Roman 'tortoise' was formed at which the barbarians hurled fire-hardened clubs. The Goths broke through the left wing: the circular formation of the Gothic wagon *laager* always caused problems to men advancing in a straight line as they reached the vehicles. The situation remained unresolved, though many were killed, split with swords through the head, pierced by iron-tipped arrows or hit by sling-shot. Many others fled, leaving the dead and dying to the carrion eaters.

One of the Roman commanders, Sebastianus, had left the Western Empire on the grounds that the emperors were youthful and controlled by their eunuchs. He was admired by his troops for his disinterest in wealth and evidently had no time for soldiers who made 'womanish pleas'.[59] Not surprisingly, Valens employed him. Sebastianus asked for 2,000 new recruits of good physique, because he considered that he would achieve more with a small, well-trained force than with any number of ill-prepared men.[60] Their training included drill in the arts of war and exercise to make up for any deficiencies discovered in tests. He praised the obedient and was severe with the perverse. With these hand-picked recruits Sebastianus enjoyed much success in harrying the Goths who were by now scattered over the countryside. It appears they were becoming over-confident, since on at least one occasion they were drunk. Modares, a Goth who had defected to the Romans, managed to slaughter a large number who were thus relaxing with their spoils.[61]

Ammianus Marcellinus recounts one incident in which Sebastianus secretly left Adrianople and came upon a 'predatory band of Goths'. He remained hidden behind mounds and thickets until, under cover of darkness, he advanced 'with light step' and killed almost all.[62]

It is a mark of the times that when Sebastianus first reached the town of Adrianople, he was barred from the gates because the townspeople feared that he might have been captured by the Goths and won over, and that as soon as he was admitted he would betray them.[63]

The Battle of Adrianople[64]

In August, near Adrianople, reports came to Valens that there were 10,000 Goths in the area. He was advised to wait for reinforcements from his nephew Gratian (who had succeeded Valentinian I as emperor in the West). Fritigern offered peace, but the terms were unacceptable.

The motivation for Valens' next decision has been subject of conjecture[65] – was it perhaps an ego trip for an older man wanting to rival his nephew Gratian? Or was Ammianus Marcellinus right when he implies that the emperor was tired of receiving letters from Sebastianus, exaggerating his magnificent deeds.[66] Whatever the truth, the emperor took aggressive action. On 9 August 378 the Romans left the imperial treasure under guard outside the walls of Adrianople and began to march in oppressive heat and dust. The Goths had purposely set fire to the surrounding countryside. The Romans certainly lacked drink as they tramped for an exhausting 11 miles before they came on a circle of wagons, formed so perfectly as though turned 'on a lathe'.[67] This could imply that it was no hasty formation. The barbarians uttered terrible cries. Since most of the Roman cavalry was still on the road, formation was difficult, but the Roman leaders drew up their battle lines so that the cavalry on the right wing were pushed forward. The majority of the infantry waited in reserve.

The Gothic cavalry, under two Greutungian cavalry '*duces*', Alatheus and Saphrax, was 'far away'. They were summoned, but time was at a premium. The Visigoths offered peace once more, but they sent envoys of such low origin that the emperor refused to negotiate. Ammianus is quite clear that these were delaying tactics so that the Romans would become exhausted in the heat. This seems to suggest that the Goths may have had a water supply or the measure would surely have been counter-productive.

During the negotiations Richomeres himself volunteered to be a hostage, but before he reached the Goths the Roman archers and the targeteers attacked.

At this dramatic point the Gothic cavalry led by Saphrax and Alatheus arrived with the additional support of some mounted Alans and rushed forward. The left wing of the Roman force reached the wagons but became detached and was crushed. The foot soldiers were therefore left unprotected and crowded together so closely that they could not wield their weapons efficiently. The carnage was appalling. The ground was covered with blood so the troops could not keep a foothold. The roads were blocked by the dying, and fallen horses lay in mounds. Richomeres survived the battle, Sebastianus did not. It is not known what happened to Saphrax and Alatheus after Adrianople, but since they had played such an important part in the victory and were not listed among the dead, they may have escaped death.[68]

A moonless night followed which resulted in the fate of Valens being unknown. He was thought to have been mortally wounded by an arrow. Certainly his body was not recovered. Ammianus recounts the story of a returning survivor who reported that the emperor had received rudimentary medical treatment in a peasant house. This was so well defended on the lower storey that the Goths burnt it down when they failed to gain entrance in search of booty.[69] They were dismayed to discover that they had destroyed such a valuable prize. The battle of Adrianople was not the first in which an emperor lost his life and it did not bring about immediate change, but to many then and since it marked the beginning of the end of Roman power. The Goths certainly dealt a severe but not incapacitating blow to the Roman forces. Ammianus Marcellinus reported that two-thirds of Valens' army was killed in the battle, which has been calculated as between 20,000 and 25,000 dead. Doubts have been cast on these figures and comparisons made with, for example, the battle of the Somme, where machine-gun fire killed 21,000 men on the first day. Given that the opposing forces at Adrianople were more equally armed, it is possible that the Roman casualties numbered 10,000 to 15,000.[70] However, if the Romans were suffering from heat and thirst as badly as Ammianus implies and the Goths were well watered, higher Roman casualties would be likely.[71]

THE SIEGE OF ADRIANOPLE[72]

The Goths did not wait for Gratian and his troops to arrive, but attempted to seize Adrianople since deserters and traitors had told them about the imperial treasure. After encircling the town walls, the Goths rushed in impetuously. Some of the imperial troops who had originally guarded the treasure had been left stranded outside the city. They wasted no time in going over to the Goths, but most were immediately butchered regardless. Peals of thunder from black clouds scattered the Goths who took the opportunity to send a threatening letter. The delay allowed the urban defenders time to repair the walls and in some unexplained fashion find a store of water (possibly storm-water).

The Goths then devised a 'clever plan'. Some of the young defecting officers whose lives had been spared the day before agreed to return in order to set fire to parts of the town. The Goths planned to break in during the ensuing chaos. These unfortunates, on being questioned under torture by the Romans in Adrianople, gave conflicting answers and were beheaded.

Lack of weapons appears to have been a problem to the Goths – the Romans noticed that the Goths were throwing back the missiles that they had hurled out. They therefore ordered that the string by which the barbs were attached to the shafts should be partially severed so that the arrows could not be reused. Psychological matters also inadvertently came into play when the Romans fired a huge boulder from an *onager* (a type of large catapult common in the Roman army). The missile fell harmlessly to the ground, but the Goths, unused to mechanised war, were temporarily appalled. They rallied, but the citizens hurled down many missiles including javelins, sling-shot, arrows and sections or even 'whole drums' of columns. It was noticed as the day went on that the Goths were showing signs of discouragement and at nightfall they retired to their tents with accusations of 'reckless folly' because they had not, as Fritigern had advised, held back from a siege.[73]

THE SKIRMISH AT CONSTANTINOPLE

After this massive waste of life, time and effort, the Goths moved on towards Constantinople, the capital of the Eastern Empire. This vast, rich city controlled traffic from the Black Sea to the Mediterranean – the traditional meeting-point of east and west. It had been enlarged by that time into 'a very great city', inhabited by people from all over the Roman world, and was well provided with walled defences.[74] Despite the city's clear strengths it is doubtful if the Goths had much choice of action at this point: they were aliens in a hostile land and their original homes had been overrun or were threatened by the Huns. Inept seafarers, useless with siege engines, terrified by catapults and so recently fighting among themselves in small bands, the Goths were discouraged. They engaged in a skirmish with a troop of Saracens who happened to be in the city. These men were specialists in surreptitious raiding expeditions, not pitched battle, so the Goths were initially able to put up a reasonable show. Extraordinarily, a long-haired Saracen wearing only a loin-cloth suddenly rushed into the thick of the battle uttering terrible cries. Having slit the throat of a Goth, he drank the flowing blood.[75]

This appalling spectacle seems to have brought the Goths to their senses. Constantinople may have contained unimaginable treasures, but its reserves were overwhelming. The city remained impregnable until it was captured by the far more sophisticated and experienced Turks in 1453. The Goths departed to find easier targets.

Changes in Imperial Attitude to the Goths

The death of the Eastern Emperor Valens at Adrianople required action and without a doubt imperial policy towards the Goths changed at this point. The Western Emperor Gratian immediately summoned out of obscurity a Spanish-born commander called Theodosius who had campaigned in Britain against the Picts (368–9), against the Alamanni (370) and against the Sarmatians in the Balkans (372–3). His distinguished career had been curtailed when his military father was executed, but he was well qualified for Gratian's purposes. After a further victory over the Sarmatians in 379 which showed he had lost none of his talent, Theodosius was made co-emperor, in the East.[76]

Within the year he had an opportunity to put Gothic–Roman relations on a new footing. The pagan Athanaric had not fared well in the Carpathians, and a warrior leader unable to provide booty or gifts rapidly fails in the eyes of his followers. Athanaric seems to have been driven out by his own people in about 380. Despite his anti-Roman vow he was forced to seek refuge in Constantinople. A splendid reception was held on 11 January 381 in the presence of Theodosius (379–395).[77] Two weeks later Athanaric was dead[78] – the circumstances of his death are not known and are therefore, in the eyes of many then and since, suspicious. A splendid funeral enabled Theodosius openly to honour the Goths. He subsequently took both Visigoths and Ostrogoths into the imperial armies in autonomous units under their own leaders – a practice that had previously been avoided as being too dangerous. He also invited Gothic leaders to dinner and showered gifts on them.

Four years later, on 3 October 382, Theodosius (by now the sole emperor of both Western and Eastern Empires) formally settled the Goths in Lower Moesia (a province in the Balkan peninsula not so very far from their coveted Thrace) where they remained federates until his death in 395.

Alaric and Stilicho: Goth and Vandal in Roman Pay

In 392 a former teacher of Latin grammar and rhetoric, Eugenius, was set up as emperor by Arbogastes,[79] the nephew of Richomeres.[80] The battle in which they were defeated – Frigidus, in 394 – was important to the careers of two men under Theodosius' command. One was Alaric, a Visigoth of the ruling Balth family.[81] His subsequent career was so unusual that he has been remembered, reviled and sometimes elevated to hero status. The second commander was Stilicho, the son of a Vandal officer in the Roman army, who, as a result of the pro-barbarian policies in the imperial court, had met and married Theodosius' niece Serena. After 395 Stilicho was commander-in-chief of the army and his daughter Maria married the Western Emperor, Honorius, in 398.[82] The relationship between the two men, both Roman commanders of barbarian blood, has intrigued many commentators, since Stilicho remained in Roman service while Alaric was effectively made redundant.[83] They were often, but not always, on opposing sides. Orosius plants suspicion by writing that he will say nothing about King Alaric and the Goths who were often defeated and surrounded – yet always released.[84]

The battle of the Frigidus left many Gothic casualties. It is even possible that the supposed 'Gothophile' Theodosius had used the Goths against Eugenius in the expectation that the two sides would reduce each other's numbers.[85] According to Orosius, 10,000 died,[86] though Jordanes doubles that number. The significance was twofold. Firstly, replenishment recruits were in very short supply (the activities of the Huns were decreasing the supplies of young, fit, ambitious Goths, although Athanaric's former supporters had been enrolled into existing units of frontier forces). Secondly, Alaric was dissatisfied because he had not been promoted.[87] He and his troops showed their anger by going on a violent rampage through Thrace that ended only at the impenetrable walls of Constantinople.

Theodosius was taken ill in the same year when on campaign against the Franks, and subsequently died (395), having arranged that the empire should be divided. The eastern half was left to his young son Arcadius in Constantinople, while the western half was bequeathed to Honorius, with Stilicho as regent.[88] Since many of the eastern troops had remained in the West after the battle of the Frigidus, Stilicho had a huge military advantage over his eastern rival Rufinus (Arcadius' regent, a Celt who had been much favoured by Theodosius[89]). Claudian clearly showed his opinions of both Rufinus and Stilicho in the titles of his literary offerings alone: 'Against Rufinus,' and 'Panegyric to Stilicho'. For example, he graphically describes the devastation that took place, categorically stating that Rufinus was pleased at the sight of women in chains and the fields ablaze. The eastern leader also demonstrated his allegiances by dressing in the furs of a barbarian.[90]

Stilicho certainly gave every appearance of wanting to take control of Arcadius and the Eastern Empire, in particular in wanting to restore the province of Illyricum to western control. He seems to have allied with Alaric to annexe the area,[91] though it is also possible that Rufinus protected himself by employing Alaric.[92] Stilicho was ready to engage Alaric in battle using troops from both Eastern and Western Empires – Armenians on the left wing, Gauls on the right. The banners waved with a 'scarlet dragon': everything was ready.[93] At this critical point, in the middle of the noise of the cavalry and the sounding trumpets, Rufinus (through Arcadius) sent 'treacherous letters' demanding the return of the eastern troops to Constantinople.

Stilicho agreed with what in hindsight may be seen as suspicious alacrity. Alaric and his supporters escaped into Greece.

THE MURDER OF RUFINUS

Stilicho returned some of the troops with a Gothic leader called Gainas. As the young Emperor Arcadius[94] came out of Constantinople to meet them, Gainas' men savagely cut down Rufinus[95] on 27 November 395. Claudian tells the story in ghoulish detail. It appears that Rufinus had regarded the return of the troops as such a victory that he should be made co-emperor. The troops surrounded him under pretence of negotiating, and dissected him while he was alive, before finally beheading him. With 'paeans' of victory, they paraded his hand through the streets, where it was offered to passers-by so they might give it money since it was 'insatiable'.[96] Rufinus had not been universally loved.

Stilicho sought new recruits on the Rhine frontier. Evidently the fate of the Goths in the 376 crossing was seen as a different matter altogether since Claudian reports with healthy contempt that 'flaxen-haired warrior-kings' were offering their children as hostages and seeking peace.[97] The death of Rufinus did not deliver the Eastern Empire to Stilicho – internal political struggles led to the rise of the eunuch Eutropius. It appears that Gainas was eventually returned to his original command in Thrace, though probably short of men. In 397–8 Eutropius personally took command against the Huns in Phrygia and Cappadocia, where they had taken advantage of the lack of troops in the east and were attacking monasteries and cities, so that (in the words of St Jerome) the streams were 'reddened with human blood'.

However, Eutropius became 'drunk with riches' and over-ambition and lost power. After his execution, Gainas became equal in power to Stilicho.[98]

ALARIC AND THE GOTHS' DISSATISFACTION

Considerable debate and argument surrounds Alaric's position at this time, but it seems that he was deprived of his command. Effectively, he was a Roman commander with no supplies, no authority and no power, but whose followers still looked to him for support and pay.[99] He could disappear into obscurity, commit suicide, or fight on. There was a perfectly good leadership mechanism ready to be put into place through Gothic traditions. He chose this option while assuming the non-Gothic title King of the Goths.

In the meantime, not everyone was wholeheartedly behind Gainas. On 12 July 400 some 7,000 of his followers are said to have sought asylum in a church from the citizens of Constantinople. They were slaughtered on the orders of Arcadius (who had presumably not forgotten the terrible death of Rufinus). Due to their unease at murdering people who had sought sanctuary and could therefore be expected to resist, the citizens stripped the roof over the altar and hurled down 'lighted kindling' until all inside were dead.[100] Gainas himself was eventually defeated with the aid of Uldin, the first Hunnic leader in the west to be known by name, and another Gothic leader (Fravitta).

On 18 November 401 Alaric moved south through the Alpine passes into Italy. Presumably he chose his time deliberately, because snow promptly stranded Stilicho in Raetia outside Italy. Honorius hurriedly moved the western court from Milan to Ravenna and Stilicho summoned troops from the already depleted forces in Britain and the Rhine. Alaric and his men had to live off the land, but it was Easter Day 402 before the two met in battle at Pollentia (Pollenza). The choice of day was important: the Goths, being Christians, did not expect an attack on a holy day, but the Roman commander (Saul) was a barbarian and a pagan. He was later condemned by Orosius for this wickedness.[101] Lack of men and supplies left the outcome undecided, and a second engagement at Verona a few months later was equally unsatisfactory.

The manpower problem was now acute – there were simply not enough men left in Raetia, Illyricum and Gothia. Disease and desertion at Verona also weakened Alaric's forces. It is probable that one of the Gothic leaders, Sarus, took this opportunity to desert to the Romans. There is dispute as to how many Goths and their associates were involved in the crossing of the Alps and the ensuing battles. It is often claimed to have been as many as 80,000 or 100,000. If these numbers were accurate they probably included civilian followers. Claudian mentions Alaric's wife, picturesquely claiming that it was her desire for Roman jewels that urged the Gothic leader onwards.[102] However, this may have been merely poetic licence and there is some doubt whether wives and families were among the Gothic numbers.

It appears that since neither could muster enough power to defeat the other, Stilicho and Alaric made an agreement. The details are obscure, but probably included a reinstatement of military power for Alaric. He was in an ambivalent position – still calling himself king, but also commander-in-chief of Illyricum. Both commanders by this time probably led the dregs of the recruitment process. An edict at the time instructed Stilicho to recruit 'laetus, Alamannus, Sarmatian, vagrant, son of a veteran'. The desperation of the recruiters is clear as the edict continued 'or any person of any group'.[103] Simply training such recruits would have caused problems.

RADAGAISUS AND THE DEFEAT AT FIESOLE

In 405 the centre of interest temporarily moved away from Alaric and the Visigoths. A vast multitude of Ostrogothic peoples and others under a pagan called Radagaisus crossed the Rhine. They quickly overran Italy and ravaged many cities, threatening Rome itself.[104] Stilicho defeated Radagaisus at Fiesole, using Huns under Uldin's command and Alans and Goths under Sarus. Twelve thousand of Radagaisus' best troops were taken into Roman pay.[105]

Stilicho's subsequent actions led to further suspicion that he wanted to take over the Eastern Empire. He instructed Alaric to hold Epirus (a coastal region in north-west Greece and southern Albania) and closed off the Italian ports to eastern ships. Before the two could join forces there was a false report of Alaric's death, and Honorius summoned Stilicho because of the urgent situation that had arisen:[106] on the last day of 406 the Vandals and many others had crossed the Rhine and were now threatening Italy. Additionally, in 407, taking advantage of the unrest, the British troops proclaimed emperor the soldier Constantine (later III).[107]

Holding out at Epirus was difficult through lack of supplies and support. In the spring of 408 Alaric marched on Noricum (central Austria) and eventually received compensation of 4,000 pounds in weight of gold.[108] With difficulty Stilicho persuaded the Senate to pay up. One senator called Lampadius exclaimed that it was a 'treaty of slavery', though once it was paid he had to take refuge in a church for fear of reprisals.[109] The equivalent in coin was 288,000 solidi – the average income of a fairly wealthy senator. Was there just the breath of suspicion that Alaric was trying to buy his way into the Establishment? It also happens to be the sum required for 90,000 people to live comfortably for a year, which might imply that Alaric's followers were indeed numerous.[110]

Fast-moving Events

The year 408 turned out to be eventful. During the summer the usurper Constantine established his base in Arles, having taken control of the armies in Gaul and Spain.[111] Stilicho's daughter Maria had died, so Honorius married her sister Thermantia. When the Eastern Emperor Arcadius also died, Stilicho's position was dangerously high. A palace official[112] spread the rumour that he was about to put his son Eucherius on the eastern throne. When Stilicho went to Ravenna he was imprisoned on Honorius' orders. Sarus treacherously murdered Stilicho's Hunnic body-guard,[113] and Stilicho himself was beheaded on 22 August 408.[114] Honorius terminated his marriage, and many (possibly 30,000) of Stilicho's supporters went over to Alaric.[115]

After this shuffle of allegiances, Alaric wasted no time in demanding hostages. When his demands were rejected, he marched on Rome.

The Goths Demand Payment

The Eternal City was the symbol of everything that was civilised and desirable. The citizens were desperate and the Senate needed a scapegoat. Stilicho's policies were blamed and it was even rumoured (almost certainly wrongly) that his imperially born wife Serena was conspiring with Alaric.[116] Accusations based on superstition were brought against her.[117] The Senate conferred with Galla Placidia (Theodosius' daughter by his second wife, whose high status added respectability to the venture), who did not intervene[118] to prevent her cousin Serena's murder.[119] This violent measure did not achieve its aim. The Goths assembled outside the walls of Rome, and Alaric's demands were typical of barbarian taste for the flamboyant: 5,000 pounds of gold, 30,000 pounds of silver, 4,000 silk robes, 3,000 purple-dyed furs and 3,000 pounds of pepper. He also demanded a lasting peace treaty.[120] These were not excessive demands since many wealthy families received an income of 4,000 pounds of gold in a year, with grain and other produce amounting to perhaps a third more.[121]

Honorius refused to make peace. Never the strongest of statesmen, he and his advisors had other things on their minds, including the fact that the usurper Constantine was still around. In 409 Constantine sent a deputation to Honorius claiming (as usurpers often did) that the troops had forced him into his actions. Distracted by Alaric, Honorius recognised Constantine as co-ruler.[122] Negotiation with the Goths could now continue, but the process was hampered by Honorius' propensity for switching allegiance. Alaric's negotiation base included land – Noricum and Venetia (inclusive of Dalmatia) – and annual payments. Honorius engaged 10,000 Hunnic troops and arranged for grain, sheep and oxen to support them to be brought from Dalmatia.[123] Alaric reduced his demands to the two provinces of Noricum and sufficient grain. This was interpreted as a sign of weakness and negotiations were broken off. Zosimus calls the negotiators dim-wits for not agreeing to those terms.[124]

Alaric marched to Rome again, gained control of the food supplies and, in late 409, persuaded the Senate to make emperor a man called Attalus who had been working with the Goths for a reconciliation. He proved less amenable once he was emperor; in particular, he refused to join the Goths in a conquest of the highly prosperous provinces of North Africa.[125] Alaric was thus left with a surplus usurper and no negotiation base. He publicly stripped Attalus of the Purple (the imperial insignia), which he sent to Honorius. Attalus remained on good terms with the Goths.[126] Negotiations were reopened and Alaric and Honorius finally met face to face at Alpes, 60 stades (8 miles) from Ravenna. They might well have come to terms, but for the arrival of Sarus with a small force of only 300 men.[127] He was fleeing from Alaric's brother-in-law Athaulf (who led a formidable force of Huns and Alans).[128] It has been suggested that the murder of Stilicho's Hunnic bodyguard was sufficient reason for Athaulf's fury towards Sarus. Whatever the truth, the 'vendetta' between Sarus, Athaulf and Alaric was powerful enough to have effect even after all three were in their graves. The prospect of being caught up in a Gothic feud frightened off Honorius. He was a fickle, quirky character whose general folly was censured by the early sixth-century writer Procopius.[129] On this occasion the emperor immediately abandoned discussions with Alaric to receive Sarus.

Alaric once more marched on Rome.[130]

THE SACK OF ROME

On 24 August 410 the Goths gained entry to the Eternal City. There was a rumour that the gates were opened to them by a wealthy Christian called Proba, because the Roman citizens were being reduced to cannibalism.[131] An alternative explanation is given by Procopius:[132] Alaric chose three hundred youths 'as yet beardless', who were, moreover, not only of good birth but brave 'beyond their years'. He persuaded them to enter Rome pretending they were slaves, and to ingratiate themselves with the patricians (nobles) in whose homes they worked. Then, at an appointed hour, they were to overpower the guards of a particular gate and let in their compatriots. Finding the teenage boys (predictably) only too ready to agree to such an adventure, he made an ostentatious show of leaving and sent them as 'goodwill' gifts to the Romans. Rome was indeed deceived and the gates were opened.

The fall of Rome made a huge impact. Honorius was momentarily aghast. The oddly domestic lifestyle he led in the remote but easily defendable marsh-bound Ravenna is illustrated by his reactions on being told (presumably by his poultry-keeper rather than by an ambassador) that Rome had perished. He exclaimed in perplexity that it had just taken food from his hands. Matters were explained to him and he sighed with relief: the very large chicken which he owned, and which was named 'Rome', was still in good health.[133]

In the Eternal City itself few people would have been so complacent, though the looters stayed only three days, and as sacks go (as even St Augustine later agreed), it was not one of the worst. Alaric ordered that the churches should be spared and human life respected, though Procopius says burned-out houses remained to his day. The Basilica lost some silver, but many riches including the Esquiline treasure were successfully concealed. Orosius (who had had to flee from the Vandals in Spain in the previous year) plays down the event, wishing to emphasise the importance of the Christian faith. The fires were not so great as the famous one in the time of Nero, he points out, and the period was a mere three days as opposed to the year the city had suffered under the Gauls (led by Brennus in 390 BC). He recounts a touching story in which a barbarian, chancing on an ageing 'virgin of Christ', asked her for gold and silver. In a rather stately exchange, she explained that she had a vast amount of treasure which was sacred to God and challenged him to defile the sacred vessels. The objects were then processed through the streets, guarded by the Goths, and a hymn was sung jointly by barbarian invaders and Romans alike.[134]

In the same year[135] Alaric died of disease, perhaps contracted in Rome. He had hoped to reach North Africa via Sicily, whence it was a relatively short trip to the North African coast, with the major towns of Tunis, Sousse and Tripoli temptingly easy to reach. However, the Visigoths failed to cross the water because some of the ships sank, probably in storms, within 12 miles of the Straits of Gades (Cadiz).[136] They began to retreat northwards.

ALARIC – HERO OR OPPORTUNIST?

Before the sack of Rome in particular, Alaric was regarded by many churchmen as being possessed by a devil. The fact that he was (at least nominally) a Christian made no odds, though his treatment of church property softened clerical views. More recently he has been seen with considerable sympathy, for it is easy to be persuaded that here was a genuine warrior in the heroic mould, leading his people against overwhelming odds. His life was coloured by blood ties, blood feuds and the desperate search for booty and honour. More cynically perhaps, his actions were those of a capable man passed over for promotion. Finding his people also in need – of land for settlement – he fell back on his barbarian upbringing and the traditional *mores* of his people, to seek redress. He can be viewed as exploiting his situation, with both the Goths and the Romans, for personal gain or as turning disaster into success for his followers, and possibly both.

He was buried in the river Busentus which was temporarily diverted to allow for the interment of his body and many treasures.[137] The grave-diggers were then killed, and expeditions have so far failed to discover the grave.[138]

ATHAULF AND 'GOTHIA'

Athaulf took over Gothic leadership. The usurper Constantine III was finally apprehended and executed in 411, and his severed head was displayed on a pole. Almost immediately a Gallic nobleman called Iovinus expropriated imperial power with the aid of the Burgundians,[139] the Alans,[140] the Alamanni and the Franks. Under his régime the Burgundians were permitted to establish a kingdom on the left bank of the Rhine.

Sarus, with eighteen or twenty men,[141] was on his way to join Iovinus against Honorius when Athaulf, evidently taking no chances, deliberately intercepted him with a force of 10,000. In the true spirit of all the most celebrated warriors, Sarus 'performed heroic deeds' which were unfortunately not recounted. He was with difficulty captured alive 'with lassoes'.[142] This method of capture was Hunnic – Ammianus says the Huns threw strips of cloth plaited into nooses in which they entangled their adversaries' feet.[143] Sarus was eventually put to death.

Athaulf established a base at Narbonne, having failed to take Massilia in late 413. In the same year Athaulf captured Iovinus after a siege but the usurper was murdered while on his way under escort to Honorius. One of the more valuable prizes found in Rome was Galla Placidia,[144] who was treated with royal dignity and courtesy.[145] Negotiations notably produced no agreement over how much should be paid by Honorius from the imperial coffers in exchange for his half-sister. It appears that neither Athaulf nor Galla Placidia was anxious for her return, because in January 414, four years after she had been captured, but without Honorius' blessing, 26-year-old Galla Placidia consented to marry Athaulf at the house of a Narbonne Roman.[146]

Since the sack of Rome it seems that Athaulf's ambitions, quoted at the head of this chapter, had changed to a desire for conciliation.[147] Athaulf later attributed this change to his new wife's influence. The Gothic leader appears to have come to realise that the State could not function without laws, and that the Goths' 'unbridled barbarism' prevented them from following the law. Therefore the Goths had to become Roman, not vice versa.[148] Athaulf was voicing a variant of the modern theories of state formation: warrior-based social organisation is simply untenable for vast confederations of people. Something wider is needed, even if the individual is in some ways more constricted.

As a symbol of his intent, at his wedding Athaulf wore a Roman general's cloak; his bride wore a (Roman) royal outfit. Among other wedding gifts, he gave her fifty handsome silk-clad youths, each carrying two huge dishes (one full of gold and the other filled with priceless stones), booty saved from the sack of Rome.[149] One of the wedding hymns was sung by the former usurper Attalus.[150] The match appears to have been happy. Jordanes says Athaulf was attracted to Galla Placidia's nobility, beauty and chaste purity,[151] and the noble Goth himself was strikingly handsome though not particularly tall.[152]

This promising union was seen by some as the marriage of the king of the North with the daughter of the king of the South that had been prophesied in the Book of Daniel 11.6.[153] It was destined to fail in its public aspirations. Honorius sent his commander Constantius against the Goths who were forced out of Narbonne into Spain in 414.[154] Their supplies were cut off and famine led to the Vandals exploiting them over grain.[155] Athaulf spent the next three years in the Iberian peninsula fighting the Vandals from his base in Barcelona.[156] An infant born to Galla Placidia died and was buried, with sorrow, in a silver coffin near Barcelona.[157] Significantly, the child was named after his illustrious maternal grandfather Theodosius, the imperial champion of the Goths. Athaulf was clearly signalling his pro-Roman policies. However, it is clear that they were not welcomed by all, whether Romans or Goths.

The Murder of Athaulf

Athaulf was murdered in the summer of 415. Two versions of this event exist. Olympiodorus relates that one of Athaulf's men called Dubius gained revenge for the death of a previous master (a king of the Goths) by killing Athaulf when he was inspecting his horses.[158] It would be dramatically satisfying to see the unnamed former master as Sarus, but no proof of this exists. Jordanes' version would have us believe that another enemy, Euervulf, pierced him in the groin with a sword because Athaulf had frequently mocked him for being short.[159]

The dying Athaulf asked his brother to return Galla Placidia to Honorius, but in fact Sarus' brother Sigeric seized power. He violently murdered Athaulf's children by his first wife and humiliated Galla Placidia by making her work in front of his horse with the other prisoners.[160] The possibility that Athaulf's murder was the result of vengeance stirred up for political reasons sounds logical but is unverifiable.

Wallia, Leader of the Goths

A week later Sigeric was deposed, perhaps because even he was more interested in peace than in war.[161] Wallia, an austere and sensible man,[162] took over the throne but also sued for peace.[163] Constantius was sent to meet him. Jordanes (probably romanticising the event with hindsight) says that the Roman general had been promised Galla Placidia in marriage[164] (as an incentive). An agreement was made with significant ease at a pass in the Pyrenees and the Visigothic widow was handed back to Honorius in return for a peace treaty and a prosaic 600,000 measures of grain.[165]

Immediately the Vandals began to ravage the Spanish territories of the Visigoths.[166] In 416 Wallia agreed with the Romans to challenge Vandal supremacy. He carried out his duties with enthusiasm, nearly exterminating the Alans and totally exterminating the Asding Vandals. Like Alaric, he too failed to make the crossing to Africa.[167]

On 1 January 417 Honorius gave the unwilling Galla Placidia to Constantius in marriage.[168] He was a considerable contrast to her Gothic husband. Though an attractive character, cheerful and affable at parties, he had bulging eyes, a long neck and broad head. He looked sullen and was prone to slumping over his horse which, apparently, gave him the appearance of a tyrant.[169] Galla Placidia's effect on both her husbands seems to have been marked, but in the case of Constantius not for the better. Until he married her he was said to be completely free from greed.[170] They had two children, Honoria and

Valentinian (later III). For seven months before his death on 2 September 421, Constantius held the Western Empire jointly with Honorius, though he was never acknowledged by the Eastern Empire. He regretted his elevation because it curtailed his former freedoms.[171] Galla Placidia was given the equivalent title of Augusta (Empress).

In 418 Wallia negotiated with Constantius for a federate settlement in Aquitania Secunda (between the Garonne and the Loire) for the Goths. When he died, the move was completed by Theodoric I.[172]

The Visigothic Warriors Settle Down

Theodoric I reigned from 418 to 451, using Toulouse as a centre. It is notable that he was the first Visigothic leader to be able to issue decrees – a major turning-point, where traditional warrior society began to metamorphose into a settled state. The Visigoths remained enthusiastic about defending themselves on the battlefield and in initiating aggression, but from this time on they were increasingly limited by the trappings of the State. Their stay in Aquitania Secunda lasted for three decades until in 451 they successfully allied with the Romans against the Huns at the major battle of the Catalaunian Plains.[173] Theodoric I died in the battle. Presumably in recompense for his help in this victory, his son Theodoric II was permitted to extend the Visigothic territories. At the emperor's request he attacked the pagan Sueves in north-east Spain, defeating them in 456.[174]

Ten years later Theodoric II was murdered by his brother Euric, who in 475 published a code of Gothic law (written in Latin and drafted by Roman lawyers). He expanded his kingdom eastwards along the Rhône and southwards to the Pyrenees.[175] In 507 the Visigoths were defeated by Clovis of the Franks in the battle of Vouillé and were thereafter mainly confined to four of the former Roman regions in Spain.[176] They lived in the old Roman cities and had no discernible urban culture of their own. They were far from being the warrior-based society of their fourth-century ancestors. Even the army was different since recruitment was not based on kinship.[177] Visigothic Spain developed culturally and has left fine architecture, but was finally destroyed by Muslims from north Africa.

Chapter 2

The Huns

A subtle man who fought with artifice before he waged his wars.[1]
        Jordanes, describing Attila the Hun.

In the space of seventy years, from the later fourth century, the Huns managed to terrify the barbarian and the Roman worlds alike. They were known as the 'Scourges of God's Fury',[2] equalled only by Genghis Khan and his Mongol hordes centuries later.[3] Unlike many of the other peoples in this book, the Huns were nomads. They were non-literate, maintained no discernible industry and left no identifiable settlements, monuments or major works of art. In short, their aims and aspirations were the exact opposite of everything the Roman Empire admired.

They came from the Steppeland, a dry, treeless area which sustains no agriculture. Humans trying to exist in such an environment need to hunt. This in turn means following the herds rather than establishing permanent bases in which to develop crafts, arts, literacy and economic stability. The nomadic lifestyle favoured those with physical prowess, who were quick and accurate with the bow, capable of outwitting the wiles of hunted animals. Not surprisingly, the Huns became known in battle for the ferocity of their mounted charges, their unexpected retreats, their skilled horsemanship and skill with bow and arrow. Such a harsh lifestyle also meant that the riches of settled communities were attractive.

This chapter covers the reputation and background of the Huns, their rise to prominence in the late fourth century and the career of Attila, after which they were quickly assimilated into the general population.

The Reputation of the Huns

The reputation of the Huns is owed to a number of factors in addition to their aggressive characteristics. First, the Huns left neither oral nor written tradition to celebrate their achievements for posterity, although they sang about their exploits. Their language is known only from a few personal names, from which it has been suggested that they may have spoken a form of Turkish. Attila had a number of Roman secretaries through whom he maintained written communication (presumably in Latin or Greek) with the empires. The result was that non-Hunnic commentators had more or less a free hand to enhance the reputations of the Huns, making them into monsters. This was done through ridicule (the notion that the Huns remained on horseback at all times),[4] disgust at their ruthlessness (the Huns were claimed to eat their parents and take blood from their horses to stave off hunger on campaign[5]) and through alluding to them in terms of literary characters such as the centaurs (half-man, half-horse)[6] who were generally represented as lawless, wild and subject to their animal passions.

Secondly, the Huns remained pagan at a time when the empire was insecure in its religious beliefs. To Christian writers, it seemed that the Huns posed a threat to political security (and eternal well-being), and were easy targets for priests determined to rally the faithful. Orosius was clear that they were sent to Europe by God as a punishment for sin. By the seventh century, when the Huns had long since ceased to exist as an entity and posed no physical threat whatsoever, propaganda against them as symbols of evil reached the level of hysteria.[7] However, when the Huns turn up in dispassionate records, it is often as fighters either in or with the imperial armies. Attila himself comes across as relatively mild-mannered, though his casual ability to order miscreants to be impaled or crucified may dismay anyone unfamiliar with the ruthlessness of Romans and barbarians alike at the time.[8]

Thirdly, ancient writers in general tended to focus on those aspects that distinguished barbarian society from civilisation rather than emphasising common factors. By definition it was virtually impossible for any barbarians to gain Roman approbation. When they were described as fierce or indomitable fighters, for example, it was usually to imply how much more valiant the victors were.

Fourthly, the Huns were physically distinctive. Through the acquisition of people as booty or hostages as well as by peaceful inter-marriage, they are likely to have had varying amounts of Turkish, Greek, Mongolian, even Persian, Chinese or Indian blood in their make-up. To Jordanes (significantly, after the Hunnic heyday) a Hun's face was a 'shapeless lump' with 'pinholes' for eyes.[9] It is not recorded what the Huns thought about the celebrated 'Roman' nose. Jordanes said that the Huns were cruel even to their children, and cut boys' cheeks with a sword so that even before they had taken their first taste of milk they had to 'endure a wound'.[10] This left the Hunnic men without good looks since the 'natural grace of a beard' was impossible in a face furrowed by sword scars. The differing comments on Hunnic appearance may be based partly on truth: in Hunnic and Gothic areas skulls have been found which had evidently been deliberately constricted from infancy so they grew excessively tall and conical.

Finally, fear of the Huns may well have been fuelled by the fact that their origins were unknown and they were buffered from the Roman world by other barbarian peoples such as the Goths and Alans. Successful generals always study their opponents. In the case of the Huns, the Romans found this impossible.

Hunnic Origins

The origins of the Huns have preoccupied many writers and caused many heated arguments. The Huns have, for example, been tenuously identified with both the Hsiung-nu of China and the Hephthalites who invaded Iran and India in the fifth and sixth centuries.[11] The problem cannot be resolved at present. It is often impossible to correlate political with cultural traits, and certainly by the time the Huns came into Europe in the late fourth century they were as much a political entity as an ethnic one.

The Huns themselves did not know where they came from though ancient writers made suggestions and archaeology has shed some light. Ammianus Marcellinus dispensed with the problem by admitting only that they came from the area 'beyond the Maeotic marshes' (the Sea of Azov),[12] near the 'ice-bound ocean' in the north. If this is true, they may have had similar origins to the Finno-Ungrians, but they may equally have been the first of the succession of Turkic nomads to reach Europe.[13]

According to one story, the Huns and Goths lived side by side, unaware of each other's existence, until one day a Hunnic heifer was stung by a gadfly and ran into the marshes at the Straits of Kerch. The herdsmen followed her and eventually came across the Goths, living in relative luxury and comfort in a mild climate with fertile soils.[14] Hotfoot, the Huns went home to tell their friends. Some versions tell of a stag. The gadfly element is to be found in Aeschylus.[15] It is possible that this is a literary method of explaining a change in climate which forced the herds and consequently the Huns into Gothic lands. The Goths believed that the Huns were created when certain witches were cast out[16] and interbred with evil spirits (the Haliurunnae in Gothic).

Whatever their origins, in the later fourth century the Huns expanded their area of control to include the Alans.

THE ALANS – SUBJECTS AND ALLIES OF THE HUNS

The Alans (also nomads) were fine horsemen. They included people who (it was said) decorated themselves with blue dye, ate human flesh and stripped the skins from their enemies to make clothing and horse coverings.[17] The accuracy of these statements is of less interest than the fact they were made close to the time and Ammianus was probably stating what his audience wanted to hear. The more reasonable part of the narrative comes at the end, once he has caught the attention of his audience with a laugh or two and a couple of gasps of horror. The Alans, he asserts more credibly, consumed meat and milk. They lived in wagons where all domestic life took place.[18] Physically, the Alans seem to have been totally different from the Huns – tall and (in Roman eyes) handsome, their hair generally blond. They were said to take delight in danger and war. Dying of old age, it seems, was regarded as cowardly. They had an unusual method of divination using 'twigs of osier', were all of noble blood (i.e., they did not have slaves) and chose their chiefs for their long experience as warriors.[19]

HUNNIC LIFESTYLE

The Huns were even more fearful, and despite the embellishments in literature the harsh realities of their lifestyle are apparent. They ate the roots of wild plants (credible) and the half-raw flesh of any kind of animal that they warmed between their legs and their horses (less credible, if only since they used saddles, though the practice has been explained in a number of ways). They were said to wear shoes made without lasts (credible) which therefore necessitated their spending all the time on horseback (exaggeration, though possibly not so far from the truth as some suggest). Ammianus Marcellinus discusses the wagons the Huns used when they were on the move, in which the young grew to puberty and the women made clothes.[20] There is no reason to believe that wagons were used either as dwellings (the Huns had tents) or as part of Hunnic warfare, although they left their herds with the women and children when going off on horseback. The wagons may have been necessary for transporting the tents and for carrying booty.[21] From this tough lifestyle they certainly learned from infancy how to endure cold, hunger and thirst – formidable attributes in an adversary.[22]

The First Huns in Europe – Negotiation, Treachery and War

In the late fourth century the Huns and Alans, under a Hunnic leader (the semi-mythical Balamber),[23] destroyed the huge, amorphous territories of the Greutungi who lived between the Don and Dniester rivers and are the subject of Chapter 3.[24] Life on the Steppes had not fitted the Huns for a static life as farmers. Very little is known about how society worked in the period when the Huns were overlords to the Greutungi, but it was clearly sufficiently menacing to send the many thousands of Tervingi and others fleeing across the Danube in 376. The death of Theodosius I in 395, the subsequent division of the empire between Arcadius and Honorius, and the activities of Alaric and Stilicho in the west meant that there was little to stop the Huns in the east. When the Danube froze in the winter of 395 the Huns crossed into Roman territory. Devastation followed in Armenia and Syria, though the nomads and barbarians alike would doubtless have described their actions as successful sorties for booty. Cappadocia in particular suffered greatly.

Uldin

By the late fourth century Hunnic lands north of the Danube were ruled by Uldin, who helped to defeat the Gothic leader Gainas. Having sent the severed head (after it had been suitably displayed) to Constantinople in a package which arrived on 3 January 401, he was rewarded with gifts and a treaty.[25] Although he had fought under Stilicho at Fiesole against Radagaisus and the Goths, he invaded Thrace in 408 with a large army; his refusal to accept offers of peace lost him the support of many of his followers. Many of the Sciri died before he finally escaped across the Danube, probably in 409.

Little is known about the activities of the Huns for the following two decades. They may have been granted (or seized) lands in Pannonia.[26] At one point, possibly between 415 and 425, they attacked Persia, apparently as a result of famine.[27]

HUNNIC WARFARE TECHNIQUES

The best account of Hunnic horsemanship in war is provided by Ammianus[28] who said that the Huns occasionally fought as individuals but more usually entered the fray in tactical formation. Like all barbarian groups they deliberately made a 'savage noise'. He says they were lightly equipped, which allowed them to move quickly and unexpectedly. One tactic especially perplexed the Romans who did not use it: the Huns would purposely and suddenly divide into scattered bands and would then rush about in disorder 'here and there' and as a result, initiate considerable slaughter. First they fought from a distance using missiles with sharp bone (instead of the usual points) joined to the shafts. Then they galloped over the intervening spaces and engaged in hand-to-hand combat with swords, without thought for their own lives. While their enemies were busy trying to fend off the swords, the Huns would throw over them strips of cloth, 'plaited into nooses', which fell down over them and fettered the legs.

AËTIUS AND THE HUNS

The empire took security measures at all points of entry to the provinces, but when Honorius died of dropsy on 27 August 423, leaving no heir, events conspired to bring the Huns into prominence through political means. A usurper called Joannes seized power, hoping to oppose the claims of the young Valentinian, son of Constantius and Galla Placidia (who had lost favour with Honorius and either fled or was banished to Constantinople).[29] The western general Aëtius Flavius was among those who supported Joannes but a man named Bonifacius allied himself with the imperial opposition. The Eastern Emperor Theodosius II (402–50), the gentle and scholarly son of Arcadius, sent Galla Placidia and Valentinian back to Italy with an army led by an Alan called Ardabur and his son Aspar, who, to judge from his long career, must have been very young at this time. During the struggles, Ardabur was captured by Joannes' men. He ingratiated himself with them to such an extent he was able to undermine the confidence of Joannes' supporters.[30] A second version of this story has the young Aspar valiantly leading his men (with the help of a messenger from God) through the treacherous marshes to capture Ravenna, where Joannes was in residence.[31] The usurper was mutilated and paraded through the streets before being executed. The seven-year-old Valentinian III was enthroned on 23 October 425.

Whether by accident or design, Aëtius missed the main action, having been sent to fetch Hunnic reinforcements on behalf of Joannes. Aëtius had a special relationship with the Huns, having spent part of his youth with them as a hostage, as well as the years between 405 and 408 as hostage to Alaric and the Visigoths. He is mentioned as having specifically learned about Hunnic warfare.[32] He was described as healthy, spare in physique, manly in his habits, an extremely able soldier but also a skilled negotiator. Having spent time with the Huns it is not surprising that he was both a good horseman and a good shot with a bow. He was contemptuous of danger and could survive hunger, thirst and lack of sleep.[33] He arrived with 60,000 Huns three days after Joannes' death. Galla Placidia, as regent, probably had no option but to employ her former opponent. The Huns departed after receiving payments of gold.

Galla Placidia kept Aëtius in Italy, but gave Bonifacius a military post in Africa (Libya) where the Moors and other tribes were causing problems. By 427 the two men were certainly strong rivals. Aëtius wrote to Bonifacius warning him not to respond when Galla Placidia summoned him, since she intended to have him killed. At the same time he told Galla Placidia that if she were to summon Bonifacius, he would not respond because he was her adversary not her friend.[34] She summoned Bonifacius. He failed to respond. They both drew their own conclusions. However, the deception was uncovered and Galla Placidia in consequence loathed Aëtius, but she was not, in the long term, capable of outwitting him. After using Huns to defeat both the Franks and the Visigoths in 427–8, Aëtius removed a rival, Felix, and moved closer to real power.

In 430–2 Aspar the Alan and Bonifacius were defeated by Gaiseric of the Vandals in North Africa, but two years later Galla Placidia recalled Bonifacius to Italy and appointed him to Aëtius's position. Battle between the two was inevitable. Defeated, Aëtius fled to the Huns who by this time were controlled by a central ruler, Rua (425–435/440). He had two nephews Bleda and Attila, the former being the more important at this time. Bonifacius died of disease later in 432 and Aëtius was able to regain power. He married Bonifacius' widow, and, when Galla Placidia's regency ended, he gained almost total control, leaving Valentinian III to enjoy a life of pleasure.

The Destruction of the Burgundians

Once Aëtius regained power, a problem arose with the Burgundians. Originally from Scandinavia,[35] they had moved into the Lower Vistula valley in about the first century AD, where the Gepids forced them to the frontiers of the Western Empire. There they served as federates or auxiliaries in the

Roman army and established a kingdom north of the Rhine. During the rule of the usurper Iovinus they extended into Roman territory south of the river where their king, Gundichar, maintained a capital at Worms. In 436, for unknown reasons, they rebelled[36] and raided one of the Belgic provinces of Gaul.[37]

Aëtius attacked them and made peace, but he seems to have sent Attila against them in the following year when the Burgundians were almost totally destroyed. The number of fatalities are recorded as being 20,000[38] and the episode has been remembered, with such inaccuracy as to be historically useless, in the complex medieval German heroic poem *Niebelungenlied*, in which the character Etzel represents Attila. This story has been adapted and modified many times, notably in the opera *Der Ring des Nibelungen* by Richard Wagner.[39] As Thomas Hodgkin wrote in 1892, the 'round and rubicund' Etzel, full of benevolence and hospitality, was most certainly not the 'thunder-brooding, sallow, silent Attila' found in the pages of the contemporaneous Priscus of Panium.

It is unknown to what extent the apparent collaboration between Attila and Aëtius was premeditated or planned and their relationship over the following two decades is as intriguing as that between Stilicho and Alaric. Certainly Aëtius gave Attila a secretary called Constantius, though such a move might have been more for surveillance than friendship.

The Huns after Rua[40]

Various Danubian groups including the Amilzuri, Itimari, Tounsoures and Boisci began joining the Romans against the Huns, so Rua engaged in negotiations with Constantinople, threatening to break the peace unless the renegades were returned.[41] Before the problems could be resolved, he died (sometime between 435 and 440), reputedly struck by lightning, and the vast triangle of Hunnic territories between the Baltic, the Alps and the Caspian Sea passed into the control of Bleda and Attila. The Eastern Empire sent an embassy that included a 'Scythian' called Plinthas to the two new leaders.

The Treaty of Horreus Margus

The two sides met at Margus,[42] probably some time after February 438. The Huns stayed on horseback, which seems to have made quite an impression on the Romans who also felt it necessary to remain mounted.[43] It was agreed (*inter alia*) that the Romans should not ally themselves with any barbarian tribe that was waging war on the Huns; that there should be markets with equal rights for Romans and Huns; that the treaty should be maintained; and that the tribute should be doubled to 700 pounds of gold. The Romans handed back fugitives who had fled from the Huns, including two children of the royal house. In the blood-feud tradition of warrior groups, all were immediately impaled.[44] Attila and Bleda were then free to pursue and subdue other barbarian groups.

However, the treaty did not last because (according to the Huns) the Bishop of Margus came to their lands and searched out the tombs of their kings. He is said to have stolen the treasures which were 'stored there' – an ambiguous phrase that could mean either that the tombs were the sites of treasuries or that he was grave-robbing.[45] The Huns demanded that the bishop and other fugitives should be surrendered, and when this was refused, the Huns attacked a large number of cities in reprisal. Some Romans began to think the bishop should be surrendered, and seeing his danger, he offered to betray the city of Margus to the Huns. Accordingly, after shaking hands and swearing oaths (each side tended to swear by their own deities), he did just that.

Following more Hunnic attacks, a truce was arranged for 442 through the negotiating skills of Aspar the Alan, by this time an experienced general. Together with other Roman commanders, however, he seems to have been defeated by Attila in the following year. In 442 the Eastern Empire made peace with Gaiseric of the Vandals,[46] possibly because of Attila's activities. It seems possible that another treaty was made in 443, revising the Margus agreement. The empire was also concerned about the danger from the east, though in 444 there was a temporary respite from hostilities with Persia.

ATTILA IN SOLE POWER

In about 445 Attila had Bleda murdered, though no details about this exist. Since Bleda had ruled over the greater part of the Huns,[47] Attila's power-base was considerably strengthened. The new Hunnic leader was described as a lover of war, though personally restrained in action. He was impressive in counsel, gracious to those asking help and generous with those he trusted. He was snub-nosed, short, swarthy and broad-chested with a massive head, small eyes and a thin grey-sprinkled beard.[48] Few could argue with Jordanes' opinion that he was born to 'shake the peoples of the world'.[49] Few people, if any, have been the subject of more distortion and more legend.[50]

While he was undoubtedly the leader of some very aggressive and persistent groups, there seems little justification for hailing him as either a genius or a hero. His reputation in popular lore has been exaggerated to an unfounded degree, though he was certainly charismatic. The least that can be said is that he was born at the right time, in the right place and with the right personal attributes to achieve more than the average in an unusually spectacular manner.

In 447 he advanced on the Eastern Empire, laid waste the Balkans and pushed south into Greece.

The Siege of Naissus

One of Attila's conquests was the town of Naissus, where the Romans refused to come out to fight. Barbarian warfare had developed through the decades and the description by Priscus of the siege of Naissus[51] illustrates how sophisticated Hunnic warfare had become. The Huns bridged the river to enable them to bring their engines of war close to the circuit wall. These were simple wooden beams, mounted on wheels, on which men stood to shoot arrows at those on the battlements. The warriors on the beams were protected by willow branches interwoven with rawhide and leather screens. They also brought forward huge siege machines. Each consisted of a beam with a metal head that was suspended by loose chains from timbers inclined towards each other. Further screens were provided. Priscus describes the mechanics: using small ropes attached to a projection at the back, the men forcibly drew the beam backwards and then let it go so that it swung forwards to crush the wall in front. They were assailed by fire-darts and boulders 'the size of wagons', but to no avail. The wall was breached through the sheer number of rams and the Huns gained entry.

If the Huns were learning how to take towns, the Romans were also learning to be devious. The garrison in the fortress of Asemus, for example, not only refused to comply with Hunnic demands, but fought outside the defences, inflicting losses. They then pursued the retreating Huns, took them by surprise and seized their booty.[52]

Attila as Negotiator

Emperor Theodosius II sent messages inviting Attila to withdraw. A major series of negotiations took place and the Huns made peace on condition that they were given 6,000 pounds of gold in compensation for the previous unpaid tributes; a further 2,100 pounds of gold was to be paid annually.[53] In addition, either the fugitives were to be returned or twelve gold pieces paid for each. The Romans were not to receive any barbarian who fled from the Huns. Priscus (who accompanied a Roman embassy to Attila's stronghold during negotiations around this time – late 449/early 450) was very censorious about why the Romans could not afford the payment. He states that they had spent the money not on necessities but on 'disgusting spectacles' and dissolute feasts.[54] To pay the Huns, taxes were raised. As a result, men who had formerly been well-off put their furniture up for sale and even offered their wives' ornaments in the markets. Many either starved themselves to death or hanged themselves. It is probable, however, that Priscus exaggerated these stories, one way or another.

Negotiations began when two of Attila's aides, a Hun named Edeco and a Roman called Orestes, were sent to Constantinople with letters.[55] Through an interpreter, the Hun admired the riches of the capital and a corrupt court eunuch called Chrysaphius, who was influential with Theodosius II, told him he too could own a room with a gold ceiling – if he would work for the Romans. Edeco intimated that this would not be proper, but when it was discovered that he was one of Attila's bodyguard, the eunuch urbanely suggested that they must have leisure to discuss matters. A dinner party without Orestes and the other ambassadors was arranged. Oaths were exchanged and Edeco agreed not to reveal what was said to him, even if nothing came of it.

The secret dinner party attracted much speculation in the summer of 449 while the ambassadors were returning from Constantinople to Attila's camp in Wallachia. Priscus describes the journey almost hour by hour and the highly complex situation ended with Edeco telling all.[56] Apparently it had been suggested that he should murder Attila. He had asked for fifty pounds of gold to pay the men he needed, but refused to take it with him for fear of arousing suspicion. The account is sufficiently detailed to lead to speculation about what was really going on behind the scenes and whether Edeco had always intended to betray Chrysaphius rather than Attila.

The accounts of the embassy show Attila as a natural negotiator. His personal demeanour was unassuming, though he undoubtedly had presence: Jordanes is clear that, one way or another, his reputation frightened people even before they met him.[57]

The question of fugitives was a sensitive one, but one incident shows clearly that Attila was very much in control, probably using anger as a deliberate weapon. When he was told that no fugitives remained, he 'railed violently' at the messenger and said 'with a shout' that he would have had him impaled and fed to the birds *if such an action would not have been an outrage to the law of embassies.*

In this way, the threat was removed even as it was made. Attila then ordered his secretaries to read out the names of the fugitives from a piece of paper.

Negotiations took a dramatic turn in June 450 when a messenger arrived at Constantinople[58] announcing that Honoria (the 31-year-old sister of Valentinian III and daughter of Galla Placidia and Constantius) had begged Attila for help. She had been caught out in a love affair with the administrator of her estates. Her lover was put to death and, kept in close custody, she was unwillingly betrothed to a politically 'safe' man of consular rank, Herculanus. Honoria reacted by sending her eunuch Hyacinthus to Attila with promises of wealth in return for avenging her marriage. She is also said to have sent her ring pledging herself to the Hunnic leader in marriage.[59]

Attila's dilemma at this point has been much discussed. He has been made out to be everything from an inept bungler to a genius and/or a power-mad maniac. Honoria had no claim to the western throne, but marriage to her would certainly have increased the Hunnic leader's power-base. From her point of view, what had she to lose? Had not her mother married a Goth and did she not, even now, surround herself with Goths?[60] Honoria was also in the potentially intolerable position of many imperial women, constrained to chastity by court etiquette and kept in check by her brother.[61] Like Attila, Honoria has been the focus of modern and ancient vitriol on the grounds that she possibly wanted imperial power for herself. Theodosius II robustly told Valentinian to surrender her to the Hunnic leader but instead the hapless Hyacinthus was arrested, tortured and killed. Galla Placidia's constant pleas to be given her daughter, to save her from execution, were eventually successful.[62]

These unruly imperial domestic matters gave Attila huge opportunity. He insisted that he was betrothed to Honoria[63] and decided that the first step should be to capture Aëtius. However, Theodosius II died on 28 July 450 and his successor in the East, Marcian, was a military man of different mould. Later legend says he was at peace with the Vandals. If this were true, he would have had one less problem to worry about, which may partly account for why, on his accession, he refused to pay subsidies to the Huns.

The situation was now highly volatile. It is probable that the Vandals bribed Attila to move against the West.[64] Since 429 they had been established under King Gaiseric in North Africa, but in 450 they would certainly have wished to divert Visigothic attention away from them after an especially sordid and depressing marriage break-up involving a Visigothic 'princess'.[65] Whatever lay behind his decision, in 451 Attila invaded Gaul. He announced to the Romans that his objective was the Visigoths in Aquitania Secunda, while he separately urged the Visigoths to break their alliance with the Roman Empire. It was in connection with this that the comment quoted at the head of this chapter was made. Subtle

Attila may have been, but Valentinian III and his advisors were not taken in. The emperor sent an embassy to the Visigoths asking that they might 'join hands', reminding them that the Huns tended to use treachery to achieve their ends.[66]

THE BATTLE OF THE CATALAUNIAN PLAINS

In July 451 Visigoths and Romans united under Theodoric I of the Visigoths and Aëtius, whose forces notably included Franks, Sarmatians, Armoricans, Liticians, Burgundians, Saxons, Riparians, Olibriones and some other Celtic or German tribes.[67] The battleground was the Catalaunian Plains (also called the Mauriacian), a large level area of some 300 acres[68] which rose to a sharp ridge and was cut by a brook. It has been argued that it would have been too hot for maintaining a large number of horses since the best fodder would no longer be obtainable. Certainly the account does not mention cavalry.[69] Franks (on the Roman side) and Gepids (fighting for the Huns) seem to have wiped each other out the night before the main battle – there were thus 15,000 dead even before the start of the battle proper.

The battle, as recounted by Jordanes, was not straightforward. Aëtius and Theodoric discovered that their supposed ally, the leader of the Alans, intended to switch sides at the last minute, so they threw up earthworks and kept the Alans hemmed in by auxiliaries. Attila was dismayed and felt it advisable to retreat. He was persuaded to continue with the battle plans only when a soothsayer suggested that an enemy general would be killed. Attila optimistically interpreted this as Aëtius and decided that even if he lost the battle it would be worth the gain.

Theodoric took the right wing and Aëtius the left, with the potentially treacherous Alans in the centre where they had no choice but to fight. Since Attila and his Huns were in the centre of the opposing force, they had to fight the very men whom they had hoped would be on their side. Attila's warrior forces included Ostrogoths under three noble leaders[70] and Gepids. He was said to have valued Valamer of the Ostrogoths and Ardaric of the Gepids more than all his other subject kings.[71] The Hunnic leader's style of command was charismatic. All the forces waited for 'Attila's nod' as if they were slaves. There was no question but that 'he alone was the supreme king'. Aëtius and Theodoric won a huge strategic and psychological advantage by gaining the ridge first. Jordanes attributes a long and impressive speech to Attila at this point. Since the battle had been joined, there was no suggestion of withdrawing or trying to negotiate. It was, the Hunnic leader told his men, the right of nature to 'gorge the soul' with vengeance. He urged his troops to despise the alliance of 'discordant races' that they faced. He urged them to attack the Alans and beat the Visigoths. When sinews are severed, he pointed out with horrible logic, the limbs soon relax and a body cannot stand if its bones are taken away. Undoubtedly a reflection of his style of command was the last exhortation that he would hurl the first spear: anyone who failed to join in when Attila fought was dead.

During the battle itself, the brook was swollen with blood so the battlers had to quench the thirst caused by loss of blood with their own diluted gore. Theodoric of the Visigoths was thrown from his horse and trampled to death by his own forces. It seems that Attila's soothsayer had been correct – only the identification of the slain general was at fault.

Attila in Defeat

Attila escaped death only because he took refuge among his prearranged wagons, and Aëtius became temporarily lost among the enemy during the night. The next day the death toll was evaluated. If the ancient figures are to be believed,[72] 165,000 lives were lost (180,000 in total). The Huns thought they had won, but on finding this was not true, they behaved courageously. Attila was likened to a lion wounded by hunting spears but still able to terrify its attackers by its roars. He was reputed to have made a funeral pyre of saddles on to which he was prepared to leap rather than be taken prisoner. This was his single recorded defeat and his method of dealing with it is, arguably, all the more impressive.

The Visigoths finally found their slain leader, Theodoric, and carried him away singing songs in his honour. A warrior burial from Pouan has been tentatively (and almost certainly erroneously) identified as being his.[73] His son Thorismund, who was noted for his valour and impetuosity, wished to gain vengeance on the Huns, but took advice from Aëtius who, interestingly, counselled caution.[74] To Aëtius is attributed the thinking that, in the long term, the empire needed the Huns. In view of later events it is as likely that Aëtius himself needed them even more. Thorismund returned to his people and continued his father's rule from Toulouse.

Attila and Rome

One outcome of the battle was that Aëtius, although the nominal victor, was not in a position to repel the Huns a year later when Attila invaded Italy and sacked several cities including Aquileia and Mediolanum (Milan). When his troops were losing heart at Aquileia, Attila noticed that some storks were carrying their young from the roof-tops. He pointed this out, saying that the storks knew the city was about to fall to the Huns. Morale immediately rose and the Huns were successful.[75] The Huns caused much destruction at this point and Rome was clearly the next logical goal.

Unlike Alaric, Attila turned back, for reasons that have caused much speculation through the centuries. Could it have been superstition because Alaric had died so soon after entering the gates?[76] Pestilence and famine were rife and were indeed likely deterrents. Pope Leo I is said to have intervened[77] and may even have paid a subsidy to the Huns. There is a marked difference between the violence and destruction which occurred and the restraint with which negotiations seem to have been carried out.

THE DEATH OF ATTILA

In 453 Attila was planning a campaign against Marcian in the East when he suddenly died, in bed though not undramatically, after marrying the latest of his innumerable 'wives'. The circumstances can be seen as either suspicious (it was whispered at the time that he had died at the hands of the bride) or sordid (he had haemorrhaged after a bout of drinking and, had he not been asleep on his back, might have survived). The scene is graphically described by Priscus: the beautiful young Ildico was found next morning, alone and distressed, with the bloodied corpse.[78]

Priscus quotes Attila's funeral song which extolled his virtues as chief of the Huns, lord of the mightiest races. It emphasises that he alone, with power previously unknown, had held the 'Scythian' and 'Germanic' territories and terrified both Roman empires. Attila was honoured in song for capturing their cities and, as a result of their entreaties, accepting annual tribute from them to save further plundering.

THE TOMB OF ATTILA

Attila's tomb has not been identified, though the literary sources describe the burial in detail. The Huns bound his three coffins with gold, silver and iron respectively. The metals were symbolically suited to a great king: iron, because with it he subdued nations, and gold and silver because he received the homage of both empires. The mourners added the captured arms of his enemies and costly fittings that gleamed with various precious stones. The undertakers were then slaughtered to prevent pilfering.

AFTER ATTILA – THE BATTLE OF THE NEDAO

Jordanes relates that Attila left many sons who, as a result of his wide-ranging libido, were almost a tribe themselves. Their disagreements over how to share out the lands were resented by the subject peoples concerned, and came to the notice of Ardaric, King of the Gepids. The Gepids first appeared in history in the 260s, when in conjunction with the Goths they attacked Dacia. Only the north-west edges of the province remained available for Gepid settlement, and during the Hunnic invasions of the area they stayed put and were left alone. Under Ardaric, the Gepids allied with Attila, campaigned with him in the Balkans in 447 and died for him on the Catalaunian Plains in 451. Notwithstanding this former alliance, in conjunction with Sueves and others, Ardaric led a rebellion against Attila's sons,[79] defeating the Huns in 454/5 at the Nedao River in Pannonia (the exact location is unidentified).

The battle was unusual and reflected the specialist warfare techniques of the groups: Goths fought with pikes, Gepids with swords. The Sueves were on foot, the Huns used bows, the Alans drew up in formal battle-line, heavily armed. The Heruli were lightly armed and the Rugi were described as 'breaking off spears in their own wounds'.[80] Attila's eldest son Ellac was killed. Marcian recognized the Gepids as his allies and gave them annual tribute and the former lands of the Huns in Dacia.[81]

Aëtius lost power relatively fast at this time and was murdered by Valentinian III. Thereafter, the Huns were neither an important nor a unified force in European affairs, though they were present when the Roman general Belisarius launched a campaign against the Vandals in North Africa in 533 and later. Two Huns, Sigizan and Zolbon, for example, commanded Huns in the army of Anastasius during the Isaurian War.

HUNNIC FOLKTALES

Although no literary tradition about the Huns exists, Hunnic folktales can be traced across Europe into the Middle Ages when they were given various embellishments. One example, available in different versions, concerns a woman who is persuaded or forced to go away with a warrior. The couple rest under a shady tree, where the warrior asks to rest his head in her lap and, with singular lack of romantic charm, requests that she should look for lice. He tells her not to look up into the tree, and then falls asleep. Naturally, she looks up – and sees eleven hanged girls dangling from the branches. She screams. He wakes up and tells her she is destined to be the twelfth corpse but she is (usually) rescued at the last moment.

In Siberian tradition, the tree is described as having nine branches. A variation of the story is current in German, and an English version appears as 'Lady Isabel and the Elfin Knight'. The story is depicted in Scythian gold plaques of the third or second century BC (where the girl is depicted with a rope round her neck). A nine-branched tree appears in Scythian art.

A related story in Germanic tradition tells how a hero waited under a tree for two 'friends', who prove to be his enemies. This figures in the story of *Alpharts Tod*, when the hero Alphart, guard of the Gothic–Hunnic army, rests under a linden tree and is killed by the traitors Wittich and Heime. A scene showing a warrior being slain by two others appears on a gold nomad comb from Solokha on the Lower Dnieper. The story is known first in Central Asia, and spread westwards, and appears to be linked with the Hunnic custom of wearing two swords (the friends/enemies).[82]

Hunnic Horses

The Huns would have gained no prominence in history at all were it not for their ability to traverse great distances. For this, the horse was vital. Hunnic horses were small and reputedly ugly but tough.[83] The animals were marked either by branding, or by cutting the ears, a very ancient custom among the nomads.[84] It would appear that they were gelded. There is no evidence for the use of either stirrups or spurs.

The Huns used saddles with a wooden frame and pillows front and rear, a type found as far afield in time and space as Hsiung-nu graves at Noin Ula and Scythian graves at Pazyryk. In eastern Europe the saddles had a wooden tree with a straight vertical bow in front and a larger bow behind.[85]

Plaques decorated with repoussé scale patterns are characteristic of Hunnic burials, and it has been argued variously that originally they were attached to saddle bows, quivers or kitchen utensils. A Korean saddle roughly contemporary with the Huns has similar decoration, perhaps pointing to an origin in the Far East.[86] It has also been suggested that the pattern is derived from the feathers of the mythical *simurgh* or *varanga* used as a protective motif on late Sassanian weapons.[87]

While it is not in question that the Huns started out as horsemen, it has been seriously questioned whether they remained so when they moved into Europe since the area west of the Carpathians could not sustain large herds.[88] No mention of horses is made at this period in the Classical sources, and while Claudian repeated in summary form what Ammianus had written about horsemanship, it was not necessarily in the context of the events in the 390s (which he was discussing). Subsequent references to the Huns in the West make no mention of their use of horses, though Hunnic horsemen are documented in the East.[89] Significantly, Orosius states that in the time of Theodosius I, the Huns, Goths and Alans had acquired Roman horses.[90]

Boats

Huns appear to have crossed rivers on rafts (to take the wagons) and boats constructed from a single piece of wood (which seems to have been common practice among river folk). Once within the empire they, like the other barbarians, would have travelled fast along Roman roads.

The Culture and Lifestyle of the Huns

The lifestyle of the Huns changed very rapidly as they moved into Europe. They became accustomed to wealth through booty and tribute and were able to buy the advantages of civilisation. No identifiable remains of a Hunnic settlement have so far been found, but by 449 Attila was living in a semi-permanent or permanent base in Wallachia. Priscus describes this enclosure as having many beautiful houses. The standard of carpentry was exceptionally high, with beams so smoothly planed that the joins were invisible.[91] This suggests the employment of local craftsmen since there are no trees on the Steppes for the Huns to have gained experience in woodwork. The houses were built on timbers laid out in circles and were of moderate height. The floors were covered with mats of felted wool.

Priscus describes Attila's house as built with 'highly polished timbers and boards' and surrounded by a wooden palisade which very notably was not functional but beautiful – a mark of the Hunnic leader's power and strength. It was graced by towers. Attila's second-in-command, Onegesius, had a bath-house – one of the major symbols of Roman civilisation. Stone for its construction was imported from Pannonia. The bath builder was a captive from Sirmium who expected to be given his freedom in return for his ingenious work. Unfortunately for him, Onegesius instead made him the bath attendant.[92]

Although there is no record of Hunnic women taking part in war, they were not without influence. Women feature fairly prominently in graves and other archaeological remains and also in the literature. The embassy described by Priscus brought gifts for Attila's wife Kreka, and found women embroidering fine linens to be placed as ornament over their barbarian clothes. The clothing of both sexes appears to have been colourful. Clothes were sometimes decorated with beads, and occasionally fastened with distinctive bow-brooches with plate heads and elongated feet, which were produced in southern Russia. Some were plain and some jewelled, while others had relief ornament.

In another episode Priscus writes about a village that was ruled by a woman who had been one of Bleda's wives. She sent provisions – including attractive women – to the ambassadors. They accepted this Scythian compliment, but after the food had been laid out, they politely 'refused intercourse'. They repaid their hostess with gifts – three silver drinking bowls, red skins, pepper from India, dates and other sweetmeats. Luxury food by this time was obtainable from the Romans, through Priscus notes that the Huns drank mead rather than wine and consumed millet instead of wheat.

It is clear from the archaeological evidence of graves and the written sources that there was a hierarchy and some ceremonial within Hunnic life. When Attila arrived at his village,[93] he was met by maidens with white linen trains under which walked seven or more girls. Onegesius' wife came out of her home and offered him food and wine, though he did not dismount when he tasted it. A description of a banquet at which Roman ambassadors (including Priscus himself) were present has been preserved in graphic detail.[94] There was a definite order in which drink could be taken, and Attila's eldest son Ellac sat apart from his father with his eyes respectfully downcast. Ernach, another son, was treated with a show of affection that clearly surprised Priscus. Attila was offered a wooden cup of wine and was remarkable for eating only meat on a wooden plate while the rest of the company ate a wider variety of delicacies from silver platters. Attila's dress, too, was plain and he was concerned only with cleanliness. Unlike those of his followers, his sword was not embellished with gems and gold. Part of his success – and certainly a mark of his real power – must surely have been that he lavished status symbols on his supporters.

On this occasion, when evening came the pine torches were lit and two barbarians sang their own composition about Attila's victories and his virtues in war. Reactions varied: some were 'excited in their souls', but others wept. After this emotive scene, the mood changed with the entrance of Zercon, a quirky stand-up comic who had been acquired by Bleda from Aspar the Alan.[95]

A Moor by origin, he put his natural lisp to good use in misusing the Hunnic, Gothic and Latin languages to amusing effect. Short and hump-shouldered, with distorted feet, he was a source of unquenchable laughter at the banquet and has therefore been afforded inordinate publicity by accident of history. It seems that his Hunnic master thought him very funny. When the comedian ran away and was recaptured, Bleda gave him a wife, since he asserted his lack of a mate was the reason for his dissatisfaction.

Attila was clearly not amused by the man at the banquet and, later, once Bleda was dead, he sent Zercon to Aëtius who restored him to his original master.

Chapter 3

The Ostrogoths

He did not rest until he had killed some in battle and brought the rest under his control ...

Jordanes, describing the warrior-leader Ermaneric.¹

In around 350 the Greutungi lived between the Rivers Dniester and Don in the south-west Russian Steppe of the Ukraine, north of the Sea of Azov.² They were primarily farmers who lived in prosperous settlements scattered throughout the lands of the nomads they had conquered.³ Their sphere of influence probably extended from the Black Sea to the Baltic and they were beginning to exercise some control over the Slavs to their north. Their immediate neighbours were the Alans and the Tervingi whose frontier lay west of the Dniester. This chapter outlines the defeat of the Greutungi by the Huns, the rise of Theodoric the Great and the change from Ostrogothic warrior-society into a settled state.

ERMANERIC

The Greutungi first come to prominence in the literature under their ruler Ermaneric – a warlike leader who was feared by his neighbours because of his personal determination.⁴ Jordanes goes further and says that some people had likened him to Alexander the Great.⁵ According to the same source, Ermaneric ruled people of both Scythia and Germania by his own valour alone.⁶ The people under his influence included the Maeotic Heruli at the mouth of the Don, the Antae and Sclaveni and maybe the Aesti along the Baltic Sea. Finns,

Slavs and Huns are also mentioned as being under his control, though current opinion favours the view that the Goths at this time consisted of a number of independent political units, only one of which was ruled over by Ermaneric.[7] The methods used to regulate what may have been many thousands of square miles are obscure. Since the Greutungi and their followers had no organised armies but engaged in skirmishes with rival war-bands, it is probable that Ermaneric had conquered his subject peoples and protectorates piecemeal. If his 'empire' were indeed so huge, he must have been encroaching on the Huns' and Alans' traditional hunting grounds. Greutungi riches would have been a magnet to any nomadic booty-hungry neighbours. The settled farming existence of the Greutungi, which sustained both crops and cattle, would not have been compatible with the traditional skills of the nomadic Huns, so conflict was inevitable.[8]

Ermaneric's régime was defeated by the Huns in the late fourth century, the events being surrounded by mystery that lies deep in warrior-band traditions of blood-feuds and vengeance. The veracity of the material has consequently been questioned by historians.[9] According to Jordanes the 'treacherous' tribe of the Rosomonni owed Ermaneric homage, so he ordered that Sunilda – the wife of a traitor who had escaped him – should be bound to wild horses and torn apart. In revenge, her brothers wounded him and reduced him to a 'miserable existence' through physical infirmity.[10] This left his territories vulnerable to attack from the Huns, in conjunction with their recently acquired subjects, the Alans. Ermaneric may have died (in 375) of his wounds, exacerbated by despair,[11] or honourably committed suicide[12] at his inability to repel his enemies. His age may have played a part – he was reputed to be aged 110, though the exact figure was probably Biblically inspired.

Ermaneric's successor, Vithimiris, died in battle, despite the fact that he had engaged some Huns to fight on his side.[13] The majority of the Greutungi and their subordinates surrendered. The two cavalry leaders, Saphrax and Alatheus, took charge of affairs on behalf of the young Viderichus,[14] the son of Vithimiris. They are termed *duces*, which implies that they were not of Amali blood (the Amals were a charismatic ruling family[15]). The Greutungi gradually retreated from the Hunnic front, first to the Dniester and in 376 found their way to the banks of the Danube. It may be deduced that Saphrax and Alatheus were involved in the dramatic river-front escape of 376 before playing a decisive part in the battle of Adrianople.

The various groups, usually termed Ostrogoths by this time, were among others who crossed the Rhine under Radagaisus in 405. Orosius quotes the numbers of Goths in this migration as 200,000,[16] while Zosimus says Radagaisus was collecting 400,000 Celts and Germans from beyond the

Danube and the Rhine.[17] They swept into Italy and besieged Florence, which was relieved by Stilicho.

Radagaisus was widely reputed to have vowed the blood of the Romans as an offering to his gods. St Augustine says he made human sacrifices to ensure his success against the Romans. When Radagaisus' forces threatened even Rome, widespread panic resulted. It was suggested that the danger was caused by Rome having given up her traditional pagan gods in favour of Christianity.[18] According to Orosius (who as a Christian had an axe to grind and must therefore be viewed with circumspection) Radagaisus was less interested in glory and booty than sheer love of cruelty, because he was a pagan. Apparently he loved killing for its own sake.[19] He was, in short, made of the kind of stuff on which Gothic infamy is based.

THE DEFEAT AT FIESOLE

The Roman forces trapped Radagaisus and his force on a ridge near Fiesole, encircling the much larger force with some 15,000 men. The Romans were so well supplied with food and drink that they were able to 'carouse', but they cut off Radagaisus' supplies so that the Goths became exhausted, thirsty, starving and afraid. As a result, according to Orosius, the victory was bloodless. Twelve thousand Gothic troops were recruited into the Roman army.

Those taken prisoner were sold at random into slavery, a factor that caused a glut on the slave market. Prices fell as low as one aureus per person[20] regardless of skills or age. The going rate in the second century (which had by this time halved, however) had been 20 for an unskilled adult and 50 for a trained clerk, with children commanding an aureus for every year of their ages up to 10.[21] Orosius takes Christian satisfaction in relating that since the slaves died from malnutrition and exhaustion, their burials cost their greedy, unprincipled owners the money initially saved on their purchase.

Radagaisus lacked Attila's panache and courage when facing defeat. He deserted his men but was later caught and executed.

THE OSTROGOTHS AFTER ATTILA

By the mid-fifth century relationships between some of the Ostrogoths and the Huns had improved, though Ostrogothic involvement in the defeat of the Huns at the battle of Nedao (after Attila's death) is obscure. They must have come to an agreement with the empire whereby they were settled in Pannonia.[22] There they were ruled by three Amal brothers, Valamer, Thiudimer and Vidimir, until one year their annual payment from Constantinople did not arrive. They sent enquiries to the Eastern Emperor and found that another Goth (Theodoric Strabo, son of Triarius)[23] was receiving an annual bounty.

The Amal-led Goths therefore began to make raids on Illyricum, and the Emperor, Leo I, rapidly sued for peace, sending gifts. By the terms of the peace treaty it was agreed that Thiudimer's seven-year-old son Theodoric be sent to Constantinople as a hostage in 461–2, despite his father's misgivings. It seems that Theodoric was a good child who gained imperial favour.[24] He was born at about the time Attila died, and his family tree included Ermaneric. He was certainly blessed by the Amal mystique – even the timing of his birth was seen as important since it coincided with news of a victorious (but difficult to identify) battle.

Warrior Skirmishes

While the little boy was wrestling with his lessons in the Imperial City,[25] the peace between Ostrogoths and Constantinople brought financial security and freed his father and brothers to engage in their traditional, warrior-based activities. The ten years which followed the peace treaty are described in some detail by Jordanes.[26] The incidents might have come from any history of any barbarian people, including the Celts, and the Vikings much later in time. Whether they represent exact historical truth or not is of less importance than the fact that the barbarians chose to preserve and relate them in detail.

Thiudimir and his brothers had begun by plundering their neighbours, the Sadagis. This gave Dengizich, one of Attila's sons, the opportunity to attack the Pannonian city of Bassiania, taking with him warriors from the Ultzinzures, the Angisciri, the Bittugures and the Bardores. The Goths under Thiudimir immediately abandoned the Sadagis and successfully turned on the Huns.

In about 465, when the chief of the Sueves, Hunimundus, was on his way to plunder Dalmatia, he picked up some stray Gothic cattle. As he was returning, 'having devastated Dalmatia', Thiudimir and his men attacked the sleeping Sueves and took captive and sent into slavery all survivors. Having made his point, Thiudimir pardoned them and adopted the king as his own son. This ingenuous attempt at peace negotiations was not a success. The Sueves did not swallow their pride, but instead plotted with the Sciri. The Goths were, it seems, surprised when their 'friendship' ended with an attack. In the ensuing battle Valamer, the senior Amal leader, was killed by spears when his horse fell. The leadership fell to Theodoric's father Thiudimir. The Goths took revenge by nearly annihilating the Sciri. Hostilities escalated as the Sueves called upon the Sarmatians, the remnants of the Sciri and the Gepids. At the River Bollia in Pannonia the battlefield was like a 'crimson sea'. Weapons and dead bodies were piled up like hills, and the plain was covered for more than 10 miles.[27]

The Danube subsequently froze over. At the time the Sueves were allies of the Alamanni, whose Alpine lands lay where several streams poured into the Danube with a huge 'gushing sound'. Despite the harsh conditions, Thiudimir 'conquered, plundered, and almost subdued' the Alamanni and the Sueves.

THEODORIC — A WARRIOR LEADER AT EIGHTEEN

In 471 Leo sent Theodoric home to his father with gifts. His father's victories over the neighbouring tribal groups could only have been a challenge to the eighteen-year-old. North of the Danube King Babai of the Sarmatians was living 'with insolent pride', having recently defeated a Roman force. Without his father's knowledge, Theodoric raised a force of almost 6,000 friends and followers.[28] Babai was killed and Theodoric returned with slaves and treasures. This clearly whetted his appetite and Jordanes catalogues the subsequent plunderous exploits of Theodoric, his father and his surviving uncle in Italy and Illyricum.[29]

The arguments for choosing raiding over agriculture as a way of life make only short-term economic sense, however. The Goths ran out of collateral and soon lacked food and clothes.[30] When his father died (c. 474), Theodoric was his sole heir. Additionally, within a year the Emperor Zeno came to power. He received Theodoric with honour and at some point adopted him as a son.[31] Notwithstanding this, within the year Theodoric led his people into Lower Moesia and his militaristic activities began to cause real concern in Constantinople. His relationships with Theodoric Strabo and with Zeno were complex.[32] Many battles and much bad feeling resulted in considerable devastation. Even making the young Amal Consul in 484 and giving the Ostrogoths lands in Moesia and Dacia was not successful – he continued to ravage imperial lands and threatened Constantinople itself in 486 by cutting one of its aqueducts.

The emperor eventually found a solution to Theodoric's behaviour by inviting him to deal with the long-standing and immensely complicated problems in Italy, which had been out of the control of the Eastern Emperors since the sack of Rome.

Italy since the Sack of Rome

Orestes (Attila's former secretary and by this time Master of the Soldiers) had driven the Western Emperor[33] out of Italy and elevated his own son Romulus Augustulus on 31 October 475. Although this child has been remembered in history as the last Western Emperor, he was never recognised by Constantinople and was, in effect, a usurper. He also had a rival. Attila's other aide, the Hun Edeco and his (probably) Scyric wife had produced a son, Odoacer. A man named Odoacer was in Gaul with a band of Saxons sometime after 463 and by the time young Romulus was made emperor in 475, the troops were dissatisfied with the arrangements made for their support, and contingents of Scyri, Heruli and Rugii chose this man as their leader. Whether the two Odoacers are one and the same is a question that remains unresolved.[34] Within a year, Romulus was deposed and the Western Empire came to an end. Orestes was captured and executed by Odoacer and his troops[35] 28 August 476. Due to his youth and beauty, the former emperor was allowed 6,000 gold solidi and a Campanian estate.

Odoacer's constitutional position has been much discussed[36] and his thirteen-year rule included considerable oppression of the local people. He assumed the new title 'Rex nationum' ('king of the nations') rather than the Roman title 'Imperator'.[37]

Hostilities between Odoacer and Theodoric

Faced with this situation, in 488 Emperor Zeno offered Theodoric a military title and the Goth arrived in Italy in late August 489; his followers were said to include a total population of 300,000 from the Balkans, desirous of settling down. Odoacer was defeated three times in pitched battle. After a defeat on the River Adda in 490 he fled to Ravenna, from which vantage point he frequently made punishing night-time sorties.[38] Most of Italy was won but the Senate in Rome declared Theodoric merely vice-regent.

Odoacer survived under siege in Ravenna for a further three years while pockets of his followers were suppressed. Eventually negotiations reached sufficient accord for him to allow Theodoric into the city, on 5 March 493. At a feast ten days later it was agreed that the two men should rule jointly. The culmination was the presentation of a formal petition to Odoacer. Two of Theodoric's men knelt before Odoacer and clasped his hands as supplicants. There was a dramatic pause. Then, as his men hesitated, Theodoric seized a sword. Such was his strength and his victim's frailty that his blow split the sixty-year-old man from collar-bone to hip. He allegedly told him 'this is what you did to my friends'.[39]

This action has been seen as totally out of character for Theodoric, though if Odoacer were a Hun, it is possible to see it as the result of long resentment against those who had made his people homeless for decades. However, it was not the act of a ruler secure in his victory and Odoacer's fate might be contrasted with those of Romulus Augustulus and Attalus.

Theodoric's action was clearly not done in the heat of the moment, nor did he regret it, because he went on to kill Odoacer's brother, son and followers wherever they could be found. He even had his widow killed in prison.[40] This was totally in line with the blood-feud traditions of the warrior society from which he came, but the incident creates unease in the modern reader. The formal ceremony and the treacherously planned execution hardly fit in with the heroic ideals of a warrior leader.

Ostrogothic Italy – Two Differing Lifestyles[41]

Once he achieved total power, Theodoric was faced with creating a workable political framework for two groups of people whose lifestyles had virtually nothing in common. Indeed, they held conflicting ideals. Even Gothic Christianity was Arian derived, and the Romans in Italy were Catholic. The new king achieved surprising success by rigid segregationalism – the exact opposite of the empire's former policy of integration under *Romania*. For thirty years after Theodoric's accession the Ostrogoths maintained a strong presence in Dalmatia and Pannonia and ruled northern and central Italy. He earned his epithet 'the Great' partly for sheer convenience (to distinguish him from the many others of that name) and partly, too, because the Goths prospered, living harmoniously on the income from the long-established Roman estates. Under Orestes, Romulus Augustulus and Odoacer a third share in all the estates in Italy had been allocated to the barbarians – this third was now confiscated and redistributed among Theodoric's men.

They may have lived on Roman estates, but the traditional gift-giving habits died hard – local Ostrogothic warriors went annually to wherever the king happened to be (usually Ravenna), to receive money. Theodoric ruled Italy as king of his own people and with a high military title (Master of the Soldiers) from the Eastern Empire. He was emphatically not the Western Emperor even though he dressed in the Purple, which was traditionally an entitlement only of the imperial house (other barbarian rulers tended to wear skins and furs). He made up for his inability to write by using a gold stencil to sign documents.

The importance of kinship, which had driven his ancestors, was now deliberately employed in establishing links with the neighbouring kingdoms. At his request Theodoric married Audefleda, daughter of the Frankish King Lodoin. Theodoric's two daughters by a concubine from his days in Moesia were given in marriage to the Visigothic King Alaric II and Sigismund, king of the Burgundians. For Amalasuintha (his daughter by Audefleda), he found a young Amal, Eutheric, who was wise, brave and healthy and lived conveniently in Spain.[42] Theodoric's sister Amalafreda was given to King Thrasamund of the Vandals in Africa and her daughter, Amalaberga, Theodoric's niece, was given to King Herminifridus of the Thuringians.[43]

Theodoric's achievements ended with the suspicion of treachery. Suspecting Zeno of plotting against him, he attacked the Roman leaders who had previously supported him. Three senators, Boethius, Albinus and Symmachus, were tried and condemned to death in 524–5. Pope John I was arrested and died in prison in 526. Before his death on 30 August 526, Theodoric deeply regretted these actions. His body was placed in a porphyry sarcophagus in a stone interpretation of the brick-built mausolea then current in Ravenna. The roof was a single slab of stone weighing 470 tons. In the tradition of Roman mausolea, the lower portion was ten-sided and the upper was circular. The ponderous roof had loops, with the names of the apostles on them, possibly designed to carry their statues, and between the first and second storeys there was a gallery.

A sixth-century writer quoted Theodoric as asserting that the Roman who imitated the Goth was without worth, though the Goth who imitated the Roman was 'valuable'. This is probably apocryphal but it none the less emphasises the admiration Theodoric displayed for all things Roman.[44]

THE GOTHS IN ITALY AFTER THEODORIC

Theodoric's grandson Athalaric was perhaps ten or twelve years old at his grandfather's death in 526. Since his father was also dead, his mother Amalasuintha acted as his regent. An educated woman, she promised to take all the Ostrogothic treasure to Byzantium (formerly Constantinople) if anything went wrong in Italy. She summoned her cousin Theodahad from Tuscany to help her but the relationship was not a success – he is said to have hired people to strangle her in her bath.[45] Athalaric died in 534.

BELISARIUS AND THE END OF OSTROGOTHIC ITALY

Theodahad certainly did not agree with Theodoric's Romanophile views – he was a Gothic 'nationalist'. There were now several excuses for the emperor in Byzantium to regain control of Italy. Justinian (527–565) sent his formidably capable general Belisarius on the mission. Belisarius had recently defeated the Vandal kingdom in North Africa: his arms were 'still dripping' with Vandal blood.[46] Eventually the Ostrogoths were subjected to Byzantine rule and ceased to be an important historical force.

Chapter 4

The Vandals

[The Vandals] were no good with javelin or bow, nor did they know how to fight on foot ... and their horses, upset by the sight of the camels, totally refused to be urged against the enemy.
    Procopius describing a Vandal defeat by the Moors in North Africa.[1]

As ideal warrior groups, the Vandals simply do not come up to scratch. Although their reputation for destruction outstrips that of any other barbarian group, they did not like fighting. There are problems in assessing them since the sources are rarely unemotional.[2] Churchmen were quick to catalogue Vandal sins, though Salvian (a fifth-century Gallic cleric) approvingly compared their chaste Christian views with the immorality of the Romans, and their reasonable treatment of the working population with the oppressive imperial tax collection policies. Overall, the small amount of archaeological and historical evidence points to a relatively peaceful enjoyment of the lands in which the Vandals settled – first Spain, then North Africa – interspersed with scandals and the most appalling atrocities.

Unlike the Franks and Visigoths (who generally honoured federate treaties) and the Ostrogoths (who paid at least nominal homage to the emperor), after the fall of Carthage in 439 the Vandals ruled a quasi-independent state in Africa.[3] No figure of the stature of Alaric or Attila emerges in the literature, though Gaiseric is described as a great warrior and a statesman. This chapter outlines their journey through Europe into Spain from where, after twenty-five years, they left for North Africa. They ceased to exist as a separate entity in the early sixth century after a campaign by Belisarius.

From the Rhine to Spain

Little is known of early Vandal development. Jordanes says they were subdued by the Goths.[4] The Emperor Aurelian was victorious over the Vandals and the peace treaty included the provision of 2,000 horsemen for federate service in the army. There is evidence that they served in Egypt. A Vandal ruler called Godigisel was killed in battle against the Franks shortly before the Vandals, Alans, Sueves and others crossed the Rhine on 31 December 406.

Stilicho is probably the most widely known Vandal (see Chapter One), but it is not known whether he was behind the migration or whether the Vandals calculated that with him in power they had a chance of success. It is also possible that neither of these explanations is accurate. Certainly Stilicho was looking for recruits at the time. But certainly, too, after the sack of Rome by Alaric and the Visigoths in 410, the Romans were in a mood to blame him for everything and anything, so the word Vandal would have seemed far bleaker than Goth.

In 406 leadership was assumed by Godigisel's legitimate son Gunderic, together with his illegitimate son by a slave, Gaiseric. The Vandal experience was very different from that of the Goths under Theodoric the Great. For one thing, neither leader had spent his childhood in Constantinople nor had either met the emperor. Gunderic is described by Procopius as still a child in *c.* 428, which may also account for the unhappy history of the Vandals during his reign.[5] In the space of three years the Vandals, Sueves[6] and Alans arrived at the Pyrenees. Their progress through Europe was coloured by the confusion which accompanied the rise of the upsurper Constantine III. As he advanced from the Channel to Arles, via Trier and Lyons, he effectively prevented the Vandals from withdrawing northwards. Illegal private armies were raised in Spain by some of Honorius' relations to prevent the barbarians from moving through the Pyrenean passes. Constantine III saw this as a challenge and destroyed them, enabling the Vandals to gain access to the Iberian peninsula.[7]

Spain had never been very close to Roman or Greek hearts despite its mineral wealth. It was difficult to reach, with three sides bounded by water and the fourth by the Pyrenees. Its wilder, mountainous areas had always harboured brigands. The following twenty years are a true Dark Age in Spain, for the invaders were non-literate and the former Roman domains attracted almost no surviving written interest. A few letters to and from the popes are all that remain, except for a slim work by Bishop Hydatius (*c.* 427–*c.* 470) who was an eye-witness.[8]

Apparently the Vandals, Sueves and Alans divided the land between themselves.[9] By tradition this was done by casting lots, though Gregory of Tours suggests that on at least one occasion the matter was settled by the use of champions to save full-scale battle. There does not seem to have been any suggestion of federate or any other status conferred by Rome. The Alans took Lusitania and Carthaginiensis, the Asding Vandals took Galicia and the Silings were left Baetica. The Sueves took land in the extreme east, near the sea.[10] The Vandals and Alans eventually (though not without bloodshed) merged as one people under Gunderic in 418, ruled from Galicia.[11] The mechanics of this are shadowy, though the native population was said to be enslaved.[12]

The stories which survive from this period are not happy, showing clearly that here was warrior society at its most distorted. The age-old ties to their kin and to their traditional lands beyond the Rhine had been swept away. The local citizens did not welcome them with gifts or annual payments, as the emperors had done to so many others in different circumstances. The main sources of booty were the towns – and the townsfolk stayed put and preferred living in the most appalling conditions to futile fighting without access to arms or military skill.

One source relates how, when the Vandals went into Spain, the Romans fled to their walled cities where a famine then reduced them to cannibalism. One woman ate all four of her offspring, each time excusing the action as being for the good of those remaining. When the last one had been consumed, the townspeople stoned her to death.[13]

Relations between the Visigoths and Vandals were bad. In 414, when Athaulf, Galla Placidia and the Visigoths were forced into Spain and cut off from supplies by Constantius, the Siling Vandals exploited the Goths over grain. They called them 'trulli' because when they were desperately hungry they bought grain at one solidus per *trulla* (Latin: scoop).[14] The vendors were demanding 48 solidi per modius instead of selling 40 modii per solidus (the price fixed for parts of North Africa by Valentinian III in 445). After Athaulf's death in the summer of 415, the Romans sent the Visigoths under King Wallia against the Siling Vandals who were totally annihilated. The Asdings moved south. In 418 Constantius recalled the Visigoths and settled them in Aquitania Secunda, leaving the Vandals free to pursue their own policies. Accordingly, in 419 Gunderic made war on the Sueves,[15] but eventually this fierce group was left in almost total isolation in Galicia until 585. Raids, battles and destroyed cities are listed, but with few or no details.[16]

In 426 the Vandals raided Mauretania and the Balearics and in 428 captured the port of Cartagena. They were a short but hazardous sea journey from the rich North African provinces.

The African Provinces

The climate in North Africa during the Roman period was cooler than it is today and the area was a highly desirable place to live. The northern coastal strip sustained vast grain fields and olive groves for oil, the control of which was of economic importance to the empire as a whole. Horses were bred in the numerous rich villas. Splendid towns, dating back to the third century BC when Carthage was a major power, controlled the administration and cultural life. The Emperor Septimius Severus had been a native of Lepcis Magna and the area had been settled and developed long before the Roman victories in the Punic wars. The present-day ruins of Hippo Regius, Sabratha, Lepcis Magna and many others illustrate the elegance and sophistication of life in these provinces. The huge mansions were adorned with intricate mosaics, wall paintings, statuary and all the usual luxuries of Roman life.

The area was divided into a number of provinces including Numidia, Africa Proconsularis, Tripolitania and Mauretania. In the east it was bounded by Egypt (which came under Roman rule in the first century BC, ending the reign of Cleopatra), and in the west by the Atlantic. Along the 3,000 miles to the south, the frontier was roughly demarcated by a series of forts (with no physical barrier) which nevertheless controlled the movements of Berbers, Garamantes and other Saharan and mountain nomadic tribes. Unlike the Rhine/Danube and the British frontiers, this was a sparsely populated area where the troops had experienced relatively little trouble for centuries. The northern boundary was the Mediterranean seaboard, an easy journey from Italy, Sicily or Sardinia for good seafarers. At Gibraltar the crossing is between 8 and 36 miles wide, but the prevailing winds are east and west. Water flows on the surface to the east but at a deeper level to the west. This deceptively easy crossing also had the disadvantage of being furthest from the most urbanised, agricultural and wealthy areas of Roman North Africa.

A major difference between Africa and other provinces was that here was a hotbed of Christian controversy. The churches were commensurately embellished with major treasures.

Bonifacius

In 428 the military commander of Africa was Bonifacius. Sent there by Galla Placidia, he was said to have left Africa free of many barbarians (he certainly had successes against the Moorish tribes in 417).[17] Probably a native of Thrace, he married a Visigoth. Bonifacius is described as heroic (as was Sarus),[18] in the sense of the Greek heroes such as Jason or Hercules. He frequently beat the barbarians, using sometimes a few men, at others many, and occasionally fighting alone. Olympiodorus tells a swashbuckling story about a peasant who complained that his 'young and pretty wife' was having an affair with a barbarian. Bonifacius slipped out in the night, discovered the two in the fields 70 stades away (about 10 miles), and next day presented the lover's severed head to the astonished husband.

In 429, when Galla Placidia was regent for Valentinian III, Bonifacius' rival Aëtius was very powerful. It is possible that Bonifacius needed all the help he could get, and that he did, as was alleged, invite the Vandals from Spain into Africa.[19] Gunderic, with Gaiseric, prepared a huge fleet. There is no evidence of how they gained experience with boats, but the journey does not seem to have caused problems. In the same year the Vandals took Seville,[20] where Hydatius tells us that the king attempted to take the church but was 'possessed of a devil' and died.

Gaiseric

Gaiseric, who was said to be the cleverest of all men and well trained in warfare (428–77), succeeded his brother, though not without the suspicion of fratricide.[21] Hydatius suggests that he may have converted to Arianism; certainly he was anti-Catholic. Jordanes describes him as of medium height, lame from a riding accident, hating luxury but greedy for gain, and shrewd in winning over the barbarians and creating dissension. He is universally agreed to have been a good statesman, but unfortunately the atrocities committed in his reign remain a hurdle to an unbiased view of his life and times. He made good his power-base by throwing his dead brother's wife, tied to heavy stones, into the river near the town of Cirta. He then killed her children.[22]

The exact number of Gaiseric's followers who moved into Africa has been much debated. Both Procopius and the fifth-century cleric Victor of Vita state that Gaiseric crossed from Spain to Africa with 80,000 followers. Because the same figure occurs in two sources, it has often been assumed to be correct, despite the fact that Procopius claimed that this figure comprised only able-bodied warriors, while Victor said it comprised everyone, including new-born babes and old men,[23] though he also points out that Gaiseric had commissioned the count specifically to create fear. Once in Africa, Gaiseric gave his men the title *chiliarchs* (commanders of a thousand) and appointed eighty of them – possibly to increase the impression of a greater force than he actually had.[24] The Vandal fighting force may have been as low as 20,000. It was still too great to withstand any resistance from the inhabitants of Roman Africa.

In 429 the Vandals and Alans crossed the Mediterranean at its narrowest point.[25] The relationship with the local landowners has been debated. It is arguable that they welcomed the Vandals because of trouble with local tribes, though Victor is categorical that it soon went wrong: old men were killed, babies snatched from their mothers' breasts and dashed to the ground.[26] The Vandals moved aggressively eastwards. In the spring of 430 Bonifacius was defeated and forced to withdraw to Hippo Regius where he was surrounded. During this siege, St Augustine (author of some 230 books on theological matters) died. The situation was totally unlike that encountered so often by the Goths a mere sixty years earlier in the Balkans – supplies for the besiegers were easy because the North African estates were rich and relatively unprotected.[27]

At about this time, Gaiseric is said to have made a useful ally.[28] Watching his prisoners from an upper window as they suffered from the sun in a courtyard, he saw that, as midday arrived, an eagle hovered over one sleeping man to create shade. Gaiseric investigated and discovered that the man was Marcian, an advisor to Aspar the Alan. Gaiseric argued that, as Aspar's '*domesticus*', Marcian was clearly on the path to royal power and that the eagle would never have wasted its time over a potential emperor who was fated to be killed. Gaiseric therefore spared Marcian's life and gave him his freedom after he swore never to take up arms against the Vandals.

In 431 the Eastern Empire sent an expedition commanded by Aspar who, with Bonifacius, was defeated. Aspar established friendly contact with Gaiseric before withdrawing. (Bonifacius was eventually recalled to Italy and was mortally wounded in battle against Aëtius.)

The Vandals focused their attentions on the rich churches. By 433 only three minor churches – at Hippo Regius, Carthage and Cirta – remained intact.

Further action against the Vandals was prevented when the Huns threatened the Balkans in 434, and an agreement was made in 435, which allotted the former Roman provinces of Numidia and Mauretania Sitifensis to the Vandals as federates.

It was not enough. Within a few years Gaiseric had broken the treaty and invaded the rich province of Proconsular Africa.

The Capture of Carthage

Gaiseric took Carthage on 19 October 439.[29] Many Vandals married and settled down near Carthage, Cherchel and Tipasa. The title of the Vandal rulers was *Rex Wandalorum et Alanorum* (King of the Vandals and the Alans), illustrating the closeness of the two peoples. Carthage was an especially rich town. It had many adjuncts of civilised Roman life, including splendid plazas, public buildings and baths. There were schools of the liberal arts and languages, centres of philosophy and many administrative offices. Salvian was scathing about the immoral ways of the Romans, seeing the town before the Vandals as the 'jewel of sin', and the Romans' misfortune as a result of their own 'vicious lives'.[30] Even as the barbarians were attacking (he wrote) the townspeople were at the theatre, at the circus or fornicating. Men were effeminate; prostitution was rife. Once the town had fallen, the Vandals imposed strict Arian-based Christian laws – prostitution was banned and all former prostitutes were to marry.

Nearby lay a particularly important acquisition for the Vandals – the shipyards for the Roman fleet. Within the year Gaiseric had crossed the Mediterranean and sacked Sicily.[31] From this vantage point he was clearly a threat to Italy itself.

The Vandals were bought off by treaty, but a large fleet sent in reprisal from Constantinople in 441 failed to make the crossing from Sicily. In 442 a similar situation occurred when Hunnic attacks elsewhere helped to turn back another imperial expedition against the Vandals. A further treaty established the Vandals in the richest areas – Africa Proconsularis, Byzacena and eastern Numidia – leaving the Romans only Mauretania, western Numidia and Tripolitania. It may be this treaty which Procopius regarded as sensible because of its moderation.[32]

The Vandals were not united and a conspiracy against Gaiseric ended in his putting to death a large number.

Relations between the Visigoths and the Vandals

Gaiseric claimed allegiance to the Visigoths by marrying his son Huniric to a daughter (her name is unknown) of Theodoric I (418–51). The exact timing of this event and what followed is obscure, but the relationship clearly went wrong since Huniric is described as being cruel to their children. Politics are likely to have been a factor since, once he was free of his marital ties, Huniric was betrothed to Eudocia, daughter of Valentinian III. (It is possible that he was a hostage to cement the treaty of 442, in which case the betrothal may have taken place then.)

Valentinian made no wedding preparations, possibly because of the method Gaiseric had chosen to free Huniric from the ties of his first marriage. On the 'mere suspicion' that she was poisoning her husband, Gaiseric had her nose cut off and her ears clipped, and then returned her to her father.[33] This action appears to have had far-reaching effects in Europe as a whole. Gaiseric may well have sent gifts to Attila, encouraging him to attack the Visigoths[34] to divert any acts of vengeance – certainly it happened around the time that Valentinian's sister Honoria made overtures to Attila and the Hunnic leader turned his attention towards the west.

The Murder of Aëtius

Imperial dynastic matters impinged on Vandal history at about this time. Procopius relates a story which has a certain credibility, but which has been hotly debated.[35] It seems that a certain Petronius Maximus had a lovely wife, 'discreet in her ways', to whom Valentinian III was attracted. The emperor summoned Maximus to the palace, won a game of draughts and received Maximus' ring as a pledge for the money owing. Valentinian then sent the ring to Maximus' wife with the message that the Empress Eudoxia wished to see her. Naturally, the lady hurried to the palace and was surprised to find herself ushered to a remote apartment where the emperor ravished her. The wife then turned her anger against her husband, saying it was all his fault in the first place. He, in consequence, began to plot against the emperor. However, he could see that Aëtius might stand in his way, so he plotted with the palace eunuchs to suggest to Valentinian that Aëtius should be removed.[36] This ploy seems to have been singularly successful because, during a discussion of revenues and taxes on 21 or 22 September 454, Valentinian suddenly jumped up and accused Aëtius of wanting the Eastern Empire for himself. He then drew his sword and with the help of the chamberlain (who had a cleaver concealed under his cloak) killed Aëtius.[37]

Vengeance was gained when Valentinian was relaxing in the Campus Martius on 16 March 455. He was cut down by two of Aëtius's barbarian retainers, Optila and Thraustila (they were Scythians – either Goths or Huns).[38] Interestingly, despite the fact that the emperor was surrounded at the time by his retinue, nobody prevented the act or avenged it, suggesting that this incident, too, may have been manipulated by Maximus. Whatever the truth, Petronius Maximus became emperor, against the wishes of Valentinian's widow Eudoxia whom he forcibly married (his wife having died).[39]

Later written sources suggest that Eudoxia asked Gaiseric to rescue her.[40] Procopius is clear that she expected no help from the Eastern Empire since Theodosius had died (28 July 450) and Marcian had now fulfilled the eagle prophecy and was the Eastern Emperor.

The Vandal Sack of Rome

Whatever the details may have been, the situation was clearly unsettled and open to opportunists. Gaiseric sailed to Italy in 455, captured Rome and allowed his followers to rampage through the city for two weeks. The buildings themselves seem to have stayed intact, but he removed a vast amount of booty, including the treasure that the Emperor Titus had carried off from Jerusalem in AD 70.[41] Gaiseric tore off half the bronze roof of the Temple of Jupiter Capitolinus on which the Emperor Domitian had spent 12,000 talents[42] (estimated in 1916 at £2.4 million) when he had it thickly overlaid with gold. The ship carrying the statues was wrecked on the way home.[43]

Gaiseric found further, valuable imperial booty: the Empress Eudoxia and her daughters Eudocia and Placidia. He took them back to Africa where he married Eudocia to Huniric.[44] Procopius says that on his return Gaiseric tore down the walls of all the Libyan cities except Carthage in case the Libyans themselves might consider rebellion or the imperial armies might take them over during an invasion.[45] This action is very much in keeping with the Vandals' reputation for wanton destruction and, although the logic behind it can be seen, it was eventually counter-productive.

It might be thought that Gaiseric would be in a strong position, having in his possession the wife of the Western Emperor Petronius Maximus. In fact, the emperor had fled as the Vandals attacked Rome, and was later stoned to death by a crowd and segmented into trophies.[46] Placidia's husband Olybrius also fled but escaped.

Ricimer and Gaiseric

In 455 it was clearly of importance to both empires not to allow Gaiseric to go unpunished, and also for Gaiseric to strengthen his position. He made regular attacks on Italy to support his claims for the estates of his daughter-in-law Eudocia and for Placidia's husband Olybrius to the Purple.[47]

Gaiseric was both helped and hindered by the power held in the Western Empire by Ricimer (the unusually manipulative and ruthless grandson of the Visigoth Wallia and son of a royal Sueve).[48] His lineage barred him from the imperial throne, but he compensated for this with extraordinary ruthlessness. He was sent by Petronius Maximus' successor Avitus, to oppose a Vandal attack on Sicily.[49] He defeated them at Agrigentum and again at sea near Corsica, but subsequently rebelled and defeated the emperor's forces on 17 October 456.[50] He placed another candidate, Marjorian, on the imperial throne, but when the new emperor failed in a sea-borne campaign against the Vandals, Ricimer deposed him on 2 August 461 and had him executed at Dertona five days later.

The new vacancy for emperor enabled Gaiseric to continue his support of Olybrius and, presumably as a token of goodwill, he set free Eudoxia and Placidia. They both went to Constantinople in 461. Gaiseric's candidate was not successful because Ricimer created yet another emperor, Libius Severus, who was not recognised by Leo I, in Constantinople and it is probable that Ricimer later poisoned him.[51] Ricimer was effectively ruler during the interregnum before the next Emperor, Anthemius (who was chosen by Leo), was invested with his title on 12 April 476.[52] Ricimer's daughter married Anthemius.

An imperial embassy warned Gaiseric not to interfere but Gaiseric's warrior instincts took over – and he prepared for war.

The Imperial War Fleet

There were rumours that Gaiseric intended to attack Alexandria. An expensive fleet was sent out from Byzantium in 468 – a cost of 64,000 pounds of gold and 700,000 pounds of silver is recorded.[53] Some 1,113 ships and over 100,000 men were said to have been involved. The imperial general Basiliscus (brother-in-law of Leo I) may have been persuaded by Aspar to spare Gaiseric and his forces in order to prevent Leo increasing his power. He may also have taken bribes from Gaiseric.[54] Procopius describes a dramatic sea battle. The Vandals asked for a five-day armistice and, as they had expected, the wind then rose in their favour. They towed out empty ships which they set on fire before allowing them to be blown into the Roman fleet. In the resultant disorder soldiers and sailors shouted orders and pushed off the fire-boats with poles. Vandal ships were also destroyed and the campaign generally came to nothing.[55] The Byzantine treasury, however, was close to bankruptcy for a generation.

Eventually (after 470), open war broke out during which Ricimer captured his imperial father-in-law Anthemius in Rome. Leo I sent Placidia's husband Olybrius with two missions – first to intercede between Ricimer and Anthemius and then to make peace with Gaiseric. Instead, Ricimer's nephew Gundobad (King of the Burgundians) killed Anthemius, and Ricimer had Olybrius declared emperor in 472 (probably in April).

This extraordinary career, making and breaking emperors, ended when Ricimer died on 18 August 472. His powers were briefly given to Gundobad who (since Olybrius had died on 2 November 472) was instrumental in putting Glycerius on the western throne on 3 March 473.

Gaiseric's Successors

Around 476 the Vandals made peace with the Eastern Emperor Zeno[56] and Gaiseric died of old age on 25 January 477. He was succeeded by Huniric (477–84), who was 'even more sadistic',[57] though in general he and his successors pursued less formidable foreign policies. Huniric persecuted Catholics from pure religious fanaticism rather than political motives. Victor of Vita does not inspire posterity to be attracted to him with his graphic stories of torture and cruelty in the name of Christianity.[58] Huniric murdered or drove out a large number of influential Vandals who had supported his brother (whom he had exiled naked and in want, his wife and son murdered).[59]

The Vandals as Landlords

Like the Huns, the Vandals were not good landlords or farmers. Gaiseric was quick to dispossess the landlords and distribute hereditary tax-free allotments to himself and his family and followers.[60] Particularly in Tunisia, landlords were totally dispossessed even though they remained free men.[61] Such displaced nobles made their way to the Roman provinces of Africa or to Italy and the East where they were in a position to agitate for reconquest. Others kept their land and were assessed for taxes with great harshness. Claiming to be unable to pay was useless because they were deemed to be hiding the money and were killed or exiled.[62] Not all those who had been dispossessed actually left. The Albertini tablets (discovered near Bir Trouch) are unique finds that show how life was endurable among remaining Romans.[63]

Inevitably there was economic decline in North Africa. The imperial authorities had to reduce taxes by seven-eighths in Mauretania owing to the amount of devastation it had suffered before being returned under treaty. The prevailing agricultural system relied on peasants being bound to the soil but the new régime also had serious effects on landowners in towns. When a drought struck, there was no support from the rest of the empire and, of course, no stores. Terrible scenes were described by Victor.[64] He attributed the lack of water to the persecution of Catholics, which Huniric had ordered in February 484. In a way, he was probably right – too much time and energy may have been spent on persecutions and not enough on good husbandry.

The whole face of the earth remained yellowish. The grain, the vines, the olive and fruit trees all failed to grow. Everything was dismal and repulsive. Rivers and fountains dried up. There was no buying and selling. No bullocks remained to pull the ploughs. There were constant funeral processions. Some people tried to leave their homes in search of a few grass roots to eat, but were so overcome by hunger that corpses littered the streets and lanes. There was a constant stench because the survivors lacked the strength to bury the dead.

A crowd went to Carthage. Huniric saw the mounds of bodies and the 'living corpses', and with awe-inspiring callousness and logic ordered that they should be herded away to avoid the spread of infection.

Conversely, life for the Vandals was pleasant, sometimes luxurious. The chaste beginning to Vandal life in North Africa had changed by the time of Huniric when the Vandals apparently indulged in all sorts of moral laxity. The Vandal kings lived in the palace on the Byrsa where the Roman proconsuls had previously lived.[65] They preserved a throne room, a dining hall and many valuables. Procopius[66] tells how, when the Romans reconquered Africa, they camped among the trees on a beautiful, Vandal-occupied estate, which clearly implied that the barbarians had enjoyed and cultivated the gardens and orchards. In Carthage the Vandals used the Roman baths and held daily banquets in the dining rooms, adorned in 'true Persian style' with ostentatious decorations of gold. They amused themselves in theatres and hippodromes. Since they had dispossessed the former owners, it can be deduced that most lived in parkland, which had trees and good water supplies.

A mosaic from Bordj Djedid[67] shows a Vandal, with typically long hair and shaven face with small moustache, riding out on a lively horse. In the background is a towered half-timbered villa. The overall picture of life for the Vandal overlords suggests the enjoyment of seaside villas, dinner parties, the hunt and all the other pleasures which had been available to rich Romans.

The Vandals and African Christians

The situation in Africa was, in one major respect, considerably different from that found among barbarian warrior groups elsewhere. When the Vandals had arrived in 429, they were a mere generation away from the tribes who had crossed the Rhine in 406. Originally converted by the Goths, the Vandals were ardent Arian Christians. A vast proportion of the portable treasures in Africa belonged to the Church, which had a long tradition of martyrs, starting at the time of St Perpetua (in the reign of Septimius Severus). It is notable that the faith was so far advanced in Africa that by the time of Constantine the

Great's conversion, a schism had already occurred with Rome.[68] The Vandals were able to exploit the differences which weakened the church in Africa.

The tales of atrocities are as shocking today as they were at the time, though historical events related by contemporaneous churchmen (who tended to drive home their points with 'hell-fire' sermons) must be treated with caution. Conversely, items should not be dismissed simply because they make unpleasant reading. The history of Vandal Africa is chronicled by Victor of Vita who, through the title of his work alone (*History of the Vandal Persecution*) emphasised the iniquities and tortures. People were tied behind wild horses,[69] beaten with sharpened cudgels that tore flesh apart like saws,[70] or had their heads so tightly bound with cords that they burst. Church altar cloths were 'made into breeches and shirts'.[71] What makes Victor of Vita so compelling is that he was writing a mere sixty years after this 'cruel and savage people' reached Africa (i.e., probably around 488/9).

Through torture, Christians achieved the ultimate prize of martyrdom. This very point was made to Gaiseric's son Theodoric, who wished to kill a Christian called Armogas after inflicting terrible tortures on him, all of which (according to Victor of Vita) were unsuccessful because of the victim's faith in God. Theodoric's priest Jucundus observed that if Armogas were killed, he would become a martyr, so instead he was made to dig ditches for vine-growing and later was made a cowherd near Carthage so that his shame would be more public. Armogas eventually died, after expressing the wish to be buried not with due reverence in a basilica, as his friend Felix wished, but quietly under a carob tree.[72] The digging was difficult – his limbs seem to have caused difficulty among the tree roots in the hard, dry ground. Finally the undertakers were successful and came across a ready-made marble sarcophagus (the inclusion of miracles in this type of story was virtually a literary form). The Christian commentators were at pains to point out that despite Christian suffering in this life, Faith would prevail. That sort of attitude would have been frustrating to any straightforward warrior band wanting a good, clean fight and some honour and booty.

The Church also produced few, if any, family ties that could be manipulated. A bishop or priest taken hostage could not be ransomed as easily as a noble scion. It was not until after the sack of Rome in 455 that this pattern seems to have been broken. Gaiseric took many hostages from Rome,[73] whom the 'Moors and Vandals' divided into groups. Husbands were separated from wives, and children from their parents. However, Bishop Deogratias (454–7) avoided the break-up of families by selling the gold and silver church plate.[74] Victor lavishes much praise on him, but it was simply another variation on the theme and in the end Gaiseric got his money for the hostages.

Gaiseric's Successors

Gaiseric's nephew Gunthamund gradually decreased the persecution of Catholics and fought against the Moors who were gaining strength. His successor, Thrasamund (496–523), continued to relax the persecutions, favouring the giving of gifts and bribes instead. Many Vandals adopted Roman culture but the group retained its identity. The Vandals seem to have been so preoccupied with their own lives that independent kingdoms began to develop in the mountains and desert areas, and Moorish tribes of Mauretania and Numidia threatened Vandal lands. A defeat at this time by the Moors in Tripolitania should perhaps have served as a warning, but the Vandals did not take it.[75]

Under the aged King Hildiric (Huniric and Eudocia's son), Vandal fortunes changed. Hildiric was the ally of Byzantium and ceased to persecute Catholics. He sent an embassy to the eastern capital which was considered to be a betrayal of Vandal interests.[76] A major defeat by the Moors at Byzacium led to his being deposed by Geilamir on 19 May 530.[77] Such family violence was by this time virtually a tradition among the Asding Vandals in power. In this case it was not a sensible measure since Hildiric's friendship with the Emperor Justinian gave the Eastern Empire extra incentive to attempt the reconquest of Africa. Belisarius was sent. Procopius says the imperial forces included 500 vessels with 92 warships, 15,000 regular troops, 1,000 barbarian allies and the commander's personal bodyguard. The landing in August was unopposed. Hildiric was murdered in September 533 as the imperial forces reached Carthage.[78]

The End of Vandal Africa

Belisarius' task was easier than it might have been since over a century earlier Gaiseric had torn down the walls of the Libyan towns.[79] By March of the following year Geilamir had submitted. Thenceforth North Africa was reorganised as part of the empire. In a single campaigning season the Vandal kingdom had been destroyed and they played no further role in history. The churches were restored to Catholicism.

Chapter 5

The Franks

Even in boyhood, the love of fighting is fully developed ... Death, but not fear, may overcome them.[1]

Sidonius Apollinaris on the Franks.

The Franks were not prominent among the people who migrated with devastating effect through Europe from north of the Rhine/Danube.[2] They had been assimilated into the empire in various guises long before the threat of the Huns was felt. As a result, during the period under review they were (by and large) the protectors rather than the destroyers of the Roman state. 'Frank' probably means 'bold' or 'courageous', though they preferred to think it meant 'free'.[3] By 289 they were a 'confederation' – Chamavi, Bructeri, Chattuari, Salii (Salians), Amsivarii and Tubantes are all mentioned at different times as being Franks. The Chamavi seem to have retained their identity up to the ninth century.[4] The Franks grew to dominate the former Roman Gaul (currently France and parts of West Germany) and eventually some settled in southern England. Frankish fortunes were often closely connected with those of the Alamanni.

FRANKISH RAIDS ON THE ROMAN WORLD

The Franks belonged to three distinct groups: the Salian (salty), the Ripuarian (river) and Chatti or Hessians. In the early centuries AD the Frankish tribes settled in the area north and east of the Lower Rhine (the Netherlands and part of north-west Germany). Frankish mythology perpetuated by Gregory of Tours (an aristocratic sixth-century bishop) suggested that they originated in Pannonia.[5]

During the third century various Frankish tribes raided Roman Gaul, often in conjunction with the Alamanni, though there was also fighting between the two warrior groups.[6] A large number of buried Roman coin hoards have been interpreted as evidence for widespread fear occasioned by such raids. Town defences were also increased in Gaul from the 270s, presumably as a response.[7] The Emperor Probus (276–82) had to deal with constant insurrections in Britain and Gaul as well as with problems in the east; a weak situation which the hostile Rhineland tribes were ready to exploit. As a matter of policy, Probus settled many barbarians within the empire. He tried to settle some Franks[8] and deported others to the east where they provoked a certain admiration in one panegyrist who commented that for a small group of Frankish prisoners they enjoyed unbelievable success when they purloined ships and pillaged Greece, Asia, the Libyan coast and Syracuse. They managed to drop anchor off Africa before a force from Carthage drove them away.[9] This episode was in marked contrast to a settlement in Thrace, in the same reign, of Bastarni who fitted in with Roman laws and customs without difficulty.[10]

The Emperor Maximian (286–310) defeated Frankish pirates in 287 and successfully campaigned against the first known Frankish leader, Genobaud. Gregory of Tours, quoting from a lost manuscript (of Sulpicius Alexander), describes how the Franks Genobaud, Marcomeres and Sunno crossed the frontier in 388 and ravaged the fields until they were turned back by imperial troops.[11] The Franks were pursued across the Rhine but the Romans found only deserted villages and townships. The Franks, however, had merely feigned withdrawal and had built defensive palisades in the woodlands. The Romans became lost in the trees and eventually came to an endless barrier of wood. The Franks showered them with arrows as if 'from war catapults'. They had, moreover, smeared the tips of the arrows with poisonous plant extracts, so mere grazes could bring death. Surrounded by Frankish warriors, the Romans fled into meadowland where the cavalry became bogged down in thick mud. Some of the infantry were trampled to death. Few Romans survived, though Marcomeres was subsequently exiled and Sunno was killed by his own men.

In the fourth century there was general unrest in the Roman province of Gaul. The future emperor Constantius Chlorus, father of Constantine the Great, settled defeated Franks around Trier, Amiens and Langres as *laeti*.[12] He defeated the Alamanni in 298 and killed a British usurper, Allectus. Emperor Julian the Apostate defeated the Alamanni at Strasbourg in 357 and was successful in expelling the barbarians from the rest of Gaul. After some hard fighting the Salian Franks were allowed to remain in Gaul as federates.[13]

SILVANUS – A FRANKISH EMPEROR

Many Franks enjoyed distinguished careers in the regular fourth-century Roman army. The usurper Magnentius (350–3) may have joined the army.[14] His mother may have been Frankish, his father British. He was defeated and committed suicide in 353.[15] Another Frank, Silvanus, was the son of Bonitus, a general who had fought for Constantine in the civil war.[16] Silvanus rose to high command in the army and defended the empire against Franks. The superintendent of the emperor's pack animals, Dynamius, plotted against him. Having obtained Silvanus' signature on letters of recommendation for himself,[17] he erased the words 'with a sponge' and substituted a new text suggesting that Silvanus was canvassing the support of friends in a bid for imperial power. An accomplice presented this to the emperor who reacted strongly. After some complex manoeuvres, the trickster then sent another letter purporting to come from Silvanus and Malarichus, the Frankish commander of part of the emperor's household troops. The recipient was disquieted to receive obscurely phrased orders that made no sense to him, so he immediately sent the letter to Malarichus, asking for clarification. Naturally Malarichus, knowing nothing about the matter, investigated and involved all the many other influential Franks in the palace. The defaced letter was examined and the top of the original lettering was discovered.

In the meantime, Silvanus was warned by his friends what was happening. He had no faith that the fickle emperor would reach the right conclusions and considered fleeing to the 'savages' (as Ammianus Marcellinus calls the Franks in this context). His Frankish supporters in the army persuaded him that by doing so he would invite death. He had no option but to be declared emperor. His term of office in 355 lasted twenty-eight days – he was hacked to death on his way to a Christian service.[18]

MALLOBAUDES, A ROMANISED FRANKISH KING

Most Franks who joined the army and rose to high command remained Romanised. An exception was Mallobaudes, commander of the Emperor Gratian's household cavalry and 'a brave man', always ready for battle.[19] Gratian's father Valentinian I (364–75) had built a fort near Basle after laying waste several Alamannic regions. The Alamannic ruler, King Macrianus, was said to have been particularly aggressive and prepared to attack even fortified cities.[20] There is a description of the two leaders meeting at the River Rhine. Macrianus was full of self-importance, standing at the water's edge, surrounded by the clashing shields of his men. The emperor, equally supported by brilliantly flashing standards, crossed the river in a boat amid the wild gesticulations and loud cries of the barbarians. Eventually peace was made. When the 'formidable' Macrianus then began to raid Frankish territory, Mallobaudes lured him into an ambush and killed him.[21]

The Alamanni broke their treaty with Rome in 378 when the Western Emperor Gratian was summoned by his uncle Valens prior to the battle of Adrianople. The news reached the Alamanni when one of their number who was an imperial armour-bearer returned home on urgent business and indulged in 'loose talk'. The Alamanni eventually gathered between 40,000 and 70,000 armed men from all the villages.[22] Gratian recalled his troops and the decision to attack the Alamanni at Argentaria (modern Horburg) was made through Mallobaudes who was keen to engage them in battle. He appears to have returned by this time to his own people as *Rex Francorum* ('King of the Franks'), though he retained a Roman command.[23] *Rex* is a Roman title, usually used for a Roman client king of a 'buffer state'.

The battle commenced when the Alamanni gave the usual 'terrifying' battle cry. A rain of arrows and javelins struck down many on both sides, at which point the Roman forces dispersed into fields planted with trees. The brilliance of their arms and general appearance seems to have caused the barbarians to disperse and their king, Priarius, was killed.[24]

Arbogastes and the Height of Frankish Imperial Power

By the late fourth century many of the key posts in the West were held by Franks. Bauto, for example, was a Frankish general sent by Gratian to help Theodosius against the Goths in the 380s.[25] After his death, his daughter married the Emperor Arcadius. Bauto was succeeded in his post by his son Arbogastes,[26] who was also Richomeres' nephew and whose physical strength and fierce temper made him 'like an inferno'.[27] It appears that he obtained Bauto's post through threats and bullying.[28] When Gratian died in August 383, his twelve-year-old stepbrother Valentinian II was the obvious successor, but his youthfulness made the situation vulnerable.

In the same year a Spaniard called Magnus Maximus was elevated to the Purple in Britain and Valentinian had to flee. Theodosius defeated Maximus in the Balkans and Pannonia in 388. He then relinquished the West to Valentinian, though he continually reinforced his right to sovereignty in both East and West. Since Arbogastes was tireless in fighting corruption and had no wish for money himself, Theodosius thought he would be a good influence on Valentinian II. He installed the Frank as the young man's chief advisor. The inexperienced Valentinian II was left in his palace almost as powerless as a private citizen, with Frankish generals controlling the army and Arbogastes' friends in charge of the administration. Valentinian disliked Arbogastes and, after writing to Theodosius many times, finally plucked up sufficient courage and support to present his advisor with official notification of his removal from office. The Frank took it, read it, and destroyed it 'with his fingernails'. Having roared with rage at the teenage emperor, he left with drawn sword.[29] Nobody stood in his way. 'You have not given me my command,' he is reputed to have announced with magnificently arrogant realism, 'therefore, you cannot take it away.'

Subsequently, Arbogastes is said to have killed Valentinian with a sword when the emperor was twenty.[30] According to another source, the emperor was taken off his guard while engrossed in games with some of his soldiers, who did nothing to prevent his murder, partly through fear of Arbogastes' power and partly because of his impressive disinterest in money[31] – a characteristic that habitually persuaded Roman soldiers of the worthiness of their commanders. A further account has the young man either strangled by Arbogastes' men or hanged by his own hand.[32] The only certainty is that he died, leaving an imperial job vacancy.

Arbogastes had been introduced by Richomeres to Eugenius, 'who held a sophist chair'.[33] When Richomeres fell ill and died, Arbogastes set up Eugenius as emperor, flattering him that he alone was clever enough to take on the great office, even though he was not a soldier. When Eugenius was killed at the battle of the Frigidus by Stilicho and Alaric, Arbogastes committed suicide.[34] The nature of Roman–barbarian relations remained complex – when the usurper Constantine III required troops in 408, for example, he sent his general, Ebodich,[35] across the Rhine to obtain reinforcements from the Franks and the Alamanni.

The Material Evidence for Frankish Warriors

History is silent about the everyday workings of how warriors were taken into Roman pay as mercenaries, federates or even regular soldiers. What arrangements were made about arms and armour, for instance? Although, in theory, new recruits were issued with Roman arms, it does not seem feasible that perfectly good weapons were given up and replaced with others that differed only in their place of manufacture and decorative design. In fact, what logic suggests to be likely – that warriors normally kept their own weapons – seems to be borne out by the archaeological remains which are abundant for the Franks though so rare for the Goths and Vandals.

The *Notitia Dignitatum* is a roll-call of officials in the late Roman Empire. It documents twelve '*praefecti laetorum*' (military officials in charge of *laeti*) in northern Gaul in around AD 400. This is a rare instance where archaeological and historical information seem to correlate, for in these areas burials have been found which are characterised by the presence of weapons (notably the *francisca*, the Frankish throwing-axe) and various belt fittings that appear to have been types of insignia. Since ordinary Roman civilians were not permitted to carry weapons, and regular Roman soldiers were issued with weapons which they handed back at the end of their tour of duty, it is assumed that these are the mortal remains of recruited barbarian warriors.

Ordinary (non-combatant) women were buried next to the men, which also suggests that these were not regular soldiers. They had been laid to rest with north European-style barbarian jewellery such as domical tutulus brooches and cross-bow brooches with flaring footplates.[36]

The Transformation of Gaul into Frankish Kingdoms

Due to the early assimilation of Franks into the empire, Gallic landowners were accustomed to the idea of barbarians being settled on their land.[37] In the mid-fifth century, after the deaths of Attila in 453, Aëtius in 454 and Valentinian III eighteen months later, the dominant factions in Gaul were the Visigoths in the south-west, the Burgundians in the south-east, the Armorici between the Rivers Seine and Loire, and possibly the territory near Soissons dominated by the Roman Syagrius.[38]

No problems over the Christian faith have been documented (despite the fact that the Salian Franks were not converted to Catholic Christianity until the reign of King Clovis (481/2–511). The reasons for this are unclear,[39] but perhaps suggest that economic and security matters were overriding.

The Earliest Frankish Warrior Kingdoms

Romulus Augustulus was deposed in 475, leaving the opportunity for the establishment of kingdoms headed by Franks but closely based on the Roman system of local administration. The transformation was so smooth that there are very few records of events or personalities. The writings of Sidonius Apollinaris (whose life revolved around Gallic villa-owning society) mention Franks who were clearly becoming integrated into Roman society.

The Rhineland and the region to the west came under the control of minor Frankish kings operating from Cologne.[40] Classic archaeological sites have produced arrays of material which would be expected from small kingdoms. Examples are at Vermand, Aisne;[41] Haillot, near Namur (which continued into later Frankish times); Krefeld-Gellep,[42] a long-used cemetery on the Rhine, with some 5,000 graves; and the recently excavated sites at Vireux-Molhain (Meuse)[43] and Vron (Somme).[44] Notably, some of these are associated with Roman military bases: 70 per cent of the burials at Furfooz in the Ardennes, for instance, contain weapons.[45] The rich array of artefacts from some of these cemeteries suggests that these were free soldiers (probably federates) and their families. The graves span the period from around 350 to 450, and show an interesting mix of Roman and Frankish cultures. Some of the finds suggest very high warrior status. Some objects, for example, are decorated in the so-called 'Vermand' style with chip-carving (a technique derived from woodwork which resulted in inverted light-reflecting facets in the metal). Designs involving slightly stylised animals, plants and abstract patterns are typically Roman. Archetypal are buckles with confronted dolphins on their loops, which are also found in late Roman and post-Roman Britain.[46]

A Warrior Chief's Burial

One outstanding grave from Vermand itself (Grave IIIB) must have been that of a warrior chief. His accoutrements included a francisca, shield, spears (one barbed with an animal head) and ornamental belt fittings.[47] No ordinary soldier's wife, either, was the lady buried in Grave 26 at Cortrat, Dept Loiret, France. She was laid to rest with a pair of gilt silver tutulus brooches, a gold finger ring, a necklace with amethyst and crystal beads, a silver dress fastener and fine glass vessels.[48]

A Frankish Warrior-Style King

Sidonius Apollinaris provides a vivid description of Sigismer, an otherwise unknown Frankish Rhineland 'prince' as he went to meet his Burgundian wife-to-be around 469. It would have been clear to anyone watching this parade that here were men whose business was fighting. They held barbed lances and throwing axes, and their shields (held at the left side) gleamed gold from the central bosses and silvery-white round the edges.[49] The barbarian love of ostentation was also very evident. A 'gaily caparisoned' horse went before him, and other horses bore 'flashing jewels'. The royal leader himself was on foot among his runners and footmen. He wore 'gleaming scarlet', and 'ruddy gold and pure-white silk' which exactly echoed the colours of his golden hair, glowing cheeks and white skin. His impressive escort of chiefs and companions were laced from toe to ankle in 'hairy shoes'. Their knees, shins and calves were uncovered and each wore a short, tight-fitting many-coloured garment with sleeves covering only the upper part of the arm. They wore green coats bordered in crimson and carried their swords suspended from the shoulders by baldrics pressed against sides girded with studded deer-skins.

AËTIUS AND THE FRANKS

The rise of Frankish groups did not go unchallenged. They suffered defeat near the Rhine in 428 and in 432, for example,[50] by Aëtius. Problems elsewhere overwhelmed Roman resources and by the early to mid-fifth century a Frankish leader called Chlogio can be identified. He captured Cambrai and occupied the territory up to the Somme.[51] There is a dearth of material for this period, though a highly detailed account exists of a wedding party that was broken up by Aëtius.[52] Subsequently, although some Franks supported Attila, others supported Aëtius, who adopted the son of one deceased king of unknown identity. Disputes between his sons over the succession came at the point when Attila was wondering whether to attack Italy (on behalf of Honoria), the Visigoths or the Eastern Empire.[53] It is possible that the unknown king was the semi-legendary Merovech (whose name was perpetuated through the Merovingian Dynasty).

CHILDERIC (456–82)

The Salian Franks seem to have been less united than those living near the Rhine and the life of King Childeric has to be pieced together from later sources which often contain conflicting information. According to a late sixth-century tradition, one of Chlogio's descendants was Merovech. Virtually nothing certain is known about this man, except that he was the father of Childeric. It is possible that Childeric was the victor of the struggles that followed the death of the unknown Frankish king (above), though his reign is usually dated to around 456. As a young man he led such a dissolute life, bringing Frankish maidens into dishonour, that he was exiled to Thuringia for eight years before he became king (probably in around 456,[54] but certainly by 463, when Gregory of Tours says he fought a battle at Orleans, the identification of which has been disputed).[55]

Six years later Childeric's name is found in conjunction with Paul, a Roman military count. Childeric besieged and took Angers, but Count Paul was killed in the process.[56] We are next told by Gregory that Childeric allied with Odovacrius (sometimes identified with Odoacer) to attack the Alamanni. It might seem that Childeric was playing more than a purely regional role in the affairs of Europe in the later fifth century. His private life was evidently eventful, for the Thuringian queen left her husband and informed Childeric (once he was king) that she knew he was a strong man and she could recognise ability when she saw it. Therefore she had come to live with him. If (she went on, presumably in case he had not yet got the picture) she had known of anyone more capable she would have gone to live with him instead. This, says Gregory of Tours, pleased Childeric, so he married her.[57] Those with a penchant for salacious gossip will no doubt suspect that there was perhaps more to their relationship during Childeric's exile than is related. The two became the parents of the pugnacious ruler Clovis.

At the time of his death Childeric probably still ruled over no more than 400–500 warriors. One of his key followers was a Hun called Wiomand.[58]

The Tomb of Childeric

In 1653 Childeric's grave was discovered in Saint-Brice, Tournai, by Adrien Quinquin, a deaf-mute stonemason. It is an unusually satisfying archaeological find because it can be certainly identified with this king. The evidence comes from a signet ring inscribed CHILDERICI REGIS. It was reported well for the time by Jean Jacques Chifflet,[59] though it may be that some of the finds came from adjacent burials. The majority of the gravegoods were stolen and melted down in 1831, though a few items were recovered from the bed of the Seine in Paris.

Clovis' Campaigns

Childeric's successor was his son Clovis (c. 482–511), who married Clothild, a Christian princess of Burgundy. Their children were baptised.[60] Gregory of Tours has provided a memorable account of this period because Clovis converted to Christianity. Like Theodoric the Great, Clovis personifies the metamorphosis of barbarian warrior into ruler of a state. The Franks began to take on the mantle of Roman civilisation while maintaining independence.

THE BATTLE OF VOUILLÉ

Clovis expanded his kingdom with ruthless single-mindedness and in 507 made war on the Visigoths in a particularly well-documented battle at Vouillé. Clovis crossed the Vienne River, which was swollen from recent downpours, and reached a plain on the Roman road to Nantes. Here he positioned his archers and spear-throwers at the rear of his forces, from which position they successfully rained down missiles on the Visigothic army. Meanwhile the front ranks engaged in hand-to-hand combat. In true barbarian tradition, Clovis killed the leader of the Visigoths, Alaric II, in single combat. He managed to escape with his life through the speed of his horse and the strength of his cuirass, as two Visigothic warriors tried to avenge the death of their leader.

At Tours in 508 Clovis was invested with the thoroughly Roman title consul. He wore a purple tunic and diadem (the insignia of Roman imperial status), and scattered coins among the crowd in a display of Roman munificence.[61] He established a capital at Paris,[62] and instituted a law code, the *Lex Salica*, and for the next two hundred years only the descendants of Clovis were entitled to reign – things had moved on from the time when a warrior leader had to win respect from his followers personally.[63] The extension of Clovis' power to the Rhineland is perhaps reflected in the very rich burials of the early sixth century at Krefeld-Gellep, in particular Grave 1782. Clovis eliminated the Rhineland Franks and also made a thorough job of exterminating his own kin. Afterwards, he lamented how sad it was to be alone. Not surprisingly, none of his surviving relatives felt the need to answer his pleas for them to come forward to comfort him.

Vestiges of the Franks' barbarian origins remained, and it is likely that the many units serving in Clovis' army contained former *laeti*, who may have included Sarmatians, Alans, Taifali and Alamannic horsemen. Despite elements borrowed from Roman and other techniques of warfare (such as the use of siege engines), Clovis was essentially the leader of many warbands. Immediately under the king were *reguli*, whose larger warbands were probably divided up into smaller bands headed by what Gregory terms *leudes*, noble warriors.

By the sixth century some Franks were settled in Kent (England) and the surrounding areas. In the sixth century the term 'Frank' was a label applied to members of a particular (Germanic) group. By the eighth century it applied to anyone living in France.[64] In Germany the name survives in the duchy of Franconia (Franken).

Chapter 6

The Saxons, Danes, Frisians and Angles

Far from frightening them, shipwreck is their training.[1]
 Sidonius Apollinaris warning his friend Namatius about the Saxons.

The Roman province of Britannia was effectively abandoned after AD 409, so its story differs from that of most of the continental provinces ('Gothia' was also exceptional in this way). By the early fifth century Britannia had lost the wealth and military strength to sustain its many rich and influential inhabitants. There are therefore no Roman or Byzantine records, but instead a relative abundance of archaeological goods and some later written material which may to relate to the fifth and sixth centuries. Probably due partly to their geographical isolation and partly to their pagan beliefs, the immigrants retained the tradition of the war-band longer than their continental counterparts. Most accounts of the period tend to concentrate on the archaeological evidence alone since it is less contentious than the historical. However, partly for reasons of space and partly because the material invites comparison with that from mainland Europe elsewhere in these pages, this chapter looks briefly at some of the written accounts where they reflect the pattern on the continent,[2] and points to archaeological evidence where it appears to corroborate them. The following pages also tentatively suggest a further explanation for the so-called and highly contentious 'flight to the west' of Romano-Britons trying to elude the Anglo-Saxons. The chapter also covers the first influxes of non-Celtic barbarians into Roman Britain, the withdrawal of troops (in response to the migrations of Huns, Goths and Vandals elsewhere and the usurpers) and the establishment of barbarian kingdoms by the early seventh century.

Warriors in Roman Britain

From the Roman conquest in AD 43, Britannia was the most northerly Roman province, with a turbulent frontier eventually fixed at Hadrian's Wall. By the late third century Saxons and Franks were raiding the coasts of Britanny and Belgic Gaul, and a series of forts gradually developed along the eastern and southern British sea-board under the control of the military commander of the Saxon Shore.[3] Sidonius Apollinaris constantly refers to the Saxons as both intrepid seafarers and ferocious. In the 'curving sloops' there were oarsmen, each of whom gave the impression of being a 'pirate captain'.[4] The Saxons were not deterred by storms. Instead, knowing that their adversaries would be feeling insecure in such weather, they were likely to attack and would risk danger among the 'billows and jagged rocks'.

A letter from Sidonius to Namatius (who was at the time at sea) warns him about his adversaries, who surpassed all others in brutality. They attacked without being spotted and if seen managed to give their pursuers the slip. They were pagans and (like the Goth Radagaisus) were reputed to make human sacrifices. When ready to unfurl their sails for the return journey, they would kill one in ten of their prisoners by drowning or crucifixion.

There is no doubt that seafaring ability was of paramount importance in the migrations of the relatively small numbers of Danes, Frisians, Sueves, Jutes, Angles, Saxons, some Norwegians and Franks who came to Britannia. Some came from near the great rivers, especially the Lower Rhine, Elbe and Weser. Others were native to the islands around Denmark and Frisia, and were certainly capable of juggling the North Sea weather and tides.

By the late sixth century a large area in south-east England was subject to Frankish control,[5] and studies have suggested a strong Frankish presence in this area from early in the fifth century.[6] There was an additional migration in the later fifth century from western Norway into Norfolk and Humberside.[7] Some Saxons settled in East Anglia,[8] and Franks and Frisians were probably present there from the outset.

The appearance of the Saxons seems to have been distinctive because of their haircuts: a close shave with the razor enlarged the appearance of the face and made the head look smaller.[9]

Warriors and the Army

In keeping with imperial policy elsewhere, some warriors were drafted into regular units in the late Roman army in Britannia. There were, for example,

Frisians (Hnaudifridi) based at Housesteads fort on Hadrian's Wall in the third century. During his campaigns against the Alamanni, Valentinian I made Fraomarius King of the Bucinobantes (a tribe of the Alamanni who lived opposite Mainz) in place of their King Macrianus. Since the entire region had been devastated so badly during the campaigns he transferred Fraomarius to Britannia with the rank of tribune in command of a particularly distinguished troop of Alamanni.[10]

British politics remained unsettled in the third century when, for example, the usurper Carausius was deposed by his own financial officer Allectus, who in turn was killed by Constantius Chlorus. After this time, troops were progressively removed from Britannia as the emperors and usurpers alike were active in the larger arena. In 367 Hadrian's Wall was breached by the Picts, Scots, Attacotti (all north and west of the Wall) with the Saxons attacking the south and east.[11] The soldiery still in Britannia revolted, put one candidate, Marcus, on the imperial throne and then murdered him 'because he did not suit their temperament'.[12] They replaced him with Gratianus, but became disenchanted with him after four months and in 407 put in Constantine III. He won over to his side all the armies in Gaul and the Italian Alps,[13] but his contribution to British security was negative since there can have been few regular troops left in Britannia when Stilicho took troops out in 408 to deal with the crisis caused by Alaric.

With the army went tens of thousands of its dependent administrators and officials. Any pursuit that required central financial control or overseas backing certainly dwindled and/or failed over the next few decades. In vain was Honorius asked for help by the Britons in 409 when the Visigoths were becoming a major threat in Italy. From this time on Britannia was independent, though not united. In Wales and the north the Celtic tribes (who had never been fully Romanised) maintained their traditional political and economic structure,[14] but further south the richer and more Romanised areas would have been vulnerable. A series of Romano-British political units arose – power cells were based on towns or (in the south-west) on refurbished Iron Age hillforts.[15] Traditionally, the Britons are said to have sent pleas of help to Aëtius in 446. This futile appeal may in reality have taken place earlier,[16] but certainly by the mid-fifth century imperial interest was negligible. Town life declined, though the sixth-century monk Gildas records twenty-eight cities in the former province of Britannia which he asserted were depopulated[17] at the time of his writing around AD 540. It is known from archaeology that Verulamium and Wroxeter, for example, survived well into the fifth century.

Mass production of pottery, the importing of luxury goods, the laying of mosaics and the commissioning of artworks or architecture all ceased by the mid-fifth century, if not before. The great villa estates were in terminal decline and the production of grain, timber, pottery and building stone ceased. The last coins brought into the former province were silver issues of *c.* 420, though a recent find suggests that a few may have reached Britain as late as 461.[18] Thereafter circulation of money ceased. Contacts with the Roman world were not totally lost – St Germanus was sent in 429 to stamp out Pelagianism.[19] The holy man led an army against the heretics and won a bloodless victory by use of what was, effectively, the *barritus*, using the word 'Alleluia'.

The Source Material

Until the publication of John Morris' study of the historical sources of the fifth and sixth centuries[20] it was common among scholars during the previous fifty years, to minimise most if not all of the sparse historical sources which relate to the following century and a half. The grounds for this were that they were written long after the time (Bede, *Anglo-Saxon Chronicle*), or were biased (Gildas) or both (Nennius). Morris' work is subject to much academic argument.[21] The overall pattern reflected in the sources, however, is in part supported by archaeological evidence. Whether the stories are the literal truth or not, they serve to illustrate the type of pattern to relationships which may well have occurred. As on the continent, treaties, treachery, violence, dynastic marriages, quiet settlement of the land, sieges and inter-group fighting certainly seem to have taken place in post-Roman Britannia before it became England.

Vortigern's Invitation to Mercenaries/Federates

In the mid-fifth century a Romano-British leader, Vortigern,[22] appears in the more credible historical records as taking seriously the former Province's vulnerable political and defensive situation. He seems to have been some kind of overlord (he is called a tyrant). He negotiated with barbarian warriors overseas and invited two Jutish (presumably from Jutland, Denmark) warrior brothers, Hengest and Horsa, into Britannia as mercenaries.[23]

The initial landing involved three keels (ships). The deal that Vortigern is recorded as making with them was typical of imperial bargains elsewhere – food and clothing in return for military help. Archaeological evidence bears out a pattern of migration based on such federate agreements: a few graves from the extreme south of England (for example, Dyke Hills, Dorchester, Oxford) contain North European barbarian warrior-style possessions.[24]

Archaeological evidence also shows that the forts at Richborough (Kent) and Portchester (Hants) were partially occupied by North European barbarians whose exact status is unknown.[25] There is no evidence that entire communities under the leadership of kings migrated to Britain (as happened with the Goths, Huns and Vandals).[26] Graves with rich contents implying the existence of élites in society do not exist until the period in which kingdoms had formed (the seventh century).[27] All this is compatible with the story of Hengest, Horsa and their colleagues arriving as invited mercenaries.

The descriptions suggest that the new arrivals came in groups of two to five ships (100 to 250 men). There is no mention of ferrying systems or huge numbers as there was at the Rhine in 376. The *Anglo-Saxon Chronicle* states that Hengest and Horsa in 449, Aelle and his sons in 477, and the West Saxons in 514 all came in three ships. The same source reveals that Cerdic and Cynric in 495 had five ships, and Port, Bieda and Maegla had only two when they arrived in 501.[28]

Clearly the size of the ships is of importance in calculating numbers. Evidence from the period is missing from Britain, though a boat from Hjortspring, Denmark, of the first/second century BC, was buried with many weapons. This plank-built warship was 58 ft (17.6m) long and may have been manned by twenty men. Next in date is the boat from Nydam, Denmark, found in 1860, which was dated to the later fourth century AD. Deliberately sunk, the boat's finds included weapons, with over 100 swords. The boat is about 70 ft (21.3m) long and a maximum of 9 ft (2.74m) wide at its greatest point; it was propelled by fifteen sailors and a steersman, the rudder being 6.5 ft (2m) long. The craft was built from eleven oak planks, and was furnished with rowlocks (fifteen each side) fixed in position. The overlapping strakes were fastened with iron nails. There was no deck but, as the rowers would have needed footrests, it may be that the bottom of the boat was filled with stones covered with woven brushwood.[29] The well-known seventh-century ship from Sutton Hoo was of similar size.

Modern opinion polarises between those who believe there was a large-scale settlement of subsistence farmers, and those who favour the view that incoming warrior élites dominated a predominantly British society. The two views are not necessarily incompatible.[30]

Relationships between Romano-Britons and Barbarians

It appears that Vortigern reneged on his side of the bargain. Hengest, however, 'was an experienced man', both shrewd and skilful. He suggested to Vortigern that he should send home for a larger warrior force. Vortigern agreed, and soon sixteen keels arrived, one containing Hengest's 'very handsome' daughter. Hengest held a banquet at which he instructed the girl to serve the wine and spirits. The entire company became very drunk and the devil 'entered into Vortigern's heart' – he fell in love. Through his interpreter he asked Hengest for his daughter's hand, offering whatever the barbarians wished – up to half his kingdom.[31]

The English asked for Kent. This was granted, even though its ruler was unaware of the deal. It is notable that archaeological investigation has found Anglo-Saxon material within the walls of Roman Canterbury. This town seems to have gone into decline in the fourth century, at least in some areas, and in the fifth century burials were made inside the walls of the Roman town, something that would have been unthinkable a century or so earlier.[32] It is possible (but as yet unprovable) that this might have been a short-term expediency (perhaps a siege). Anglo-Saxon sunken-floor huts, associated with what has been termed 'Jutish' pottery, were put up within the town towards the end of the fifth century – some have argued that by this time the town had been deserted by the Romano-Britons, but the evidence is open to dispute. It fits the general pattern suggested by the historical sources of some barbarians living in former Roman areas.

The evidence of cemeteries in general shows gradual cultural integration which might reflect intermarriage, as symbolised by the wedding of Hengest's daughter with Vortigern. Roman objects are found in what are clearly pagan graves. Many objects, such as beads or brooches, are too humble and mundane to be credible as booty and occur in female graves. While current thinking favours the idea that they were 'substitutes' for Anglo-Saxon objects,[33] it does not negate the fact that Roman objects (including complete glass vessels) are unlikely to have been collected from abandoned Roman settlements, and are most likely to have been acquired through marriage or trade.

Hadrian's Wall in the Fifth Century

Hengest is said to have offered to defend the northern frontier and expeditions were made in the north. Nennius suggests that Hengest asked Vortigern to settle Saxons in the neighbourhood of Hadrian's Wall to help fight the Irish.[34]

There is growing evidence that Hadrian's Wall was indeed redefended in the fifth century. The forts at Birdoswald, South Shields and Vindolanda (which lay slightly to the south of the Wall) seem to have been reoccupied and possibly redefended at this date. In north Britain as a whole there is growing evidence for the re-use in the fifth and sixth centuries of forts which in the fourth had been under the command of the Dux Britanniarum. Of sixteen sites with fifth–sixth century occupation, fourteen had been under this command.[35] Of the Hadrian's Wall forts, the best evidence comes from Birdoswald, where timber buildings were constructed on top of the old granaries.

MASSACRE BY BARBARIANS AT A CONFERENCE?

The situation in Britain was not static. More keels arrived. Vortigern's son Vortimer evidently did not agree with his father's policies, and fought against Hengest and Horsa, driving them back into Thanet, before fighting four battles. Vortimer died, and Vortigern proved less resolute in attacking the English who did, after all, include his son-in-law. Hengest suggested that his people should make peace with the Britons, and called for an unarmed meeting to make a treaty.

The sort of conference that survives in the annals for fifteen hundred years tends to have been eventful. Hengest did not trust the British negotiators. They are described on the day as friendly in their words but wolfish in heart and deed. Intriguingly, he instructed his followers to hide their daggers in their shoes 'under their feet'. This apparently went unnoticed because, at the appointed time, when Hengest cried out to the English to draw their knives, the revellers took out their weapons and attacked Vortigern and his men. As instructed, the attackers stood firm. As instructed, they did not kill Vortigern, in consideration of the fact that his wife was Hengest's daughter – and (much more prosaically) because it was deemed better to ransom him. All 300 'Seniors of King Vortigern' were killed.[36]

This story is not corroborated in other historical sources, and scholars looking for direct archaeological evidence, in the form of mass graves, multiple bodies with knife wounds next to discarded shoes with slots for daggers and so on, have been disappointed. There are none to date, though there is evidence for battle wounds.

However, archaeology has produced a body of evidence of a much less dramatic nature which at least does not negate the story. The 'senior' Romano-British followers of Vortigern would undoubtedly have lived in villas and fine town houses. After about 450, villa buildings (as opposed to the farming land around) definitely show archaeological signs of no longer sustaining a Roman way of life. Some were totally abandoned. This is compatible with the more influential Romano-British being deprived of power in some way – perhaps the situation was akin to that under Gaiseric in North Africa where landowners were forcibly dispossessed. General violence against the local population is described in the works of Gildas. He was notably as critical of the Britons as he was of the Saxons, seeing the Romano-Britons as reaping the deserts of their wicked, non-Christian ways. He asserts that the citizens were torn to pieces like 'lambs by the butcher' and their life deteriorated to that of 'beasts of the field'.[37] Yet there are many excavated early barbarian-style settlements which are undefended – surely illogical if the inhabitants were in the habit of warring with their immediate neighbours. These villages fit in far better with the pattern of billeting that was found in Gaul, in which land was given in exchange for local 'policing'; this was the basis of Vortigern's arrangement with Hengest. There may well have been isolated acts of violence which, by their very rarity, would have appeared overwhelmingly shocking.

The Flight to the West, or the Colonisation of Britanny?

Gildas (and other later writers such as Nennius) states categorically that the incomers killed or pursued to the west the majority of the population. He may, however, have been concerned not with the majority of the population, but only with the rich and influential elements for whom he was writing. English historians (particularly in the nineteenth and early twentieth centuries) assumed he meant literally everybody.

Early historians, too, assumed that there was a mass flight to 'the west' – interpreted as Wales. Archaeological records have disobligingly shown no such influx of people. It is a possibility, however, that the flight to the west refers to Britons who are known to have moved south-west to Armorica. By the end of Sidonius Apollinaris' life these people were known as Britanni. There may have been three phases of migration of Britons to Britanny/Armorica. Later British sources support this view, suggesting that the first took place in the time of Magnus Maximus in 383, and was composed of the followers of Maximus and their families who never returned to their homeland.[38] The second may have taken place around 458–60, and is attested in Latin sources.[39] The third migration began in the sixth century and was probably quite prolonged.[40]

The earliest mention of the term 'Britanni' in connection with the inhabitants of Britanny/Armorica occurs in a letter written by Sidonius. From him it is known that their chief was Riothamus, who is also mentioned by Jordanes as the leader of '12,000 Bretons' who appealed to the Emperor Anthemius around 470 for help against the Visigoths.[41] This migration is alluded to by Gildas, who relates that after the Saxon revolt people went overseas. Clearly they were not going willingly for they 'loudly wailed' against the sound of the sails.[42] The historian also comments on the fact that they took from Britain those books which were not burnt.[43] The implication is that the exiles comprised or included some of the educated élite.

Sidonius refers to the Britanni in a letter to Riothamus[44] which asks him to listen to the complaint against one of the 'Bretons', presumably a follower of the king, from the unassertive and humble bearer of the letter. By the latter half of the fifth century Armorica was regularly described as Breton, and it is likely therefore that the first settlements of Britons there pre-dated this.

The later colonization of Britanny in the sixth century seems to have been from the south-west peninsula of England (the Breton language is closely related to Cornish), but Welsh clerics seem to have been among the leaders.[45] The process of colonization was prolonged, extending through the sixth and seventh centuries. It has been argued that the impetus behind this migration was fear of Irish raiding rather than Anglo-Saxon pressure,[46] but this explanation does not necessarily account for the two previous folk movements.

Two Lifestyles Side by Side?

Whether or not there was a dramatic massacre at a conference, or exile of at least some members of the ruling class, it is evident that a Romano-British lifestyle continued after a fashion well into the sixth century. It is equally clear that people living typically barbarian lifestyles (living in wooden-built houses in undefended villages, using hand-made pottery and bartering rather than using coins) were farming the countryside alongside the old estates. Several sites have been excavated, with a similar number of cemeteries showing a pagan, subsistence farming lifestyle. Some graves suggest that intermarriage and cultural exchange occurred to a limited degree.

Only a few Roman villas have been examined for evidence of barbarian usage in the period. Barton Court (Oxfordshire) and Orton Hall Farm (Northants)[47] show signs of having been taken over and farmed by people using goods of North European barbarian origin. Such a pattern would fit a federate type of relationship with the local landowners. One very good reason why the two populations might have remained apart on an everyday basis was that the Anglo-Saxon incomers were, and remained until the late sixth century, pagans.

Interestingly, the language adopted was that of the incomers – notably not the case elsewhere. French, Italian and Spanish, for example, remain Latin-based. Romanian (modern Romania is approximately the province of Dacia which was abandoned to the Goths) very notably remains today closer to Latin than to any other language including Italian. It is difficult and dangerous to make inferences about the spoken word, but there may be an implication that (unlike the Goths, for example) the dominant factions did not aspire to Roman life as they found it in Britannia. Conversely, without the economic and financial backing of the empire, Romano-British life would increasingly have been forced to depend on barbarian producers of everyday necessities: most farm produce, pottery, metal and leather goods, for example. The occurrence of such goods therefore does not necessarily imply barbarian origins of the users.

THE EARLY CAMPAIGNS

Whatever the truth about the first settlements, and whatever the precise origins of the first migrants, the *Anglo-Saxon Chronicle* – with notable economy of detail – tells of conflicts in the late sixth century. According to the *Anglo-Saxon Chronicle* (which is very unreliable for this period), Hengest and Horsa were followed by Aelle (trad. arrived 477) and Cerdic (in the 490s) and undoubtedly many others. In 552 Cynric fought the Britons in Searoburh (Old Sarum) and put them to flight. In 556 Cynric and Ceawlin 'fought the Britons at Beranburh (Barbury Castle)'. In 571 Cuthwulf fought the British at Bedcanford, and took four settlements, Limbury, Aylesbury, Benson and Eynsham. In the same year he 'passed away'.

The most famous warrior from this period was the legendary foe of the Anglo-Saxons, King Arthur. Generally believed to be a late Romano-British leader, his combative prowess prevented the advance of Anglo-Saxon culture and people into the south-west of England in the opening years of the sixth century. Both archaeological and historical evidence suggests that westward expansion of the Anglo-Saxons was delayed for much of the first half of the sixth century until the newly established kingdom of Wessex expanded. Some areas, such as the Chilterns, remained predominantly Romano-British until the battle of Bedcanford in 571.[48]

In 577 Cuthwine and Ceawlin fought the Britons and killed three kings – Coinmail, Condidan and Farinmail – 'in a place called Dyrham'. They took three cities – Gloucester, Cirencester and Bath. In 584 Ceawlin and Cutha fought the Britons at Fethanleag (near Stoke Lyne) and Cutha was killed.

Ceawlin took many villages and innumerable spoils and went back to his own lands 'in anger'.

THE KINGDOMS

By the seventh century the wars, skirmishes and more protracted campaigns (some against Britons, some against other Anglo-Saxon groups) produced seven major Anglo-Saxon kingdoms: the Heptarchy. Of these Kent,[49] East Anglia (the East Angles), Essex (East Saxons) and Sussex (South Saxons) were important in the seventh century. Northumbria (Angles north of the Humber) flourished in the seventh–eighth centuries, Mercia (Middle Saxons) in the later eighth–ninth and Wessex (the West Saxons) from the ninth century onwards.

SUTTON HOO

Some time in the seventh century a king in East Anglia died and was buried with a splendid and now very famous set of gold- and garnet-decorated possessions at Sutton Hoo in Suffolk. The find illustrates two factors. First, the armour was never meant to see real service in battle, so here we may have a very different leader from, for example, Attila, who was humbly dressed in everyday life (though he was buried with many treasures). Secondly, there are objects from both pagan and Christian iconography which illustrate the merging of the two societies.

Mound 1 at Sutton Hoo is the finest Dark Age burial to survive from Europe. The deceased, usually identified as Redwald, King of the East Angles, was laid to rest around 625 in an oar-powered ship over 27 metres long amid the panoply of his elevated status. In addition to these essentials and the gold-and-garnet regalia appropriate to a king were exotic objects such as a silver dish from the Byzantine imperial workshops of the Emperor Anastasius (AD 491–518), already old when it reached the grave, a fluted silver bowl with a small silver bowl inside, both East Mediterranean (as was a large bronze bowl with drop handles), and a hoard of Frankish gold coins in a purse. The deposit also contained a set of burr-walnut cups, an otterskin cap, combs, knives, a wooden box, folded textiles, leather clothing and shoes, a horn cup, bronze hanging bowls, drinking horns, maplewood bottles, buckets, a cauldron with its wrought-iron suspension chain, an iron standard and a ceremonial stone whetstone surmounted by a bronze stag.[50]

The World of the Hero Warrior from Literature

Britain has produced more heroic literature extolling the virtues of the warrior lifestyle than anywhere else at the time, though the Goths, Huns and others also used poetry and song. The British epic material includes the poem *Beowulf*[51] and the more fragmentary stories about *Finn* and *Waldhere*, *Widsith* and the *Elegy of Deor*.[52] These poems date back to the eighth century. The most recent assessment of *Beowulf* suggests that it was composed at this date by the Angles.[53] These stories contain references to characters who appear in the other tales. There is likely to have been another body of heroic tales, now lost, relating to the period of the Anglo-Saxon settlement of England, most notably a story about Hengest and Horsa which provided material for Nennius' *Historia Britonnum*.[54] Additionally, preserved in the *Anglo-Saxon Chronicle* is a group of later Anglo-Saxon poems that are historical. These start with the *Battle of Brunanburh* (fought by Aethelstan in 937), and include *The Battle of Maldon*.[55] They are contemporary with the events they describe, and make no reference to the characters who figure in the first group.

Beowulf provides clues to some aspects of Anglo-Saxon warriorship. The scale of gift-giving can be seen exemplified by the fact that Healfdene's son gave the hero a golden standard, an ornamented banner, a helmet and mail-coat and a famed ancient sword (lines 1020–4). The acquisition of booty is clearly described. In the account of one battle, lines 2985–7 state that one warrior plundered the other and took from the dead King Ongentheow his iron byrnie, his helmet and his 'tempered hilted sword'.

In lines 2361–2 we are told that Beowulf managed to carry off thirty battle-shirts, even though on that occasion he was fighting on the losing side.

Warriorship as a Career Option in Early England

There was an Anglo-Saxon saying that warfare was proper 'for a nobleman'.[56] Warriorship was certainly a career option only for those of the right birth. Even those of the right social class, however, had to be fit for the work. It would appear that kings or chiefs if necessary recruited top warriors by head-hunting from neighbouring areas. As has been seen repeatedly in this book, allegiances among barbarians often changed and loyalties could be bought or won.

In *Beowulf* we are told that Hrothgar attracted men from other areas. One such was Wulfgar, a Scandinavian Vendel (not to be confused with Vandal!)

chief, and another was Beowulf himself. Beowulf asserts that such was his service to Hygelac, his first lord, that there was no need to seek recruits from among the Gifthas (the Spear-Danes) or the Swedes.[57]

THE NEW ROMAN CONQUEST – CHRISTIANITY

The situation in Britannia changed through the deliberate introduction of Christianity to Kent after a mission by St Augustine (not to be confused with St Augustine of Hippo) in 597. The Kentish king was married to Bertha, a Christian Frankish princess, and undoubtedly, as on the continent, the adoption of the faith was intended as a demonstration of loyalty towards the remnants of the Roman Empire. With its panoply and ceremony, Christianity was a useful medium through which to channel diplomatic gifts and discussions. A common bond such as shared beliefs helped to break down political, social or trade barriers. From that time on the links with the continent which had never been severed were reaffirmed on increasingly organised levels.

Gradually all the barbarian kingdoms adopted Christianity. Under Penda, King of Mercia, there was a resurgence of paganism in the second quarter of the seventh century, but the warrior ideal gradually deteriorated into myth through epic poetry. Formal laws were established and, for the purposes of this book, society failed to live up to the warrior ideal.

By the time of Aethelstan of All England (895–939), trade and industry, the arts and learning gave young men something other than aggression on which to focus their attention. The kingdoms still went to war, but now they had organised armies. They battled against the Vikings, the Celts and, eventually, the Normans.

Theodoric the Great, as depicted on the Sennigallia gold medallion. A sixth-century writer quoted Theodoric as asserting that the Roman who imitated the Goth was without worth, though the Goth who imitated the Roman was 'valuable'. Probably apocryphal, this remark none the less emphasises the admiration Theodoric displayed for all things Roman. (Deutsches Archaologisches Institut, Rome)

The Projecta casket from the Esquiline Treasure, Rome. This bridal casket dates from the second half of the fourth century and commemorates a wedding – of Projecta and Secundus. (British Museum)

Part of a battle sarcophagus, currently in the National Museum, Rome. It depicts Roman soldiers defeating barbarian warriors. (Deutsches Archaologisches Institut, Rome)

One of the earliest relief sculptures from the Frankish world was found at Hornhausen and depicts a horseman. It dates from the late seventh century and is now known to have been part of a screen, with other figures and what may have been a hunting scene. The warrior carries a spear and a round shield as well as a sword, and appears to be riding without a saddle but with a bridle and reins. He has long hair and a beard. (Landesmuseum fur Vorgeschichte, Halle)

Silver coin of Trajan Decius (249–251).

Gold coin of Aurelian (270–275).

Gold coin of Valentinian I (364–375).

Gold coin of Valens (364–378).

Gold coin of Gratian (367–383).

Gold coin of Theodosius II (379–395).

Gold coin of Flavius Victor (387–388).

Gold coin of Priscus Attalus (409–410 and 414–415).

Gold coin of Honoria (c. 425–454).

Gold coin of Valentinian III (425–455).

Gold coin of Galla Placidia (d. 450).

Silver coin of Odovacar (d. 493).

Gold coin of Theodoric (c. 493–518).

Silver coin of Thrasamund (496–523).

Gold coin of Athalaric (526–534).

Gold coin of Swinthila (621–631).

The Frankish helmet from the warrior burial at Morken, *c.* AD 600. This is perhaps the most famous example of the Spangenhelm helmet, which was constructed with an iron framework to which leaf-shaped iron plates were attached, giving it a conical shape. Cheek-pieces and a chain-mail neck-guard were hinged to the frame, while the nose-guard was rivetted in place. The plates were coated in gilt bronze, and the helmet was lined with leather. Such helmets were probably made in northern Italy, but were ultimately modelled on an Asian, possibly Iranian, source. They were adopted by the Ostrogoths and Byzantines. The Morken helmet had certainly seen use in battle – it bore several dents, the nose guard had broken off and the gilding was worn away in places. (Rheinisches Landesmuseum, Bonn)

Reconstruction of the Frankish warrior burial at Morken. The shield fittings can be seen bottom right. Early seventh century. (Rheinisches Landesmuseum, Bonn)

The Plieshauzen gold disc-brooch. This depicts a mounted warrior, possibly modelled on a saint. Seventh century. (Wurttembergisches Landesmuseum, Stuttgart)

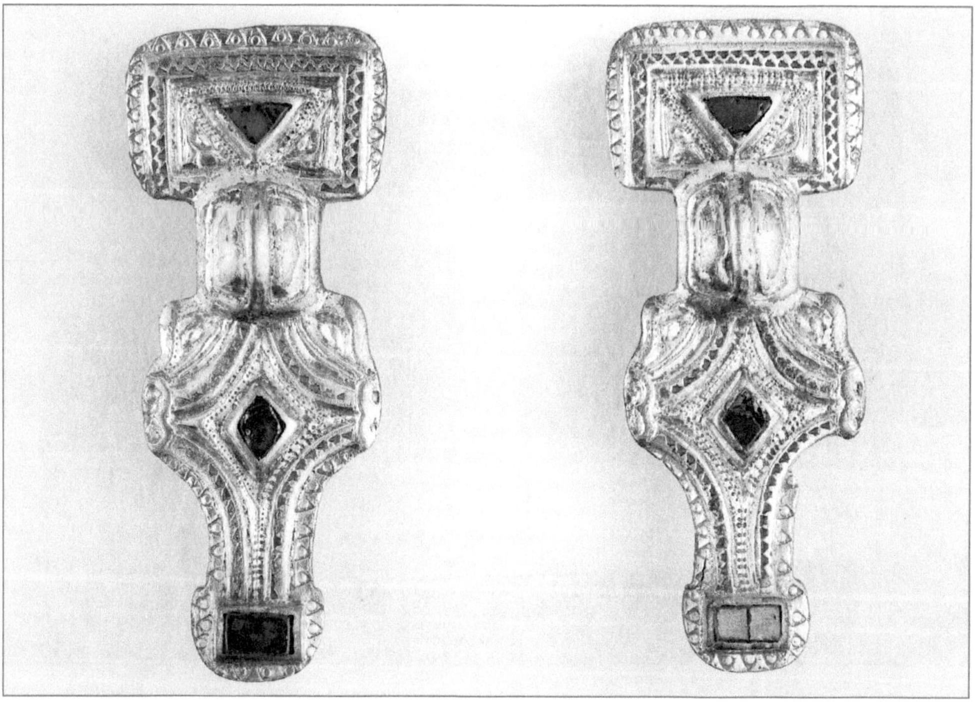

Square-headed brooches with inlays. Sixth century. Brooches like these have been found in Kent and at Herpes, Charente, France. (British Museum)

Tombstone from Niederdollendorf, near Bonn, showing a barbarian warrior with scramasax, combing his hair. This side is pagan in character, the other side depicts Christ. Seventh century. (Rheinisches Landesmuseum, Bonn)

Alamannic helmet from Grave 12, Niederstotzingen, Germany. (Wurttembergisches Landesmuseum, Stuttgart)

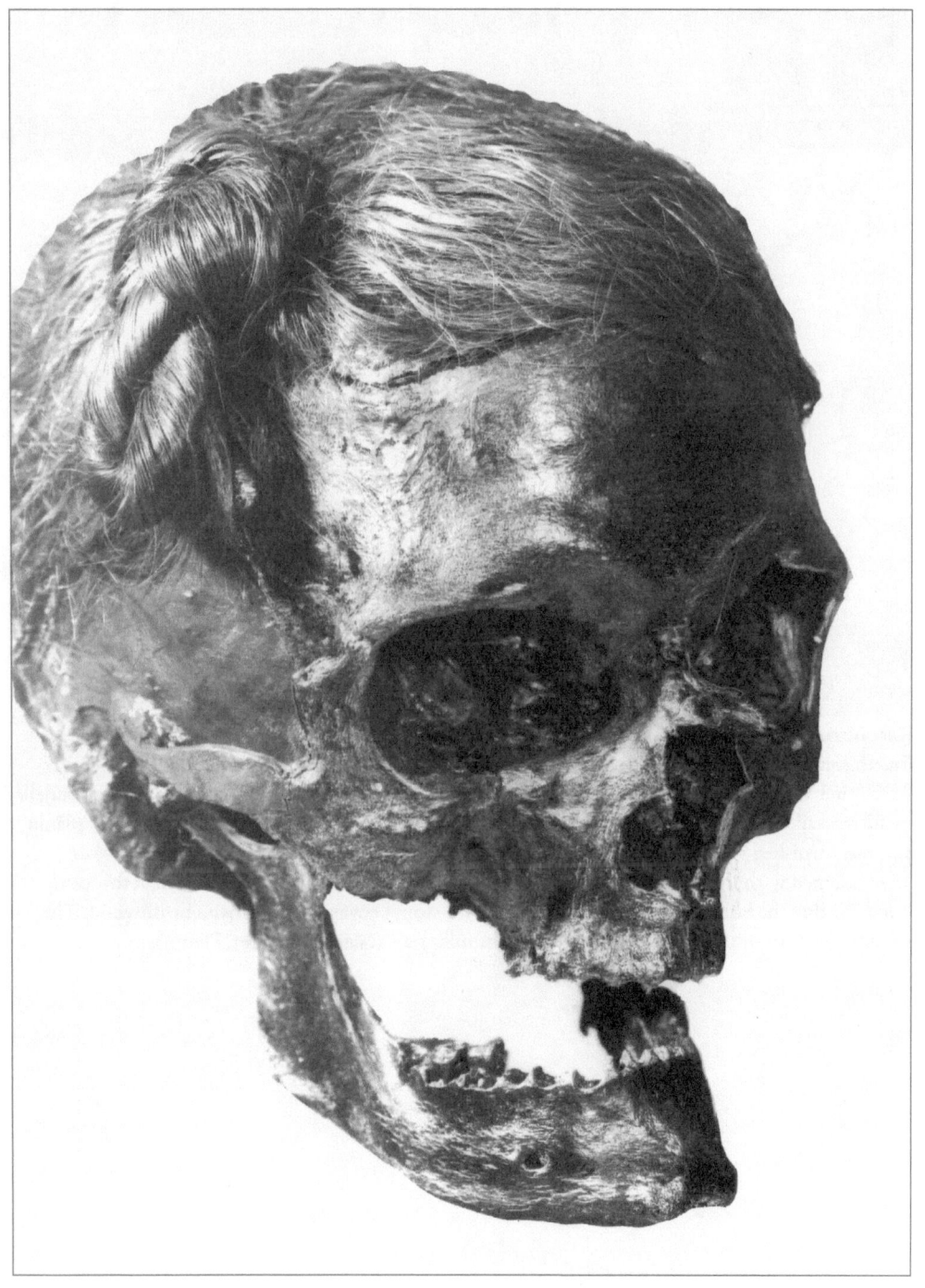

Preserved head from a peat bog at Osterby, showing Suebian hair-knot. (Stiftung Schleswig-Holsteinische Landesmuseum Schloss Gottorf, Archa[um]ologisches Landesmuseum)

Reconstruction of the Nydam ship. Found in 1860, this ship had been deliberately sunk in the later fourth century. When it was excavated, the finds included more than a hundred swords, together with other weapons. The boat was about 70 ft long and 9 ft wide at its greatest point; it was propelled by fifteen sailors and a steersman, the rudder being 6½ ft long. The craft was built from oak planks, and was furnished with rowlocks (fifteen each side), fixed in position. The overlapping strakes were fastened with iron nails. There was no deck but, as the rowers would have needed footrests, it may be that the bottom of the boat was filled with stones covered with woven brushwood. The seventh-century ship from Sutton Hoo was of similar size. (Nationalmuseet, Denmark)

Wooden shields recovered from a ship burial at Hjortspring, Denmark. This plank-built warship was 19.2 m (58 ft) long and may have been manned by twenty men. It was buried in the late first/early second century BC, with many weapons. (Nationalmuseet Denmark)

The Thjorsberg phalera. This decorative disc was made in the third century AD in a provincial Roman workshop, and native details were added. From a votive deposit in North Germany.

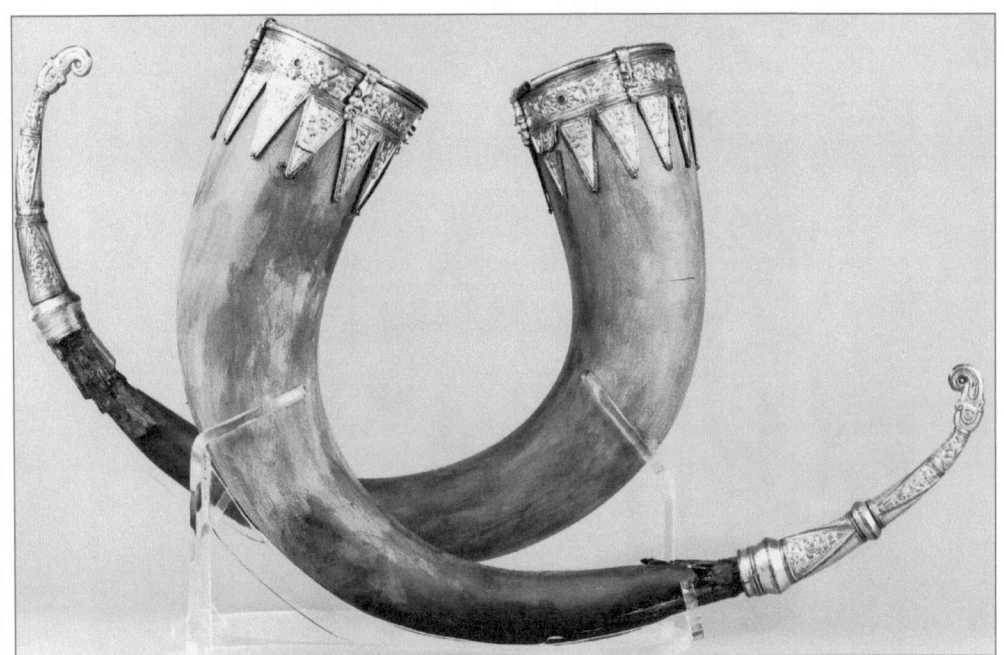

Drinking horns from a seventh-century grave at Taplow, Buckinghamshire. A helmeted warrior, his hand in the typical thumbs-up position, is apparent in the decoration on one of the horns. (British Museum)

Ring swords became fashionable in the sixth century and it is reckoned that the ring was an honour bestowed on the sword-bearer from his overlord, and symbolised the warrior's loyalty. Rings are sometimes found attached to other objects, for example on the Sutton Hoo shield. At first the ring was fastened through a staple, but later it sometimes took the form of a lateral attachment, cast in one, as for example on the Sutton Hoo 1 sword. (British Museum)

Ivory diptych of an empress, possibly Amalsuntha, *c.* 530. Amalsuntha was the daughter of Theodoric the Great and his wife Audefleda, daughter of the Frankish king Lodoin. Theodoric arranged a marriage for their daughter with the young Amal, Eutheric, who was wise, brave and healthy and lived in Spain. (Kunsthistorisches Museum, Vienna)

This fine painting, *Landscape along the Rhine*, by Joseph August Knip (1777–1847), painted in the early nineteenth century, illustrates why major rivers proved to be such important barriers, physically and notionally, in Europe during the Dark Ages. Both Julius Caesar and Tacitus referred to the barbarians living north of the Rhine–Danube frontier as 'Germani' and distinguished them from the Celts. (Haags Gemeentemuseum, Netherlands/Bridgeman Art Library)

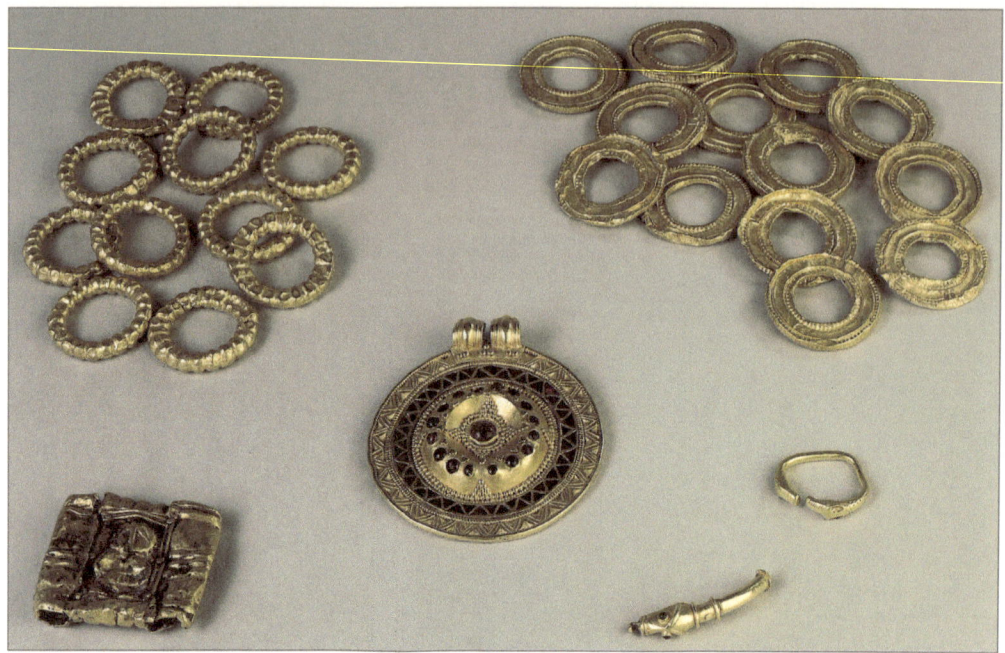

Items from the Szilagysomlyo treasure, found in Transylvania. This hoard, deposited around AD 400, contained twenty-four gold medallions of Constantius II, Valens and Gratian. Other objects included cabochon gem-studded bow brooches and an ornate circular brooch with onyx. (Kunsthistorisches Museum, Vienna)

Imitative medallion depicting the Roman Emperor Valens, from the Szilagysomlyo treasure. (Kunsthistorisches Museum, Vienna)

Ostrogothic treasure. Warrior burials are rare among the Ostrogoths, but hoards such as the Cesena treasure, found near Domagnano, can give an insight into this elusive warrior society. Finds included two cloisonné necklace pendants, a heavy gold ring, an ear-ring with garnets and pearls, a pair of mounts from knife sheaths, a large hairpin, and two gold and garnet mounts with crosses flanked by fish, one of which can also be interpreted as a representation of a facing helmet. Also found there was a superb example of an eagle brooch, a type often associated with the Goths, in gold and garnet cloisonné work. (British Museum)

Friedrich Tüshaus's (1832–85) dramatic depiction of a battle between Roman soldiers and barbarians on the Rhine. (Westfalisches Landesmuseum)

Items from the Desana treasure, found in 1941. The contents of the jewel chest were clearly influenced by Roman traditions and included a gold armband from the late fourth century, a gold rouge-jar, studded with amethysts, from the fifth century, and several brooches from the early sixth century. There were also several silver spoons of a type found in noble Roman households in the fifth and sixth centuries. (Musei Civici, Torino)

The mosaic from Bordj-Djedid in North Africa. This shows a Vandal, with typically long hair and shaven face with small moustache, riding out on a lively horse. In the background is a towered half-timbered villa. It seems that the Vandals adopted many Roman traditions, enjoying seaside villas, dinner parties and hunting. (British Museum)

Reconstruction of the Frankish prince's grave at Cologne. The boy, aged about six, was laid on a wooden bed with a chair at the head (the only two reconstructable pieces of Frankish furniture), accompanied by his weapons and other items, including glass vessels, a gold ring and a coin. Whether the boy was a member of the royal family or not has been disputed.

Finds from the above burial. Weapon sets from this period often consisted of two or more weapons, suggesting that among the Franks, as among the Anglo-Saxons, weapon burial was connected with status as much as with warrior service. The boy was buried with a helmet, shield, angon, sword, spear, francisca, and bow and arrows. The helmet had a gilded frame of narrow strips, cheekpieces, mail neck guard but no nose guard. There was also a wooden staff, assumed to be a sceptre. (Dombauarchiv Koln)

Female burial finds from Cologne: the sumptuous finds include an armring, rings, brooches and a small dagger. (Dombauarchiv Koln)

Personal ornaments from the grave of the high-status Frankish female, sixth century.

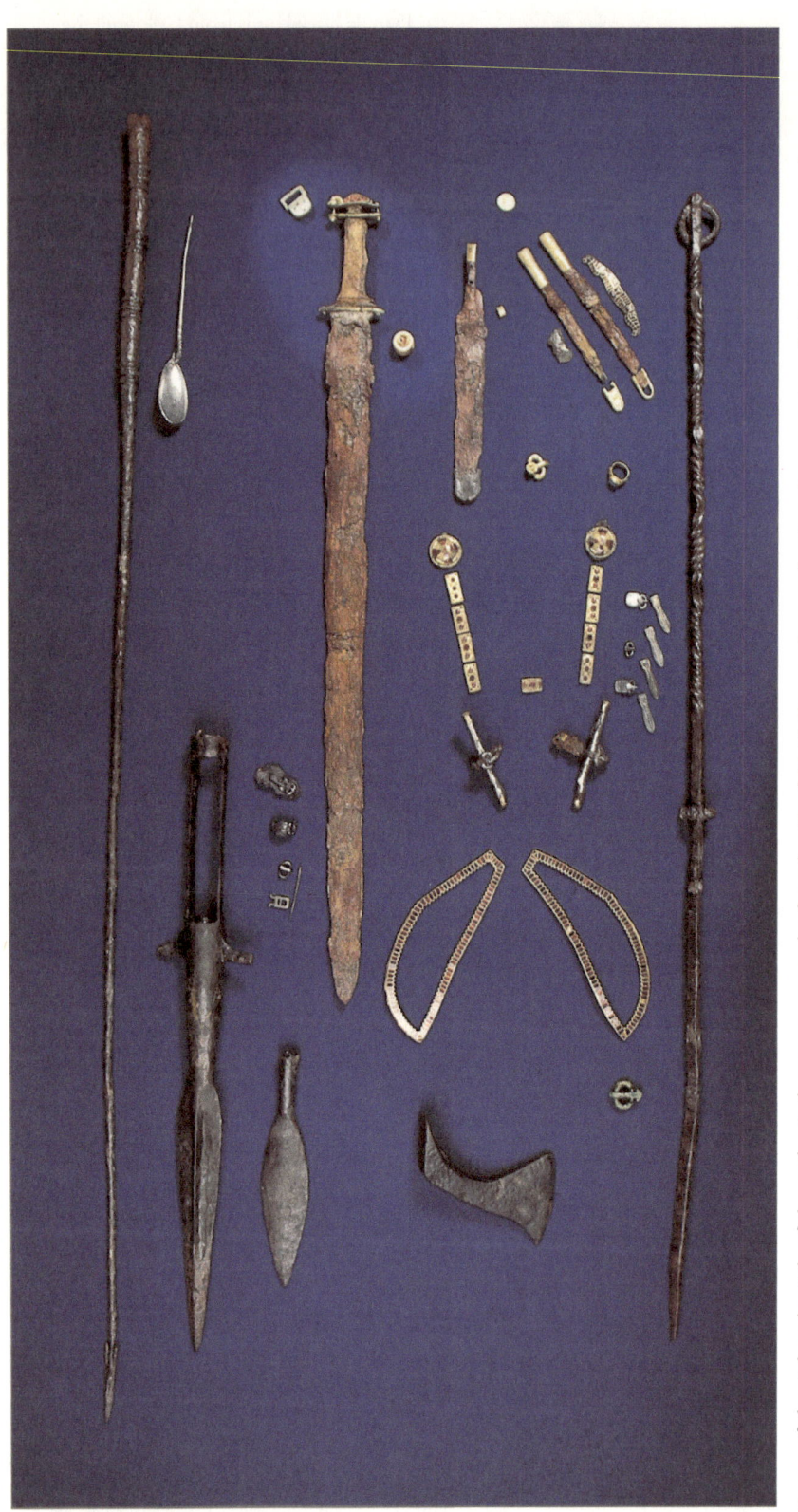

Some of the richest burials of the early sixth century are to be found at Krefeld-Gellep, perhaps reflecting the extension of Clovis' power to the Rhineland. Grave 1782 was especially rich, and seems to have been a founder's tomb in a new part of the cemetery. Deposited around 525, the grave contained a number of splendid items including a gilded Byzantine spangenhelm, long sword, angon, spear, francisca, a gold finger ring with antique gem, a Roman silver spoon, gold and garnet jewellery, including harness fittings, eating knives with gold filigree on the handles and vessels of glass and bronze. (Reiss-Museum Mannheim)

A reconstruction of the saddle from grave 446, Wesel-Bilich, dated to the seventh century, and decorated with eagle appliques. Although warriors were sometimes buried with horses, this custom may have been more representative of status than of actual use in battle. (Reiss-Museum Mannheim)

The shoulder clasps from Mound 1, Sutton Hoo. These were part of the exquisitely made gold and garnet decorated insignia buried with a king of East Anglia, possibly Redwald, in the seventh century. Such insignia was never meant to see real service in battle and was primarily symbolic of the king's status. (British Museum)

The Sutton Hoo helmet is the most ornate of the three Anglo-Saxon helmets known in England. Modelled on Roman parade helmets and furnished with a vizor, it was made by an armourer of exceptional ability. The cap was made from a single piece of iron, to which were attached ear flaps and a neck guard. It seems to have been lined with leather. Tinned bronze foil plates, fastened on top of the iron base, would have given the helmet a silvery appearance. These plates were held in place by fluted bronze strips, and binding strips also edged the sections of the helmet. The panels were die-stamped, some with intertwining animals, others with scenes from northern mythology. The whole helmet has a crest of iron with silver wire inlay, ending in ferocious animal heads with garnet eyes. The eyebrows on the helmet cap above the vizor end in boars' heads. The vizor has a high-relief moustache, and a hollow nose with nostril holes. The vizor, which is fixed to the helmet cap (in contrast to the ear flaps and neck guard, which are hinged), has die-stamped sheets of foil with animal interlace ornament. There is gilding on the crest, nose and moustache. (British Museum)

Silver and gold beaker from Himlingøje, Denmark, which shows Roman influence in its design. Dating from around the third century AD, it came from a rich burial. There is a Roman pointed glass vessel from this site. (Nationalmuseet, Denmark)

Chapter 7

The Panoply of War and Ostentatious Display

> Wisps of hair are trained over the tips of his ears, in the National fashion.[1]
> Sidonius Apollinaris writing to his friend Agricola about
> Theodoric II of the Visigoths.

Barbarian fashions were different from those of the Roman world and a constant source of comment, for they were considered to be in bad taste. Long hair in particular was frowned upon. The warriors of the early centuries AD loved gold, precious stones and bright colours – they came from northern Europe where the light is thinner, colder and bluer than that of the Mediterranean sun which creates vibrant yellows, blues and reds. They proclaimed their status with sumptuous adornments in what the Romans considered garish colours. Such objects, the 'symbols of power', had had a role to play in European society from the Neolithic onwards.[2] It was a trait shared with the civilised world, but its manifestations differed.

Barbarian warriors retained and displayed as symbols of their achievements items made in alien cultures – Roman or Persian, for example.[3] Booty and tribute were also a source of raw materials out of which new treasures could be fashioned in line with the flamboyant taste of the kings, chiefs and warriors of the barbarian tribes. Roman gold coin, for example, was recycled into brooches and buckles as well as other items designed for personal adornment.

A number of richly furnished royal or noble burials in early medieval Europe have shed light on the symbols of power of the barbarian leaders. Some of the interred are identifiable (Childeric, for example) while some are probably identifiable (Redwald at Sutton Hoo); others remain the subject of debates (the anonymous young prince found under Cologne Cathedral).

Documentary sources describe the sumptuous burials of Attila and Clovis, and the accounts of the finery worn in the barbarian 'courts'.

The Barbarians at Play

Barbarian men had long hair, wore furs and trousers and many had moustaches. Their love of ostentation was illustrated by Sidonius Apollinaris when he described a Frankish wedding party which was broken up by Aëtius. Scythian dancers and a chorus accompanied the nuptials of a blonde bride and bridegroom, but the gifts had to be hurriedly bundled into wagons. The event turned into any bride's nightmare, with salvers and food being 'randomly flung together'.

Servants with perfumed garlands on their heads carried wine-bowls on their 'oily top-knots'.[4] The bridegroom was at his Frankish best: his blond hair had been drawn toward the front of his head from the crown, exposing his neck. Sidonius said that the guests' eyes were faint and pale, with a 'glimmer of greyish blue'. Their faces were completely shaven except for moustaches, which they combed. They wore close-fitting garments over their lanky limbs, with the knees exposed and broad belts round their narrow waists.

There is a sketch of Theodoric II of the Visigoths written by Sidonius Apollinaris who seems almost to have been giving a character reference for the man, including an inch-by-inch physical description. He had a sinewy neck, long eyelashes (half-way down his cheeks when his eyelids were drooping), delicately moulded lips and milk-white skin. He had a prominent chest and receding stomach, well-girt loins and a thigh which was as 'hard as horn'. His knees were completely devoid of wrinkles. His guards wore skins. He gave quite a show of being religious, was constantly in the public eye and was certainly competitive and sporty. His dinner parties sound less than amusing – the talk was either non-existent or on weighty intellectual matters – and the wine definitely did not flow freely. The food, however, was praised for its attractiveness rather than its bulk.[5]

The Sumptuary Arts of the Barbarians

The Saxons in England, the Goths in what is now Romania, the Lombards in Italy and the Visigoths in Spain have all left examples of fine bejewelled treasures which bear striking similarities. The gemstones are set into cloisons (clasped by gold on all sides). Some debate has surrounded the derivation of the *cloisonné* work – one school of thought suggested that it was developed by Black Sea craftsmen entering France, while another has seen influence from Visigothic Spain. A third has suggested that the technique originated in Italy and was brought across the Alps. Two further possibilities are that it developed in the earlier fifth century in Pannonia and was disseminated by the Huns,[6] or that it was developed under stimulus from the Persian (Sassanian) Empire in the imperial workshops, and reached the barbarian world from the latter source. Research has suggested that the garnets came from south-west Bohemia, and that there was a production centre at Trier.[7]

Szilagysomlyo Treasure

This major treasure hoard was found, partly in 1797 and partly in 1889, in Transylvania. It contained twenty-four gold medallions depicting Constantius II, Valens and Gratian, one with a barbarian addition of a frame of garnets, and was deposited around AD 400. Despite its Hunnic appearance it has been claimed as a Roman gift to a powerful local dynasty.[8] Other objects in the treasure included cabochon gem-studded bow brooches, and an ornate circular brooch with onyx.[9]

Visigothic Gold

Although the archaeological remains of the Visigoths are not abundant, there are some fine treasures. A superb hoard of gold vessels and other items, found at Pietroassa in Romania in 1837, was probably a tribal religious treasure.[10] Probably buried around 450, it contained 18 kg of gold which included cups, handled vases, a bowl, a plate weighing 7 kg, two polygonal openwork cups with animal handles (Pontic or possibly even Persian in origin) and brooches (four in the form of an unusual type of eagle). A warrior with three hair-knots is among the depictions on a huge gold dish. The treasure shows great craftsmanship with Persian, German and Greek connections.

From Spain have come the typically Visigothic eagle brooches, such as the pair from Estremadura inlaid with garnet, opal, glass and quartz. Buckles with square plates and *cloisonné* inlays are also a feature of Visigothic cemeteries, but the finest treasures are Christian, such as the hoard of crowns found at Guarrazar near Toledo in 1858. This remarkable cache comprised nine crowns; two more were found later but were destroyed. The crowns are made of gold studded with sapphires, pearls, agates and rock crystals. They were intended not for wearing but for suspension in a church, and most may have been made for coronations. Some bear letters suspended from chains that spell out names: they include Recceswinth (653–72), who was a Visigothic queen; Swinthila (621–72), a Gothic king; Sonnica (unknown, but probably a queen) and one with the name of an abbot, perhaps made for his consecration.

Hunnic Treasures

Since there is historical evidence for huge amounts of gold passing into Hunnic hands, it is not surprising that stunning treasure has been found in graves during excavation. The best known Hunnic objects are cauldrons, which are found widely in Hunnic raiding areas.[11] Made of bronze, they are reminiscent of those found in Shang and Chou Dynasty China,[12] but given the fact that the Chinese examples are over a thousand years older the resemblance is probably fortuitous. The Hunnic cauldrons are cast bronze, deep, bag-shaped single-footed vessels with pairs of handles, often with a 'mushroom' on top, and relief-modelled linear ornament. The distribution is almost exclusively Asiatic and East European, though two western finds have been made, one in France near the Seine, and the other in Germany near the Rhine. They were suitable for fastening to a pack animal.

Seven gold-plated (on a bronze core) diadems have also been found with a distribution from Kazakhstan to Hungary. These are decorated with cabochons of almandines (from India) and glass, and were worn over hoods or veils.[13] Gold and silver ear-rings and pairs of gem-studded clips, with filigree, which were worn at the temples have also been found.[14] Die-stamped gold plaques, worn on clothing, are also a feature of Hunnic fashion – in one find from Szeged-Nagyszeksos twenty-six square electrum plaques and sixteen fragments were found.[15] Similar clothing plaques were worn by the Vandals. This ornamental metalwork may have been produced in Pontic workshops, and cannot be said to have been exclusively Hunnic.

The distribution of plate-headed bow brooches in Europe is concentrated in the east, but there is a group in Iberia, an area not associated with the Huns, and a number of finds in northern Italy, France and Germany, and it is probable that such brooches were used by many different peoples, including the Goths and Vandals.[16] An early example, in silver, is represented in the late Roman silver hoard from Traprain Law, East Lothian (which also contained other items of probably East European origin), and two fine brooches of this type with gold mounts were found with a mirror in a princess's grave at Hochfelden in Germany, pointing to the wide distribution.[17]

The mirror at Hochfelden echoes the fact that mirrors are a feature of Hunnic graves. They are discs of whitish bronze, with a loop or perforated knob on the back through which a cord was slotted. On their backs they are decorated, like the cauldrons, with uninspiring patterns of lines. They are believed to be of ultimately Chinese inspiration, by way of Sarmatian intermediaries, and the earliest examples date from the fifth century AD.[18]

Hunnic graves have produced no evidence that the Huns in Europe should be associated with the Eurasiatic animal style of art, which arguably played an important role in the development of the art of the barbarian warriors. Arguably it had antecedents in the art of the Scythians and their predecessors,[19] and many attempts have been made to link it to the Huns, but the question is too complex for inclusion in this book.

Ostrogothic Material

The Ostrogoths are not easy to define archaeologically. Warrior burials are not major features of Ostrogothic culture, and the artefacts found in Italy display mixed traditions. There is no distinctive type of Ostrogothic brooch in Italy; the eagle brooch, often associated with the Goths, is relatively rare, though two superb examples in gold and garnet *cloisonné* work were found near Domagnano (part of San Marino) in the cache known as the Cesena Treasure. The characteristically Gepid eagle-headed buckles, found also in Ostrogothic communities before the migration, are relatively rare in Italy, but are sometimes found.[20]

Rich treasures occasionally come to light from this period in Italy. The Cesena Treasure contained a gold chain, two *cloisonné* necklace pendants, a heavy gold ring, an ear-ring with garnets and pearls, a pair of mounts from knife sheaths and a large hairpin. Apart from the eagle brooches there were two gold and garnet mounts with crosses flanked by fish, one of which can also be interpreted as a representation of a facing helmet.

The contents of a jewel chest found in 1941 at Desana consciously imitate Roman traditions; there were several silver spoons of a type found in noble Roman households in the fifth and sixth centuries, and a rouge-jar studded with amethysts.[21] Table services of silver and gilded bow fibulae seem to have been made at Ravenna and exported.

A find from Golognano contained tableware of the late sixth or seventh century. It includes several chalices, one of which bears a name that belongs to an East 'Germanic' language. A platter proclaims it was made by Swegerna whose name had similar origins.[22]

Noble Ostrogothic heads were often covered with spangenhelmen (frame and plate helmets), many of which may also have been produced at Ravenna, and sometimes taken north of the Alps through trade links.[23] A bronze 40-nummi coin of Theodahad (d.536) shows the king wearing one, and examples include a fine one from Lake Geneva.

Frankish Goods

The range of the external contacts of a Frankish warrior chief at this time is demonstrated by objects which originated in Byzantine, Gallo-Roman, possibly Hunnic and certainly North European barbarian workshops.

Childeric's grave seems to have been one of the earliest, if not the earliest, in a cemetery which continued to be used into the seventh century. Excavations in 1983 found a series of three pits with multiple horse-burials adjacent, one containing as many as ten skeletons, datable by radiocarbon to 490±50, and cut into by sixth-century graves,[24] which has been taken as evidence that Childeric was, as Gregory of Tours indicates, a pagan. However, it was not uncommon for Christian converts to be buried with gravegoods at this time. Childeric's grave goods included a gold- and garnet-decorated sword, a gold crossbow brooch (erroneously identified by the excavator, Chifflet, as a stylus), thirty gold and garnet bees or cicadas, a gold armlet, a series of gold and garnet buckles and an array of coins, gold, silver and bronze, Greek, Roman and Byzantine, commencing with a Greek silver stater of Lysimachus of Thrace, datable to the third century BC. Chifflet was convinced that Childeric was buried with the severed and caparisoned head of his horse, and subsequent commentators have suggested that a golden bull head and possibly also the gold 'bees' originally adorned a harness. A horseshoe is among the finds illustrated by Chifflet. Childeric also had a spear, francisca, and gold- and garnet-decorated scramasax, as well as a crystal ball. Of these items, an impression of the ring survives along with part of his sword hilt, two of the 'bees', a gold buckle loop and his crystal ball. As Childeric died in 482, it provides a firm date for his treasures.

Childeric's sword hilt was constructed with *cloisonné* which employed pieces of garnet cut to fit the framework. The grip was gold plated, and garnet adorned the flattish pommel. The sword is possibly not the earliest of the sumptuous swords from Frankish lands. A similarly late fifth-century sword came from Lavoye, France, with similar gold and garnet work, and another from Pouan.

Childeric's is not the only tomb with rich furnishings belonging to the late fifth century. A fine example of a gold- and garnet-decorated sword comes from a rich weapon burial at Planig, where the associated finds include a gold scabbard chape, gold filigree work, gold buckles, gold-mounted eating knives and a garnet *cloisonné* mount in the form of back-to-back eagle heads, as well as a helmet. A gold solidus of the Byzantine Emperor Leo I (457–74) was also associated.[25]

Anglo-Saxon Treasures

Many rich treasures have come from Anglo-Saxon graves, the finest perhaps from the royal cemetery at Sutton Hoo in Suffolk, discussed elsewhere. But mention may also be made of the rich seventh-century burials at Taplow (Bucks), at Broomsfield (Essex) and Swallowcliffe Down (Wilts), the last of a lady buried on a bed. Individual finds of outstanding pieces of jewellery also characterise Kent, where one of the finest treasures of the Dark Ages, a gold and garnet composite disc brooch, was found in a woman's grave at Kingston Down in the eighteenth century.

Chapter 8

Warfare and Society

The minds of young men are often excited by ambition for power.
Jordanes on the sons of Attila the Hun.[1]

WARRIOR SOCIETIES[2]

Warrior societies are found worldwide from many periods. In the 1960s it was thought that there was a killer instinct in all mankind, and that war could be avoided by finding other outlets for aggression.[3] More recently it has been suggested that external factors are relevant.[4] Views about warfare have polarised into two main camps with many variants. One emphasises sociobiology, arguing that humans become warriors in order to increase the opportunities for their posterity, in other words that the phenomenon is a response to innate psychological factors and drives.[5] The second school sees warfare as the outcome of social relations, and draws parallels with the animal kingdom and the need for territory.

There have been wars and warriors since early prehistory, with particular emphasis in the Bronze and Iron Ages, when there was growth of ritual and superstition about warfare. In most modern views the development of warfare (and warrior societies) is seen as concomitant with the development of the state. Anthropologists argue that evolution of the state occurs in stages: from band to autonomous village, to tribe or chiefdom, and then to confederacy followed by fully developed state. Despite its Darwinian flavour, this evolutionary scheme appears to be broadly applicable in many societies, and certainly to the heroic society of the Dark Ages. In the transition from one stage to another, war takes on a particular role – bands have been seen as very egalitarian, states as very centralised.[6]

The Development of the Hero

It is into this scenario that the hero who fights for his people most readily fits. This concept seems to have a universal and enduring allure – modern films and television characters often differ from their Dark Age equivalents only in the technology available to them in performing surprisingly similar superhuman, magical or miraculous deeds. The use of the media to promote ideals of individual and collective physical prowess in support of the general good of the community is not new. All specialists need the support of their communities. Military specialists are no exception – war bands or armies need considerable goodwill and supplies of complex material goods from the non-combatants. Warfare therefore requires that both those who are risking their lives for the community, and those who are supporting them, should feel good about the endeavours.[7] Traditionally, this was achieved through art, music and literature. It is notable that great 'military' figures are not popularly remembered as heroes unless there is literature or song to support this view. They may instead be regarded as good or even brilliant soldiers, but the emphasis is on duty rather than glory.

Accompanying the idealistic portrayal of war and warriors is grim realism, with the result that ritual and superstition and/or religious beliefs become interlocked with the pursuit of war. Thus most warring societies developed gods specifically devoted to war. In some cases beliefs moved subtly from fighting with the support of pagan gods to fighting in the name of the deity.

The Image of the Warrior

The ideal of a warrior is expressed at its best in epic poems which are common to 'Dark Age' societies – Greece and Rome produced Hercules, Jason and Hector, for example. A period of political chaos where the original system breaks down has been observed in many civilisations. Out of such chaos, when communication was almost entirely oral, the chanting and repetition of stories from the past had multiple functions. It was unimportant if the stories were conflated or distorted and if the details of peoples and places were blurred or totally fabricated. These poems are not history, but they do contain useful data which supplements modern archaeology, linguistics and epigraphy.

Essential to the flourishing of the warband was the poet, bard or minstrel (in Anglo-Saxon, *scops*), whose task it was to reside in the court and compose paeans of praise for the lord and his followers. Some poets seem to have been permanently attached to the warband, others seem to have earned their living travelling round – their travels enabled them to build up a flexible repertoire of tales, which were enjoyed not only by the pagan kings but also by Christian clerics. The cleric Alcuin, in reference to the interest shown in such tales by his fellow clergy, peevishly asked the Bishop of Lindisfarne what Ingeld (the pagan god Ingui-frey) had to do with Christ.[8] The earthy and bloodthirsty nature of some of the songs would certainly have fuelled the many diatribes hurled by the Church at the barbarian warriors throughout Europe.

Poets accompanied the warriors to battle as chroniclers, though they could also ridicule and scorn.

Dark Age Epics of Europe

There are two main bodies of epic literature concerning the barbarian warriors of the Dark Ages.

The first, and most comprehensive, group is Anglo-Saxon. The second major source, more fragmentary and mostly later in date than the Anglo-Saxon, is from non-Celtic northern Europe. Generally speaking, it relates to all the groups of people who later formed France, Germany, the Netherlands, Italy and Spain as well as England. The earlier examples include a fragment preserved in a manuscript of about AD 800, which resembles the English *Finn* fragment, and a later poem describing a victory of a Frankish king in 881. There is evidence that there was a thriving tradition of native poetry in France in the time of Charlemagne (early ninth century) – Einhard, Charlemagne's biographer, said the king collected old poems relating to the deeds and battles of former kings.[9]

In addition, there are some references to early migration period heroes in contemporaneous or near-contemporaneous Latin literature, and a body of lore that was set down from the twelfth century AD, including the *Niebelungenlied*.[10]

Warrior Training

Superstition and belief were acknowledged to be insufficient for success, and training began very early. One possible explanation for the huge numbers of warriors that are quoted as gathered together and then slaughtered might be their youth and inexperience. Young Alans grew up in the habit of riding from their earliest boyhood and went through various forms of training so they were 'all skilled warriors'.[11] Commonly boys as young as fourteen or even twelve went to war. The fifteen-year-old Guthlac (an early eighth-century Anglo-Saxon who later became a saint) was fully engaged in warfare and indulged in 'pillage, rapine and slaughter' at the head of a band of youths.[12]

Archaeology provides corroboration (particularly from Anglo-Saxon England) of the early age at which boys were trained for war (or at the very least were regarded as budding warriors). Young boys who died before the age of 8 might be buried with miniature weapons in pagan Anglo-Saxon cemeteries; full-size weapons accompany the burials of youths in their early to mid-teens.[13] A study of weapon burials in Anglo-Saxon cemeteries has shown that there seem to have been three landmarks in the life of a boy: at 3 (possibly related to weaning), at 12–14 (puberty) and at 18–20 (full adulthood). Arrowheads are found in children's graves prior to the age of 14, but almost never from adult burials. Two spears, a shield and a sword might be put into the grave with young males from the age of 12 (though they are usually only found in adult graves), and seaxes and axes are found only in adult burials, predominantly of those aged 35–39.[14]

The weapons found in the graves were clearly not chosen solely because of their practicality for the young – a heavy sword may be found with an adolescent, but the lighter seax or francisca never.[15] This confirms the fact that weapons were a mark of status. The earliest royal burials at Sutton Hoo comprised a group of cremations of young warriors. Mound 5 contained the mortal remains of a young man who had been hacked to death – his skull bears nine sword slashes. He had been cremated, apparently with horses or other animals. The ashes had then been wrapped in cloth and deposited in a bronze bowl within a pit. This also contained bone gaming pieces, a silver-mounted cup, an ivory box with sliding lid (perhaps a stylus case) and shears, as well as other objects which were later carried off by grave-robbers. A mound was raised above the grave, and while it was being constructed a man was killed and his body dumped in one of the quarry pits – perhaps as a human sacrifice, though this can only be a guess. For 500 years unfurnished burials were deposited around the mound.

A group of cremation burials of (mostly) young adult males, similar to that of the young warrior in Mound 5, followed.[16] They display a remarkable variety of gravegoods and cultural contacts – a bone box with Christian Chi-Rho inscription, a bronze jug from Nubia and a limestone plaque with an angel or figure of Victory from Alexandria and board-games. Mound 17 covered the burial of a young prince. Two pits alongside one another contained the man and his horse, the larger pit (for the man) having been furnished with two spears at the bottom, on which had been laid a shield, with an iron-bound bucket and bronze cauldron at the north. A haversack contained lamb chops, and at the west end the harness for the horse had been buried next to him, richly decorated and gilt. One boy of about 6 at Sutton Hoo was given a weapon burial, and one female burial was richly furnished.[17]

WOMEN AND GIRLS

The sources do not reveal whether girls were trained as warriors. If so, they must have been in the minority, though female warriors were certainly not unknown in barbarian society and one mythical (Celtic) trainer was a woman.[18] The wives of the Gauls (Celts) are described by Ammianus Marcellinus as outstandingly impressive in combat, but history is notably silent about, for example, female Goths, Huns or Vandals in fighting mode. While many women must have been actively involved in the way society moved during the Great Migrations, they are rarely individually recorded; when they are, they are usually the Roman consorts of barbarians or vice-versa. The Thuringian queen who went to Childeric is unusual in the records for her assertiveness, but by no stretch of the imagination was she a warrior. Galla Placidia accompanied an army to claim the birthright of her son, but at one point (notably unlike Attila when facing defeat) she was passively 'in despair'.

Logic suggests that at least a few women must have taken part in battle, but if so, their deeds went unrecorded. Indeed, an unplaced fragment of Eunapius shows clearly the interests and biases of the readership of the time. It seems that a woman 'of manly virtue' achieved a feat of such courage and nobility that, he continues tantalisingly, he would not be believed if he recounted it.[19]

In the absence of adequate contraception and gynaecological help (both of which were relatively highly developed in the Roman world), it is likely that many women were preoccupied with child-rearing before dying young. This in turn would have resulted in a surplus of males. Whether these postulations are correct and were a factor in the rise of aggression through male rivalry for suitable mates (and female acquiescence to this, one way or another), as the present writer suspects, is an area where research would be fruitful.

A mythical story related by Jordanes in his *Gothic History* refers to the women of a village taking up arms and casting lots to see who should be responsible for defence and who for the 'devastation of other lands'.[20] The underlying assumption – that laying waste the neighbours needed no further explanation – is a typically barbarian viewpoint. Two leaders were chosen: one remained at home, the other went into Asia. They are later referred to as Amazons, destroying any credibility in the historicity, and the reader is left pondering whether this is a story used to explain real if rare occurrences, or was simply included for its preposterous amusement value to Goth and Roman alike.

Literary tradition among the north European barbarians alludes to female warriors (shield maidens). The classic examples are the legendary Valkyries. There are also a few allusions in Anglo-Saxon literature which perhaps suggest that female fighters were not unknown. For example, in *Judith* we are told (lines 77–80) of a woman with braided hair who drew a sharp sword 'hard in battle' from a sheath with her right hand.[21] Heroic literature accords women equal status with men: significantly, they indulged in the major status activity of giving gifts.[22] The medieval German folktale, *Niebelungenlied*, includes the vengeance taken by the Burgundian princess Kreimhild – a rare occasion where a female character of the period wields an axe to bloody effect.

A few burials of women in pagan cemeteries contain spears.[23] It is unknown to what extent these were marks of honour and status and to what extent they were used.

THE SCALE OF WARFARE

The duel was a method of saving life while settling disputes, particularly when the groups were small. It was popular among the people of northern Europe, including the Celts – Tacitus wrote about the custom – and it is clear that it continued down into the Viking Age.

Gregory of Tours recounts how the Vandals and Suevi/Alamanni quarrelled once they had entered Spain in 409. They were about to attack with their armies when the King of the Suevi/Alamanni suggested that combat between two chosen champions was a more sensible method of settling their grievances.[24]

The sizes of the warrior bands that crossed the Roman frontiers in the third to fifth centuries is fiercely debated. It is essential to distinguish between raiding parties or specialist groups of mercenaries and refugee populations including babes-in-arms. The figures given by ancient authors are increasingly seen as distorted for political or poetic gain.[25] Interestingly, both the small figures listed for England and the huge numbers for the continent have been regarded with suspicion. Sometimes the figures sound so precise that they have been taken at face value.

Goffart has suggested that the larger numbers are based on the 'ideal phalanx', often expressed in multiples of 40,000.[26] Thus Ammianus talks about 40,000 Alamanni, while Dexippus recorded that in the time of Aurelian (in the third century) the Juthungi fielded 40,000 cavalry and 80,000 infantry. It would seem logical that fighters formed groups in direct response to the numbers they would have to face in the Roman forces. Honorius engaged 6,000 Dalmatian horsemen, for example. Texts tend to quote the number 3,000.

Smaller groups were also commonplace – several bands of Franks were encountered by the Emperor Julian in a fourth-century campaign in Gaul. The total number given was 600 warriors, which was considered by the Romans to be a substantial force.[27] In 457 an Alamannic army of 900 men is reported as having crossed the Alps. The numbers of men were not as important as their condition and ability, as evinced by the desperate plight of Radagaisus' troops.

In Britain the situation was in many ways different. The *Anglo-Saxon Chronicle* repeatedly quotes bands of immigrants crossing the Channel in two to five ships (groups of fewer than 250 men).

Once the barbarians settled down, the parameters changed. For legal purposes at least, it was important to show that any type of aggression was not acceptable. In the Laws of King Ine of Wessex (688–726), 7 men in a raiding party were classed as thieves, 7 to 35 as a band and 36 men or more as an army.[28]

The Weapons of War

The range of weapons used by all groups was generally similar: swords, spears, bows and arrows, axes, hammers and different types of seax, knife or dagger. Occasionally the full array of barbarian weaponry comes to light, though often finds are single, frequently in graves.

The sword was highly prized and figures prominently in heroic literature and myth; more universal was the spear, which seems to have been possessed by every fighting man from king to peasant. Bows and arrows were of less frequent use, while axes, hammers and different types of seax, knife or dagger make up the list. As time went on, this repertoire was increased – the Huns used battering rams, and a type of siege engine at Naissus for example.

For defence the shield was universal. Although some form of protective clothing was probably worn by most fighting men, coats of chainmail were rare and helmets seem to have belonged only to the élite.

Evidence of Battles

The historical records of battles in Anglo-Saxon England are in part substantiated by an undatable cemetery at Eccles in Kent. This shows that wounds were certainly sustained in battle by some men. A study of injuries to six men aged between 20 and 35+ showed that there were linear injuries to brow, temple and crown, mostly to the left, which resulted from a downward chopping action.[29] One victim had suffered eleven such blows to his head, five more to his neck, ten to his back and three to his arms. Another had a projectile point wedged in his spine, which had gone in from his right side. The lengths of the cuts suggested they were mostly caused by swords, though one could have been caused by an axe. From this it was inferred that the injuries were the result of combat between swordsmen – three of the six had injuries consistent with duelling, though they could have been sustained in battle. Whether all were the victims of one battle or had died at different times is not known.

Weapons in Texts and Archaeological Contexts[30]

Documentary sources provide comparatively little information about the use of weapons. The most graphic description of Frankish weaponry comes from the writing of Agathias, a sixth-century Byzantine who said, for instance, that the Franks did not use the coat of mail or greaves, and rarely used a helmet. The Franks left their chests bare and backs naked to the loins, covering their thighs with leather or linen. He said that they had few cavalrymen, but that the infantry were bold and experienced in war.

Sidonius Apollinaris states that the Franks used throwing axes.[31] Gregory of Tours, writing about the same Franks, mentions axes being thrown, and makes many references to spears; he also disagrees with Agathias and Procopius by asserting that the Franks used bows, and cites Sulpicius Alexander as evidence that they had used the bow since the fourth century.

There is archaeological evidence for the use of the throwing axe, angon, spear, and bow (as attested by arrowheads) from Frankish warrior graves, and of horsemanship.

Weapons in Graves

Weapon burial is a feature of the barbarian societies with which this book is concerned, but it was not universal among the barbarian tribes and seems to have been fashionable at a particular stage in their development. Weapons made a statement about the status of the individual buried with them, and not all people buried with weaponry were necessarily warriors. Weapon burials are not found among the Vandals, are rare among the continental Anglo-Saxons, and comparatively rare among the Goths. They are not particularly common among the Franks, but provide a wide range of counterparts for those in Anglo-Saxon England. In the most richly furnished Frankish graves there is evidence for all the weapons mentioned by the ancient writers.

An analysis of the gravegoods on the Rhine, especially round Cologne, shows the changing fashions in the choice of weapons for graves, if not for battle. The earliest graves seem to have contained narrow-bladed scramasaxes, but after about AD 600 these were ousted by broader-bladed types. Long swords only appear commonly after the mid-sixth century, and franciscas are typical of the late fifth to early sixth centuries, after which they disappeared from graves. Spears were fashionable from around AD 520.[32] Sixth-century weapon-sets were often of two or more weapons, suggesting that among the Franks, as among the Anglo-Saxons, weapon burial was connected with status as much as with warrior service, and reached a peak of fashion in the sixth century, a fact borne out by the complete array of weapons in the six-year-old boy prince's burial at Cologne. The extension of Clovis's power to the Rhineland is perhaps reflected in the very rich burials of the early sixth century at Krefeld-Gellep, in particular Grave 1782.

This princely burial included a gilded Byzantine spangenhelm, long sword, angon, spear, francisca, gold finger-ring with antique gem, Roman silver spoon, gold and garnet jewellery, including harness fittings, eating knives with gold filigree on the handles and vessels of glass and bronze, conveniently associated with a gold coin and deposited around AD 525. It seems to have been a founder's tomb in a new part of the cemetery to be opened.[33]

A study of Anglo-Saxon cemeteries predominantly in south-east England showed that 47 per cent of adult male burials contained weapons. Female weapon burials are known, but their possible significance is debatable. There are marked regional variations, even between adjacent cemeteries, with the evidence pointing to 'rich' areas having fewer weapon burials than 'poor', which is somewhat surprising.[34] The peak period for weapon burial in England was in the first half of the sixth century, with a decline thereafter and a disappearance around AD 700.[35]

Spears are common, occurring in most Anglo-Saxon weapon burials; shields appear in about half. Swords occur in one weapon burial out of ten, while the seax, the axe and the bow and arrow are relatively rare. Spears are frequently found on their own, with the spear-plus-shield combination the next most common. Seaxes are rarely associated with a shield, while axes and arrowheads are rarely associated with other weapons.[36] It would seem also that types of weapon combination became fewer with the passage of time, and the seax and possibly the shield took over from axes and swords. This suggests that the weapon sets found in graves do not represent the weapons actually used, since the seax is unlikely to have replaced the sword in battle.[37]

Two cremations in the recently excavated cemetery at Spong Hill, Norfolk, contained sword pommels, four graves had possible scabbard mounts and three or four contained arrowheads out of about 2,300 burials.[38]

In the homelands of the Anglo-Saxon settlers weapon burial is very rare. In a fourth/fifth century cemetery at Hjemsted in south Jutland, eighty-eight graves had no weapon burials, while even the large Anglian cremation cemeteries only have a few weapon burials out of hundreds of graves.[39]

Rich Weapon Burials

Archaeologists have defined a 'Flonheim-Gultlingen' group of weapon burials characterised by gold and garnet decoration, distributed in the region south of the Somme and the Ardennes.[40] Although assumed to belong to the time of Clovis, they could equally well be testimony to early, and otherwise unrecorded, successes of Childeric's war-bands.[41] Among the rich finds from these burials mention may be made of the sword with gold-decorated hilt and garnet-inlaid guard from Arcy-Ste-Restitue (Aisne), associated with a scabbard button, and the burials at Lavoye (Meuse) and Chaouilley (Meurthe-et-Moselle).[42]

Swords

Swords were symbolic of everything that was important in a warrior's life.[43] They were not only useful, but also had social connotations. They were valuable, not everyone had one, and few of them went into graves. A sword was often given as an indication that manhood had been reached. It could have been an heirloom or trophy which carried the 'luck' of its previous owners with it.[44] It was customary for a king to have a ceremonial sword on which oaths were sworn and with which duels were fought.

All the Migration Period swords are descended from the Romano-Celtic and Sarmatian cavalry swords.[45] They were broad two-sided weapons used for cutting and thrusting. They required only one hand, and had blades of between 81 and 97 cm in length.

The blades were usually fullered (in other words they had a shallow and wide median groove which the Victorians imaginatively called blood grooves). Blades in the fifth to seventh centuries were often pattern-welded and later blades were sometimes inlaid, but in general terms the blades did not vary much throughout the Migration Period and variations are found instead in the design of the hilt.

The main area for the production of sword blades in the early Middle Ages seems to have been the Rhineland, from where blades were exported for the addition of local hilts. Analysis of some blades suggests that there may have been local production centres in pagan Saxon England, notably near Faversham in Kent; the place-name means 'smith's village', and incorporates the Roman word for a smith, *faber*.[46]

Hunnic traditions, related by Jordanes in the sixth century, narrate how the Huns worshipped a sacred sword. Such traditions were also current among the Hsiung-nu.[47] Later medieval sources referred to a type of curved single-edged sabre in central Europe as a *gladius hunniscus* (literally, 'Hunnic sword'), but there is no evidence that the Huns used such weapons – they preferred straight 'proto-sabres'.[48]

In 1932 at Altlussheim near Mainz in Germany a princely grave was excavated which contained a sword with a detachable guard which was identified as Hephthalite (White Hun). In keeping with Migration Period jewellery, it had a gold hilt with garnet and lapis lazuli (the latter probably from Afghanistan) which was probably manufactured in the Rhineland. The parallels for the detachable guard, however, are Chinese, and some dispute surrounds its origins, a Hunnic identification being just one possibility.[49] A distinctive type of sword associated with the Huns has a round pommel inlaid with a glass bead.[50]

Pattern-welding was a feature of many Migration Period swords. This technique was known from the second to ninth centuries AD in Europe.[51] By this process iron rods were twisted together and forge-welded, to give strength and flexibility. They were usually built up in layers of pattern-welded metal, suggesting that making a one-piece blade was too difficult.[52]

A reconstruction of a pattern-welded sword took twenty-five hours to complete, including the belt fittings.[53]

Inscriptions on Swords

Although not common, some swords do carry inscriptions. Those on the blades are usually maker's marks, and may be names (such as those on some of the blades at Nydam, Jutland) or symbols. They occur in very early finds, but are then extremely rare until the ninth century: there is one on a seventh-century find from Nordlingen, but the blade may have been Roman.[54] Some Saxon swords are inscribed. The hilt of a sixth/seventh-century example from Gilton, Kent, bears a series of runes explaining that 'Sigimer named this sword'.[55] Some sword pommels, notably one from Bifrons, Kent, has the symbol associated with Thunor: a swastika.[56] A number of swords have runes on them.[57]

Stamps occur on some blades. One from the Thames seems to have been stamped with a die similar to one used for striking coins (sceattas) in the eighth century.[58] Another, from the Lark, now in Cambridge, has three figures of boars stamped into the blade. This has been dated to the seventh century.[59]

Sword Hilts

Hilts were added locally to accord with individual taste. They comprised three elements: a guard, which protected the hand from opposing sword cuts sliding up the blade; a grip; and a pommel. Construction had to be sound, for if a sword's grip were to come off or shatter in battle, the sword would be virtually useless. The sword blade normally had a tang which passed through the guard and grip to the pommel. The grip was usually made of some organic material, wood, or plates of horn. The grip often seems too small to be grasped in a man's hand, and it may be that the pommel was gripped as well, or perhaps the index finger extended over the guard down the blade.[60] Two swords from Petersfinger, Wilts, had wooden grips.[61]

The earliest swords (fifth century) had simple hilts. A good example was found in the disused baths of a Roman villa at Feltwell, Norfolk. It did not have a pommel as such, but rather a disc of metal through which the end of the tang was passed and then hammered flat.[62] This feature is found on some early Frankish weapons. Another early Anglo-Saxon example comes from Cumbria, and is inlaid with gold filigree and garnet panels which may have been added in the seventh century to an old hilt.[63]

The standard design for pommels in the sixth/seventh centuries was the 'cocked hat' profile.[64] These often had upper and lower guards of wood, bone or horn, or were constructed with two layers of metal riveted to an organic core.[65] Usually of bronze, the same design is found in gold and garnet work, for example in the sword from Sutton Hoo Mound 1. This design is widespread in Europe, from Pictland in the north of Scotland to Sweden, the Rhineland, Italy and Hungary.

In the later seventh century the pommel profile was less angular, but still of 'cocked hat' shape, rising up in the centre. A good example is the pommel from Crundale Down, Kent, which had a solid iron upper guard and silver gilt pommel, decorated with long-jawed animals reminiscent of some at Sutton Hoo.[66]

Ring Swords

In the sixth century the ring-sword became fashionable.[67] It is reckoned that the ring was an honour bestowed on the sword-bearer by his overlord, that symbolised the warrior's loyalty. Rings are sometimes found attached to other objects, for example on the Sutton Hoo shield and on a drinking horn from Valsgårde, Sweden, but the earliest (free-running) rings are found in England and southern Scandinavia, from where the idea of solid rings probably spread to the rest of the continent, including Lombard Italy.[68] The hilt of the sword from the Chaouilley weapon burial was ring-hilted, as was one from Grave 1782 at Krefeld-Gellep.[69] At first the ring was fastened through a staple, but later it sometimes takes the form of a lateral attachment, cast in one, as for example on the Sutton Hoo 1 sword.

The origin of the ring-hilt on the continent has been actively discussed, and one theory sees its genesis in the use of beads and balls of amber, glass and other materials found with Alamannic and Frankish swords from the fifth century onwards. The manner in which these were attached to swords was debated, until one was found with a strap attaching it to the upper part of the scabbard below the mouthpiece at Klein-Huningen near Basle, dated to the sixth century. Here the ball was of amber, with a knob of silver gilt. Similar balls were found in the cemetery at Bullach fastened to straps, and some were found associated with ring-hilted swords, notably at Chaouilley.[70] Werner suggested that such balls were charms, and that they had originated among the Alans and Persians and were then transmitted to the west by the Huns, who introduced the fashion to the Alamanni and thence to their neighbours, the Franks.[71]

Scabbards

Swords were kept in scabbards made of thin plates of wood lined with wool (so the lanolin would keep the blade in good condition).[72] These sometimes had a chape at the bottom to protect the point from scraping on the ground and a metal mount at the top to prevent splitting or damage when the sword was withdrawn or sheathed.

The sword from Lavoye had a leather scabbard on top of a linen one. A scabbard from Zobingen in Germany was made of wood covered with birchblast, which was also used on Alamannic scabbards found at Herbrechtingen and Oberflacht.[73] At Lavoye linen was used on the outer cover of the scabbard.[74]

The scabbard from Altlussheim was made of thin wood (probably poplar), held together by metal bands down the edges and covered in gold leaf. The sword had a gold hilt with a straight guard made of lapis lazuli, fastened to a silver chape.

Scabbard Harness

The scabbard was suspended by means of a harness, normally on a baldric slung from the left shoulder. The hilt was high, above the waist, and the scabbard was at an angle. The finds from Sutton Hoo Grave 1 include a Y-shaped gold and garnet strap distributor, probably to hold the scabbard at the correct angle, and two gold and garnet pyramids with grooves underneath, which may have been strap adjusters (not unlike the slides on car seatbelts). Such harness pyramids are more or less unique to Anglo-Saxon England.[75] Later scabbards seem to have been suspended from a belt at the waist.

According to the Byzantine Emperor Leo VI, the Franks wore swords suspended by a strap, though some preferred to hang them from belts. At Bullach, in the early graves, swords seem to have been worn from a strap over the right shoulder, hung by side-fastenings. From the seventh century, swords seem to have been suspended from wide belts worn at the waist.[76]

Gregory of Tours[77] said that the Frankish King Gunthram was given a sword by the sons of Waddo: 'They appeared before the royal presence, offering as a gift a great baldric enriched with gold and gems, together with a marvellous sword, the hilt of which was covered with gold and stones from Spain.'

The early nomad swords were contained in *scabbards* suspended from a sword belt with a scabbard slide or loop to hold the scabbard vertically and take the strain of a heavy weapon.

A scabbard suspended from two straps from the sword belt was a later innovation intended to support a single-edged sword at an adjustable angle. It was developed in the eastern Steppe lands and may have been taken up by the Hephthalites.[78]

In addition to a sword, the Western Huns had a second long dagger or short sword, probably of central Asian derivation. This was hung horizontally across the midriff, and may have inspired the *seax* of the Anglo-Saxons and Franks.[79]

THE SEAX

Perhaps significantly for their later reputation, the Saxons took their name from the single-sided weapon known as the seax, which none the less was not used much in the Migration Period — they are most commonly found at this time in Frankish graves, though prototypes are found in Scandinavia in the Early Iron Age.[80] The seax (*scramasax* in Gregory of Tours) was essentially a short sword or substantial dagger: the longest are 54–76 cm long (the equivalent length to a sword) but a shorter variety is also found, 8–36 cm, the majority of which are around 24 cm. The smaller examples may have been domestic knives rather than weapons.[81]

Although comparable with Frankish seaxes, the English versions were generally lighter, with a longer grip and an upper guard curved away from the blade, perhaps for use as a two-handed weapon.[82]

The blades were commonly pattern-welded, with an angled back. The hilt was of wood, horn or bone, and affixed to the tang; pommels rarely survive. The seax appears to have been worn across the stomach, blade uppermost, with the hilt at the right, to make it easy to draw.[83]

ANGONS AND SPEARS

The angon was a specialist form of spear with barbed spikes and a solid shank. Angons were intended to be used as missiles which when hurled embedded themselves in shields and then bent under the weight, so that the shield had to be discarded. A spear bent in this way is known from a cemetery at Prittlewell, Essex.[84]

The angon is commonly represented in Frankish burials, from the most elevated to the humble. Some of the earliest have a distinctive lateral barb in the form of an animal head — these were fashionable in the fourth and fifth centuries, and are mostly found in graves north of the Seine.[85] A good example comes from the famous cemetery at Vermand in France.[86] There is reason to suppose from their distribution that angons originated east of the Rhine.[87] Angons were represented in the Sutton Hoo ship burial, where a group of three had been passed through the drop handles of an East Mediterranean bronze 'Coptic' bowl.[88]

Although long-socketed spears were fashionable among the Franks in the sixth century, barbs are less apparent, but pairs of lateral barbs well down the socket were a feature of Merovingian spears down to the eighth century.[89] Simple spears of various types were current from the fourth century to the Carolingian Age.[90] The spear is the most common Anglo-Saxon weapon, and is certainly a common grave find. Every free warrior was equipped with a spear and a shield. The spear was ceremonially bestowed on the warrior, taken with him everywhere and buried with him on his death.[91] There is evidence that the deceased was often buried grasping his spear, while other weapons were laid round him.[92] Boys were sometimes buried with a spear, even when they were too young to have carried one, and where a spear is absent from a male burial it may well be that they are the burials of the unfree or the excessively poor. On occasion spears seem to have been bent or broken for the grave – whether this was to 'release' them for the afterlife (an explanation often given for bent swords) or simply to fit them in the grave because they were too long is not always certain.[93]

There were six spears in the Sutton Hoo ship burial. One had been laid beside the sword, and was clearly the king's special weapon; the other five lay in an untidy heap where they had perhaps fallen off a low shelf. It is very rare to find more than one spear in a grave: there were seven at Garton, Yorks., and six at Hardown, Wilts.[94]

The Goths seem to have had spears with runic inscriptions, dating back to the third century AD, such as one from Suszyczno, Kreiz Kowel, which is inscribed *tilarids* ('Assailant'). Another, from Dahmsdorf, has the inscription *renja*, meaning 'One rushing to attack'.[95]

In a Hunnic grave at Hobersdorf, Austria, a lance with a head 28 cm long was identified,[96] and another has been recognised at Pecs-Uszog, Hungary, a site which also produced a bow.[97]

BATTLE AXES

It is not easy to distinguish between axes used as weapons and those used in everyday life. The axe as a weapon seems to have been developed from the second century AD onwards in the Elbe basin, and throwing-axes thereafter became increasingly popular with Germanic warriors.[98] The axeheads of the earlier part of the Migration Period are furnished with a shaft-hole and have a blade that is flatter in profile at the top than at the bottom – this type of axe continued into the full Middle Ages and beyond.

The Franks had a distinctive throwing axe, called after them the *francisca*. These had short hafts and an unusually shaped head, with a cutting edge set well above a line at right-angles to the haft, giving it a delicate curve. A fine example came from the tomb of Childeric, and there is an example with its original wooden handle in Rouen.[99] The earliest mention of the weapon is among the Alamanni in the fourth century, and the Franks using franciscas triumphed over the Visigoths with lances at Vouillé in AD 507. Classical writers commented on the great skill of the Franks in using this weapon, and attributed their success to it.[100] A dress-pin in the form of a *francisca* is in the collection at Namur, France.[101]

Axes do not seem to have been used very often by the Anglo-Saxons, but the *francisca* is occasionally represented in English graves. A type of axe-hammer is represented in the finds from Sutton Hoo, Mound 1. It has a slightly downward-curving profile to the blade, with a hammer-like extension on the other end. The shaft is 78 cm long, and ends in a swivel ring for a strap attachment. As Pollington notes, its heavy iron shaft would have meant that there would have been a painful recoil down the arm of the wielder when it was swung at the adversary.[102] There is no continental parallel for this axe, which was found associated with the mailcoat, suggesting it was a weapon rather than a tool.[103]

Bows and Arrows

The main type of bow used by barbarian warriors was the longbow, which is generally poorly represented in archaeology.

Arrowheads, usually in groups of three, start to appear commonly in rich burials north of the Rhine–Danube frontier in the third century AD. From the fact that they are often made of silver or bronze, it is assumed that in such contexts they are status symbols rather than actual weapons, but there is also evidence that bows were being increasingly used by ordinary people around this time. It has been suggested that the barbarian warriors took up the use of the bow after seeing examples employed by Sarmatian archers in the Marcomannic wars.[104]

In Frankish contexts the bow is mainly attested by arrowheads. In the cemetery at Krefeld-Gellep one grave (43) had both leaf-shaped and barbed varieties in the fifth century,[105] and both leaf-shaped and barbed arrows were apparent in a sixth-century burial at Chaouilley, Meurthe-et-Moselle, France, along with angon, sword, francisca and shield.[106] At Inzing-Hatkirchen in Germany, Grave 21b contained a barbed angon, sword and shield as well as a group of tanged arrowheads reminiscent of Roman ballista bolts,[107] and a socketed leaf-shaped arrowhead was present along with shield, angon, sword, spear and francisca of the sixth century in a warrior burial at Alach, Erfurt, in Germany.[108]

The main weapon of the Huns was the composite bow,[109] which had greater power than the longbow and could penetrate armour at 100 metres. Hun nobles gave gilded bows to one another as a mark of status.[110] A few Hunnic bows have been identified and listed, most notably one from Jakuszowice in Poland and another from Pecs-Uszog, Hungary, with gold mounts.[111]

The composite bow had a core of wood, backed with layers of sinew, and plated on the inside with horn, the whole glued together with a type of animal adhesive. This was done in winter, when the cooler weather slowed the hardening of the glue, though sinew was found to be better glued on a warm spring day. After gluing, the bow was left for at least two months to harden.[112]

The bows were 140–160 cm long. They were usually asymmetrical, with a long arm to which the bow-string was permanently tied.[113] Seven bone plaques were used to stiffen the ears and the handle, with a pair on each ear and three on the handle (two on the sides and one on the top). The nock in the ear of the shorter arm was round, the string being looped round it.[114]

The composite bow was used throughout central Asia, and developed from Scythian prototypes of the first millennium BC through Parthian and Hunnic versions into the bows of the Sassanians and finally those of the Turkish cavalry in the later Middle Ages.[115]

Continental grave finds often have arrows associated with axes, perhaps suggesting that axes were used once the volley of arrows had been discharged.[116] The bow was designated the weapon of the lowest class of society in both Thuringian and Lombardic law, though the Alamanni employed mounted bowmen to some effect – perhaps the outcome of contact with the Huns and Avars.[117] A bow and three arrows were placed with the Frankish boy prince found buried under Cologne Cathedral.

Bows and arrows are represented in finds from Danish peatbogs from the later fourth century, from which it can be seen that the average longbow was between 1.5 and 1.8 m, the arrows ranging from 61 cm to 91.5 cm.[118] There are around forty longbows from the deposit at Nydam, Jutland; they are made of yew, with strings in notches near the ends, and the stave ends are tipped with ferrules of iron or antler. The hand grip was sometimes bound with fine thread.[119] The arrows appear to have had four flights bound in with tarred twine, and to have been decorated with gold and on occasion with runic inscriptions or the names of their owners.[120] Quivers have been found in Danish bog deposits which appear to have contained about twenty or more arrows.

Arrowheads are comparatively uncommon as grave finds in Anglo-Saxon England, and bows are even rarer, though remains of them were found at Chessel Down in the Isle of Wight.[121] The Chessel Down bow was 152 cm long. Arrowheads were also found at Chessel Down, some with hazelwood shafts. An archer's brace is known from Lowbury Hill, Berks.[122]

Armour

Hunnic nobles apparently wore *body armour*, as attested by Pacatus in the fourth century, Sidonius in the fifth and Procopius in the sixth.[123] Sidonius implies that Hunnic helmets had nose-guards.[124]

The most useful clues to the appearance of Hunnic armour comes from China, where helmets and lamellar armour composed of small plates joined together for flexibility are attested in the Six Dynasties period (AD 220–589) – a pottery tomb model now in the British Museum shows the type worn by one of the warlike Toba or Wei, a nomad dynasty who were assimilated into the Chinese civilization.[125] Another Toba model of the same period shows a helmeted warrior on a horse which itself seems to have had lamellar armour and a chamfrein (head plate).[126] This type of armour is widespread in Asia.

The *mailcoat* (known in Anglo-Saxon as a *byrne*) seems to have been used but rarely in pagan Anglo-Saxon England. Made of iron links, it was intended to be flexible but able to deflect weapons. A mailcoat was found at Sutton Hoo, in Mound 1, carefully folded. It was very rusted and could not be unfolded, but to judge by its mass it probably reached at least to the wearer's knees. The links were 8 mm in diameter, but jointed or riveted with copper rivets in alternate rows.[127] There are other examples of surviving chainmail, one associated with the seventh-century 'Pioneer' burial from Northants.

Mail is mentioned in *Beowulf* (lines 405–6): '[Beowulf's] mailcoat shone on him, the net of armour linked by the smith's ancient craft.'

Mailcoats are fairly well attested in continental Europe, notably in the Swedish cemeteries of Vendel and Valsgärde of the sixth and seventh centuries.

It seems probable that chainmail was case-hardened by rolling the finished armour in charcoal, and heating it until it was red hot, thereby carburising it (in other words turning the outer layer into steel). Armour, however, was rarely made of solid steel, as it was liable to crack.[128]

Helmets

The main type of helmet that has been recovered from archaeology is the *Spangenhelm*, which was constructed with an iron framework to which leaf-shaped iron plates were attached, giving it a conical shape. There were cheekpieces hinged to the frame, and a chainmail neck-guard – a nose-guard was also furnished, riveted to the frame. The plates were coated in gilt bronze, and the helmet was lined with leather.[129]

Such helmets were probably made in north Italy, but were ultimately modelled on an Asian, possibly Iranian, source. They were taken up by the Ostrogoths and Byzantines.[130]

The most famous example comes from the warrior burial at Morken, Euskirchen, Germany, which has been dated to around AD 600. The nose-guard had broken off, and the helmet had seen use in battle – it carried dents, and the gilding was worn away in places.

Particularly fine, too, is the helmet from the boy prince's burial discovered under Cologne Cathedral in 1959. The boy, aged about six, was laid on a wooden bed with a chair at the head (the only two surviving pieces of Frankish furniture), accompanied by his shield, angon, sword, ordinary spear, francisca, bow with arrows, glass vessels, gold ring and coins. In addition there was a wooden staff, assumed to be a sceptre. The sword pommel still retained part of its wooden grip. The helmet had a gilded frame of narrow strips, cheekpieces, mail neck-guard but no nose-guard.[131] Whether the boy was a member of the royal family or not has been disputed.[132]

A Spangenhelm of Byzantine manufacture was found in a sixth-century grave at Planig, Bad Kreuznach, Germany. This helmet lacked nose-piece and mail neck-guard, but had gilded bronze decoration with arcades containing birds and bunches of grapes, and a cross incised on the front. The Planig grave also produced a solidus of the Byzantine Emperor Leo I (457–74) and a gold and garnet *cloisonné*-decorated sword hilt, scramasaxes with gold-mounted hilts, a gold buckle and other items.

Frankish helmets are rare finds and presumably were rarely worn except by the most socially elevated. Frankish laws suggest that a helmet was worth two horses or six oxen, and Gregory of Tours, describing the Frankish noble

Leudast, said he had a coat of mail, a gorget at the throat and a helmet. Leudast carried a spear, and he had a quiver suspended from a baldric, implying a bow.[133]

Until the late Saxon period helmets seem to have been extremely uncommon, the possessions of the rich. None the less finds from England suggest that there was a thriving tradition of helmet-making, each being an individual product created to meet the requirements of the patron. Three helmets are known from the period under review in Anglo-Saxon England, one of them ornate.

The Sutton Hoo helmet[134] is the most ornate. Modelled on Roman parade helmets and furnished with a visor, it was made either in Sweden or more probably in East Anglia by an armourer of exceptional ability. The die-stamped panels on it are closely related to Swedish examples, and may in fact be Swedish, but the overall design of the helmet is different from Swedish examples and closer to that of the undoubtedly English York helmet. The cap was made from a single piece of iron, to which were attached ear-flaps and a neck-guard. It seems to have been lined with leather. On top of the iron base, tinned bronze foil plates were fastened, which would have given the helmet a silvery appearance. These were kept in place by fluted bronze strips, and binding strips also edged the sections of the helmet. The panels were die-stamped, some with intertwining animals, others with two scenes from northern mythology. In one of these a mounted warrior rides down another dressed in a mailcoat (the type of scene encountered frequently in Roman sculpture and coinage in many guises); in the other there are dancing helmeted warriors, brandishing spears.

The whole helmet has a crest of iron with silver wire inlay, ending in ferocious animal heads with garnet eyes. The eyebrows on the helmet cap above the visor end in boars' heads. The visor has a high-relief moustache and a hollow nose with nostril holes. The visor, which is fixed to the helmet cap (in contrast to the ear-flaps and neck-guard, which are hinged), has die-stamped sheets of foil with animal interlace ornament. There is gilding on the crest, nose and moustache.

Also belonging to the pagan period is the helmet from Benty Grange, Derbyshire,[135] which was found in a barrow in 1848. The grave had already been looted so it is unknown if it originally contained weaponry. The helmet was composed of an iron frame with two crossing iron bands riveted to the brow ring, 2.5 cm wide. The wider of the two crossing bands extended 5 cm below the brow ring to form a nose-guard, inlaid with a silver cross. It was covered with horn plates fastened diagonally in a herringbone pattern. There was a crest in the form of a boar, of complex hollow construction, with inlays of gold, garnet and silver. A strip of fur may have formed its crest.

The 'Pioneer' helmet (dated to 650) was found at Wollaston, Northants., in a richly furnished Anglo-Saxon grave. Constructed like the Benty Grange helmet and the (later) Coppergate helmet from York, it had a nose-guard, cheekpieces and a boar crest, and traces of textile showed it had been lined.[136]

SHIELDS

Shields were fairly universal among the barbarians of the Migration Period; they are usually represented by the iron bosses that protected the fist and by the grips. No Hunnic shields exist so it has been suggested that they were of wickerwork.[137] The Anglo-Saxon word for a shield was *bord* (literally 'board'), or sometimes *lind* (linden wood – the material from which shields were habitually made).[138]

Detailed study of pagan Anglo-Saxon shields has shown that they were of quite complex construction.[139] The board itself rarely survives even as fragments, but appears to have been composed of lathes of wood. The boards on the whole appear to have been comparatively small, ranging from 34 cm to 92 cm, the average being 50 or 60 cm.[140] Very small boards may have been carried by younger men, while large boards were appropriate not only to strong heroes but also to men of high status such as kings.

The Sutton Hoo shield is reconstructed as 91.5 cm.[141] In the centre was a hollow iron boss, which protected the hand holding the grip behind – the grip was flat, and the centre of the shield was cut away (in a circle or less commonly a D-shape) behind the grip to accommodate the fist. The rivets fastening the grip to the board sometimes had decorative attachments on the outside. Metal mounts were sometimes added to the rim of the board – the shield could be used as a weapon as well as a protection.

When not in use, the shield was slung over the shoulder or back. Only in the case of one shield (from Grave 94 at Pewsey, Wilts.) was there evidence for a leather thong attached to the metal grip for carrying it, though some buckles associated with shields may have come from carrying straps.[142]

The bosses from the centre of shields are the most distinctive items to be found in Anglo-Saxon graves. The earliest examples have carinated profiles, and were made out of a single billet of metal, formed first into a cone which was then thinned to form the flange and wall. Larger bosses were made in two pieces. In the seventh century the 'sugar loaf' shield boss became widespread, fashioned from iron bands infilled with plates.[143] Grips were of varying sizes, from about 11 cm to 40 cm, and were usually covered with leather or cloth, though more elaborate wooden covers occur.

From a few pagan burials have come decorative shield mounts, such as the boar appliqué from Berg Apton, Norfolk.[144]

The finest shield from Anglo-Saxon England is that reconstructed from Sutton Hoo, Grave 1. This was shaped like a watch glass and made of limewood and leather, the rim bound by a gilt-bronze strip fastened with clips associated with pairs of dragon heads with garnet eyes and rectangular panels of gilt bronze foils with animal interlace. The boss had a cast bronze knop with animals (notably pairs of confronted horses), and is likely to have been made in Sweden. Apart from this richly decorated boss, there were on either side gilt bronze mounts, one in the form of a dragon, the other a raptor. Bosses on the outside of the shield cover the rivets fastening the fittings on the back of the shield. From them extend strips of die-stamped gold foil with alderwood underlays. These compare with examples from Vendel in Sweden, and may have been made by a Swedish craftsman, if not the same craftsman who worked at Vendel. A ring similar to those on ring-swords was found with the shield and had been attached to it.[145]

Horses in Battle

Except among the nomads, horses played a minimal role in barbarian warfare, being used more for taking warriors to the battlefield than for cavalry charges. Warriors were sometimes buried with their horses, though the custom of horse burial, well represented in the case of Childeric's tomb, may have been a symbol of status and unconnected with its use by a warrior. Horse armour is mentioned in Claudian.[146] A number of early graves have horse harness associated with them, for example in the cemetery at Bernering in Basle. Here Grave 33 of the sixth century contained a bit, mounts for a bridle, a spear, shield, sword and scramasax. Merovingian Frankish burials have two-link bits from the fifth century, for example from Grossorner, Hettstedt, Germany.

A Hunnic type of saddle with gold feather-pattern mounts was found in 1881 at Mundolsheim. Dating from the fifth century, it was possibly an exotic Hunnic or Ostrogothic object. Even more interesting is the saddle from Grave 446, Wesel-Bilich, dated to the seventh century, with eagle appliqués.[147]

One of the earliest relief sculptures from the Frankish world, which dates from the late seventh century and was found at Hornhausen, depicts a rider (one of a frieze, as is now known, with other figures and what may have been a hunt scene). The warrior carries a spear and a round shield as well as a sword, and appears to be riding without a saddle but with a bridle and reins. He has long hair and a beard.

Horsemen sometimes appear in the form of brooches, for example on one associated with radiate brooches from a fifth-century find at Heilbronn-Bockingen.

Chapter 9

Ways of Looking at the Period

It has long been debated how small, non-literate warrior groups with near subsistence-level lifestyles and little unity could have brought about the total transformation of a civilisation complete with fine cities, lavish art and architecture, major defensive works, central control, rapid communication, high levels of knowledge in medicine, science and philosophy, and efficient armies.

The question has never been answered satisfactorily, probably because it makes assumptions that were not true – society did not disintegrate around the time that the warriors moved into the Roman world. Many of the changes were concurrent with the presence of the warriors, but were not directly caused by them. Many changes can be seen to have begun years before and lasted for centuries after the 'Great Migrations'.

Since the period is so enigmatic, with such fragmentary historical and archaeological sources, it can be repeatedly reinterpreted as each successive generation ponders on new aspects. Very diverse factors have been studied in trying to understand how simple warrior societies could become so dominant. Answers have been found in the economic problems of the Roman Empire, changes in population figures, variations in climate, top-heavy bureaucracy, the numerous emperors in the third century, the constant challenges from usurpers and rebels in the later fourth, 'systems collapse', the rise of Christianity, famine, disease, pestilence and sheer moral decadence. The cyclical theory visualises states going through periods akin to childhood, puberty, young adulthood, middle age, old age and finally death. On this analogy the period of the Great Migrations/Dark Ages is the 'teenage' stage, characterised by challenge, novelty and eventual transformation.[1] Modern society is at present undergoing a major transformation in which many traditional skills are being replaced by new. Perhaps significantly, computer technology was invented and driven by young people in their teens (supported and encouraged by the previous generation).

One of the results of twentieth-century technology is, coincidentally, also found in warrior societies – much information is disseminated orally through the media of television and radio rather than by the written word. The warriors had to rely on the memories of gifted individuals. Roman and other writers of the period were just as capable as modern ones of deliberately or subconsciously manipulating material.

THE CONCEPTS OF BARBARIAN AND ROMAN

The Romans, Greeks and Chinese, for example, defined their own identities in terms of not being 'outsiders'. The Classical world called these people barbarians (because the unintelligible noises they made sounded like 'bar bar'). It was rare for writers to take an interest in the details of such people, and when they did it was usually for military purposes, both in order to know the enemy and to elevate their own achievements by describing their fierce opponents.

TERMINOLOGY

Julius Caesar and Tacitus both refer to the barbarians north of the Rhine–Danube frontier as Germani and distinguish them from the Celts. Both barbarians groups led broadly similar lives, used broadly similar objects and held similar beliefs, so it is likely that a major reason for the military interest in distinguishing between them was to establish which interpreters to employ.

Mostly as a result of the comments of Caesar and Tacitus, which were followed by all Roman writers thereafter, the warrior groups have been categorised as 'early Germans' on the grounds that their dialects and languages shared a common root that was eventually developed into modern German. From the nineteenth century on, the issue became tangled with German and Celtic nationalism and the ethnic origin of nations and races in Europe. The standpoint is now looking old-fashioned, if only because the same linguistic roots also led to modern Yiddish, English, Alsatian, Netherlandic, Finnish and Swedish, Norwegian, Danish, Icelandic and Faeroese (Vandalic, Gothic and Burgundian became extinct). These people might just as reasonably be called the early Norwegians or Finns. Archaeologists perpetuate the terminology by using the words Germanic or Teutonic to distinguish certain types of material, mostly in order to distinguish it from Celtic, though the two cultures (in the archaeological sense) had more common features than differences. In this book the term north European has usually been favoured on the grounds that it may be (fractionally) less misleading. As time goes on the different groups can be seen to have some distinctive features though there is no doubt that they also have much in common with each other and with the Celts, with whom they shared a common Bronze Age ancestry and the rigours of the barbarian lifestyle north of the Roman frontiers.[2]

Throughout the debate two major camps have taken opposing sides in a dispute that reached its peak in the nineteenth century but left an important legacy for twentieth-century historians. According to the 'Romanist' viewpoint, the barbarian warriors were a destructive force which brought an end to Roman civilisation. According to the 'Germanist' viewpoint, the incursors of the world of late Antiquity respected Classical traditions, and kept them alive as the legacy of the medieval world, while laying the foundations of a new order based on Germanic social organisation.[3]

ETHNICITY

Contemporary political attitudes have had an important part to play – the question of ethnicity, and national feelings about supposed racial identity and origins have been foremost. The question of whether Europe was basically German or Celtic was raised and by the nineteenth century the Celts were increasingly deemed to have been the original occupants of Europe (at least south of the Rhine) with the Germans as intruders who raided Celtic 'civilisation' in the way that they later allegedly pillaged the Roman.[4]

A reaction to this came with Otto von Bismarck (1815–98), who led Germany to greater unification. German scholars emphasised the importance of the Germanic peoples in the affairs of Europe, and from the 1880s up to the Third Reich, people such as Gustav Kossina interpreted archaeology to argue in favour of the early origins and superiority of the Germans.[5]

Kossina's nationalism lay in wider nineteenth-century attitudes – since the development of Darwin's ideas on evolution (*The Origin of Species*, 1859), the ideas of white supremacy and within that, 'racial' superiority, became popular. Later nineteenth-century thinkers believed that 'superior' cultures spread their ideas to those less fortunate, invasion being the main vehicle for the dissemination of a more 'developed' lifestyle. In this way the contemporaneous colonial acquisitions of Britain, France and Spain in particular could be justified.

Thus it was but a small mental jump to see the barbarian inroads on the Roman world as being not the influx of inferior people destroying civilisation, as some Romans asserted, but rather a superior race taking over a degenerate system. The concept of the *Völkerwanderung* (literally 'Folk Wandering') can be traced back to Wolfgang Lazius, who published a book called *De gentium migrationibus* in 1557. The image of attendant violence and large-scale invasion has been constantly reinforced by historical writers subsequently, using a vocabulary of words such as 'floods' or 'waves' of invaders.

Similar attitudes were fostered in England where the debate raged over whether the Anglo-Saxon settlements marked the end of Roman civilisation or the beginnings of medieval England and the true 'start' of English history. From the middle of the nineteenth century onwards historians favoured a literal interpretation of the texts and a view of the mass migration of Germans to England in the fifth century, wiping out all that had gone before.[6]

By 1870 Stubbs, the author of *Select Charters*, explained that the 'new race' was the main ancestral root of the English and shared the 'primaeval German pride of purity of extraction'. (1870, 1–3).

Although two world wars showed how volatile such nationalistic thinking could be, the 'fire and sword' view of the Anglo-Saxon conquest of England persisted during the 1950s and 1960s.

Since the Renaissance, and more particularly since the eighteenth century, the fifth and sixth centuries have been seen as a great divide between the flourishing of Classical civilisation and the emergence of the medieval world. The Belgian historian Henri Pirenne (1862–1935) saw this taking place in the eighth century AD, when the Mohammedan conquest of the Mediterranean took place and the Frankish Empire of Charlemagne was formed.[7] It is notable that many of the discussions from this time on are couched in emotive and subjective terms – Gibbon's *Decline and Fall of the Roman Empire* exemplifies this approach. Words such as 'disintegration', 'collapse' and 'fall', abound; and imply a superiority over the system so 'destroyed'.

This might be seen as no more than a common response of age to the new generations and new challenges. Through the medium of classical education these attitudes and responses were brought almost undiluted and often unchallenged into the twentieth century.

Spengler (in *Decline of the West*, 1926–8) and Toynbee (in *A Study of History*, 1934–61) drew parallels between the end of the Roman Empire and our own time.[8] For Rostovtzeff, a pre-Revolutionary Russian racist, the 'pure' stock of the Roman Empire had been too diluted by 'inferior' peoples; for the Marxists, the oppression of the many by the few was the explanation.[9]

In the last twenty years there has been a move away from seeing this period as one of 'lost centuries' and towards recognising it as a stage in the development of European civilisation in its own right. Contemporary writers are questioning many of the long-held assumptions about the barbarian 'invasions', in particular doubting the scale and violence of the settlements, the origins of the incomers and the 'ethnic' labels used. A few people at the time saw the period as one of change and transformation rather than an end – St Augustine wrote *The City of God* when he learned of the fall of Rome.[10] Bintliff and Hamerow suggest that the Migration Period should be seen as 'the result of a growing convergence between barbarian communities *increasing* in complexity and Late Roman Society that in many or most provinces was *deconstructing* in complexity' [their italics].[11]

Chapter 10

Primary and Secondary Sources

'Being clever is appropriate to rhetoric, being inventive to poetry but only truth is appropriate to history.'

Procopius, sixth century historian, on his own aims

Since the warriors were non-literate and each area has different resources, each with in-built charm, biases and problems, study of the different groups differs from area to area and topic to topic. For the early Goths, there are detailed stories of battles but few surviving weapons; for the early Saxons, there are no stories about identifiable people, but numerous swords; for the Huns, no settlements and many bizarre descriptions; for the Vandals and Visigoths in Spain, mostly biased historical records and virtually no archaeology.

The historical sources range from gossip and hearsay to first-hand accounts written in poetically florid style to amuse the audience at the time. Political correctness was unknown – though many writers were often constrained for political reasons. Sometimes the accounts read like the more lurid modern tabloids – a fact which has often unnecessarily discredited their validity.

EVALUATION OF THE DOCUMENTARY EVIDENCE

Some frequently cited writings have often been preserved only in the narratives of others. Plagiarism and copyright were not a problem, and while sometimes the original authors were given credit for what they wrote, at other times they were not. Thus Olympiodorus of (Egyptian) Thebes, a source often referred to in this book, is only known from fragments summarised by

Photius in the ninth century and incorporated into some Byzantine manuals of later date. Frigiderius is known only from quotes found in the writings of Gregory of Tours.

Some writers were close to the events described, and may even have played some part in them. In other cases they were remote both in time and location from the events narrated. However, proximity to an event does not guarantee accuracy. Political or career considerations might also colour views, for example. Later writers might have had a wider range of sources upon which to draw. Greek and Roman writers had a habit of using conventional 'set piece' accounts of events. These have to be first recognised and then evaluated by modern historians.

HISTORICAL SOURCES

Roman Pagan Historiography

These were usually written by men who held office in the Roman army or administration and therefore had all the prejudices and interests of their class, but generally did indulge in literary allusions. They include Tacitus, Ammianus Marcellinus, Zosimus, Procopius, Eutropius and Aurelius Victor.

Histories of the Church

These were concerned with the history of ideas and the lives of key personages (for example, the lives of St Germanus or St Jerome). Eusebius was a fourth-century bishop from Caesarea who wrote about the early centuries of Church history.

Regional Histories

Written mostly but not exclusively by churchmen, these include the works of men such as Gregory of Tours, who generally confined himself to the Franks, and Isidore of Seville, who was concerned with Spain. Jordanes wrote primarily about the Goths. Victor of Vita and Salvian wrote about the Vandals, Priscus of Panium concentrated on the Huns and Gildas on the Anglo-Saxons.

Letters, Poems and Law Codes

The letter-writers include the erudite and infuriatingly whimsical Sidonius Apollinaris, whose works included allusions to Goths and Saxons. The most notable Law Codes are those of the Burgundians,[2] the Salian Franks,[3] the Lombards,[4] and the Anglo-Saxon law codes of Aethelberht of Kent, Ine of Wessex and Aethelberht of the Hwicce.[5] Often the poetic or more literary sources are vague and filled with fanciful allusions which were not to be taken literally but were a means of establishing the credentials of the author who was writing for a highly educated élite with certain expectations of traditional, literary style. Total factual accuracy was rarely the aim.

Heroic Poetry
This was typically set down a long time after the events it purports to describe but does provide insights into the society and values of the barbarian peoples. These sources are best exemplified by the Anglo-Saxon poem *Beowulf*.

Miscellaneous
These include the *Passion of St Saba*, which has important information about the Goths, and the *Gallic Chronographer*, who provides a list of events in Gaul. Annals are year-by-year lists of events, such as the *Anglo-Saxon Chronicle*.

Linguistic and Place-name Studies
For this period studies in Europe are generally not well developed, though progress has been made in the interpretation of English place-names as evidence for the pattern of settlements. For long it was believed that names with an *-inga* element (meaning 'the followers of', such as Mucking in Essex – the people of Mucca – or Sigmaringen in Germany – the place of Sigimar's people) belonged to the first period of settlement, but it is now understood that such place-names did not come into existence until around the conversion of the settlers to Christianity.[6]

Place-names have been used to plot the settlement of Goths in Spain, but since similarly derived place-names were also current in much later periods the evidence is ambiguous.[7] Similarly, the place-name evidence for north European barbarian settlement in Italy has often been taken at face value. Certain Italian place-names may be Gothic, Lombardic, Frankish or even later Ottonian.[8]

In northern Europe place-names dating from the Migration Period reflect the emergence of the new landowning military élites. Place-names meaning 'X's land, held by inheritance,' appear in southern Scandinavia (where the suffix is *-lev*) and in Thuringia (where the suffix is *-leben*).[9]

Language and Ethnicity
Considerable progress has been made in recent years in studying loan-words. The growth of contact between the non-Celtic barbarians and the Romans in the first three centuries AD is reflected in borrowings from Latin – these are names for specific items such as 'wine', 'cellar' and 'pillow'.[10] Names for

the days of the week were first borrowed from Latin in or before the fourth century AD in two areas, the Lower Rhine and the Lower Danube, the former when the Romans were pagan, the latter when they were Christian.[11] 'Loan-meanings' are also sometimes found, when the word is native but copies the idea and construction of the original. The Romans borrowed some words from the barbarians. The study of loan-words shows the nature and extent of barbarian respect for Classical Antiquity on the one hand and Christianity on the other.[12]

Principal Historical Sources Mentioned in the Book

AMMIANUS MARCELLINUS: fourth-century pagan Greek officer in the Roman army, who wrote about his own time and was personally acquainted with the situation on the Rhine frontier. The last eighteen of his thirty-one books survive (covering AD 353–78).

BEDE: Northumbrian monk, who wrote the *Ecclesiastical History* (finished 731), the most reliable account of early Anglo-Saxon England.

CLAUDIAN: the last poet of the Classical tradition, flourished in the late fourth century. His works included praise of Stilicho and strong criticism of Rufinus. He wrote panegyrics, epistles, epigrams and idylls.

EUNAPIUS: born in Turkey, he wrote at the end of the fourth century for an educated audience. He was not averse to adding liberal allusions to previous works to enliven the text.

GILDAS: (fl. 540) British monk, who wrote a diatribe called the *Ruin and Conquest of Britain*, condemning both Anglo-Saxons and Britons. Contains historical material.

GREGORY OF TOURS: a Gallo-Roman aristocratic bishop of the sixth century who wrote a *History of the Franks* (ten books, 575–94).

HYDATIUS: fifth-century author of Iberian origin who attacked the Vandals in Africa, in a *Chronicle* which ends in 469. His work contains obvious mistakes (such as the date of St Augustine of Hippo's death), and exaggerations (he gives 300,000 killed at the Catalaunian Plains). Christian Courtois in 1951 extracted the credible parts of this.

ISIDORE OF SEVILLE: Saint (*c.* 560–636) and prolific writer, who was concerned among other subjects with the Visigoths in Spain.

JOHN OF ANTIOCH: probably two men, living in the seventh and tenth centuries respectively, but using earlier material.

JORDANES: a Goth who wrote a Latin history of his people from a base in Constantinople. The *Getica*, completed in 551, drew heavily on the work of Cassiodorus, a sixth-century historian.

NENNIUS: (fl. 796) Welsh monk, supposed author of a compilation known as the *Historia Britonum (The History of the Britons)*, incorporating material both historical and mythological. This is one of the most problematic of the sources and included much that is clearly fiction. One of Nennius' sources, however, seems to have been a chronicle composed in Kent, perhaps in the sixth century. He himself confessed that he was making a 'heap' of all the material he could find rather than attempting to evaluate it, which has not endeared him to historians.

OLYMPIODORUS OF EGYPTIAN THEBES: in the time of Theodosius II (early fifth century) he wrote twenty-two books of history in Greek which are now almost totally lost, but which contained what was probably a reasoned and erudite account of the Huns.

OROSIUS: an Iberian parish priest with a good knowledge of both pagan and Christian cultures. He wrote *Seven Books Against the Pagans*, completed in 418.

PRISCUS OF PANIUM: wrote for an élite audience, in keeping with the best Byzantine style, and was concerned with literary effect as much as with accuracy. His work, of which only fragments remain, originally covered the period AD 433 to 474, and discussed among other topics Hunnic lifestyle. Confusingly for new readers, the fragments have been numbered differently according to translator. The conventional numbering is to be found in, for example, Gordon, 1972, though Blockley, 1983, has been used throughout this book.

PROCOPIUS: sixth-century secretary to the great general Count Belisarius, who had witnessed some of the events he was describing. He wrote in Greek.

SALVIAN: fifth-century Gallic cleric, who wrote *On the Government of God* between 439 and 455, a work containing useful historical material.

SIDONIUS APOLLINARIS: Gallic bishop who wrote letters and poems commenting on events in fifth-century Gaul.

VICTOR OF VITA: fifth-century cleric who wrote a vitriolic *History of the Vandal Persecution in Africa*.

ZOSIMUS: sixth-century Greek official concerned with the eastern provinces, who wrote an unfinished *New History*, covering the period to 410.

Notes

Abbreviations:

Am. Mar. – Ammianus Marcellinus
Claud. – Claudian
Claud.in ruf–Claudian *In Rufinum*
Claud. De Cons. Stil.–Claudian *de consulatu Stilichonis*
Claud. BG.–Claudian *de bello Getico*
Eunap. – Eunapius
Greg. Tours. HF – Gregory of Tours, *History of the Franks*
Hyd. Lem. – Hydatius Lemicensis *Chronicon*
J.A.–John of Antioch
Jord. Get. – Jordanes, *History of the Goths*
Oros. – Orosius
Olymp. – Olympiodorus
Prisc. – Priscus of Panium
Procop. – Procopius
Procop. BV–Procopius *de bello vandalico*
Procop. BG–Procopius *de bello Gothico*
Sid. Ap. Ep/Carm. – Sidonius Apollinaris, *Letters/Poems*
Vict. Vita – Victor of Vita
Zos. – Zosimus

Introduction

1. Jord. Get. 22 and 24.

Chapter One

1. Oros. VII, 43.
2. The Goths have left their name, to be used and abused, distorted, extolled or vilified according to need or bias. It has been used in twentieth-century grafitti to show specific political displeasure (in, for example, the Canary islands: 'Goths go home'). Wolfram, 1988, 1–18 discusses the historical reputation of the Goths.
3. General surveys of the Goths are those of Wolfram 1988, and Heather, 1991, 1996; Heather & Matthews, 1991 and Thompson, 1966 and 1969 are also important. Readers should refer to the bibliographies and references in these.
4. The *Origo Gothica*.
5. The Goths sang of the exploits of their ancestors accompanied on the cithera, a type of harp which was effectively a bow with strings. Jord. Get. 43.
6. Jord. Get. 25–8. Movements of people who are identifiable as probably ancestral to the later Goths are traceable through archaeology only from Poland. The Wielbark culture in northern Poland, the Cernjachov in the northern hinterland of the Black Sea and the Pzeworsk culture of Greater Poland and adjacent areas are relevant in this connection. Constantinescu *et al.*, 1975; see also Heather & Matthews, 1991, ch. 3, and Heather, 1996, ch. 2.
7. The geographer Ptolemy, Tacitus and archaeological evidence corroborate a location north of the Black Sea in the first century AD.
8. Heather, 1995, 43–7.
9. The Gothic army and kingship are discussed in Wolfram, 1988, 96–9.
10. The early Gothic campaigns are discussed in Wolfram, 1988, 43ff.
11. Zos. I, 21.
12. Zos. I, 20ff.
13. Gallus (251–3).
14. Much of what is known about their lifestyle in the fourth century is incidental to the main story in the *Passion of St Saba*, Thompson, 1966.
15. The only known exception is the fort at High Rochester, England.
16. Burns, 1984, 186.
17. Later 'Gothicus' for his victories against the Goths.
18. Discussion in Wolfram, 1988, 52ff.
19. Zos. I, 42ff. and Am. Mar. XXXI, V, 15.
20. Cannabas-Cannabaudes.
21. Wolfram, 1988, 97.
22. In 297, for example, Goths were among the Roman troops under Emperor Galerius who attacked the Persians.
23. Discussed in Wolfram, 1988, 75f. and Thompson, 1966.
24. Discussed in Wolfram, 1988, 75.
25. Named after Arius (*c.* 256–336) who by 311 was a priest in Alexandria.
26. The religion of Ulfilas is often termed 'semi-Arianism'; although it followed many of the same precepts, it was undoubtedly an adaptation – see Heather, 1996, 60–1.
27. Jord. Get. 41.
28. Jord. Get. 48.
29. Am. Mar. XXXI., vii, 11.
30. Am. Mar. XXXI, vii, 11.

Notes

31. Eunap. frag. 48 (2) (Blockley).
32. Eunap. frag. 48 (2) Blockley).
33. Am. Mar. XXVI, iv, 3.
34. This campaign is in Am. Mar. XXVII, v, 2–6.
35. Am. Mar. XXVII, v, 9.
36. See Thompson, 1966, 13.
37. Thompson suggested that they were an excuse for Athanaric to punish the poorer and weaker elements of society (who tended to be Christian) for criticising his leadership. Thompson, 1966, 102.
38. Under the command of Munderic, Am. Mar. XXXI, iii, 5.
39. Am. Mar. XXXI, iii, 7.
40. Burns, 1984, 187.
41. Heather, 1996, 100.
42. Am. Mar. XXXI, iii, 8.
43. Am. Mar. XXXI, iv, 13. Interestingly, a statue to his father had been erected in Constantinople by Constantine.
44. Am. Mar. XXXI, iv, 12.
45. Heather, 1996, 151ff, for discussion.
46. Goffart, 1980, 33.
47. Am. Mar. XXXI, iv, 6.
48. Am. Mar. XXXI, iv, 5.
49. Eunap. frag. 42 (Blockley).
50. Am. Mar. XXXI, v, 3.
51. Am. Mar. XXXI, iv, 11.
52. Jord. Get. 134–5.
53. Jord. Get. 135.
54. Am. Mar. XXXI, v, 6. Heather argues that Lupercinus would not have deliberately planned this assassination on his own initiative, but had imperial direction. Heather, 1996, 131.
55. Jord. Get. 137.
56. Am. Mar. XXXI, v, 7–9.
57. Am. Mar. XXXI, vii, 5ff.
58. Claud., *In Ruf.*, ii, 127ff.
59. Zos. IV, 23.
60. Zos. IV, 23.
61. Zos. IV, 25.
62. Am. Mar. XXXI, xi, 4.
63. Am. Mar. XXXI, xi, 3.
64. This battle is discussed in detail in Burns, 1994, page 1ff., and is found in Am. Mar. XXXI, xii–xiii.
65. See Burns, 1973, 336–45, for a discussion.
66. Am. Mar. XXXI, xii, 1.
67. Am. Mar. XXXI, xii, 11–14ff.
68. They could have been employed in the Roman army.
69. Am. Mar. XXXI, xiii, 11–14.
70. Heather, 1996, 135.
71. See Burns, 1973, 336–45, for a discussion in which the heat is understated.

72. Am. Mar. XXXI, xv, 2ff.
73. Am. Mar. XXXI, xv, 15.
74. Zos. II, 35.
75. Am. Mar. XXXI, xvi, 4–6.
76. Hyd. Lem. 2.
77. Jord. Get. 142ff.
78. Hyd. Lem. 6.
79. Oros. VII, 35, 10–11, Eunap. frag. 60 (1) (Blockley).
80. The general who fought at Adrianople.
81. Jord. Get. 42.
82. Claudian refers to Stilicho and Serena's son Eucherius as the emperor's grandson in order to show the closeness of the relationship. When he was very young the child was betrothed to Galla Placidia.
83. A convenient account is to be found in Wolfram, 1988.
84. Oros. VII, 37.
85. Discussed in Heather 1996, 138ff.
86. Oros. VII, 35.
87. Zos. V, 4–5.
88. Zos. IV, 59.
89. Zos. IV, 51 and 57.
90. Claud., *In Ruf.*, ii, 36–85.
91. Zos. V, 26.
92. Zos. V, 5.
93. Claud., *In Ruf.*, ii, 170ff.
94. He was about eighteen.
95. Claud., *In Ruf.*, ii, 410.
96. Zos. V, 7.
97. Claud., *De cons. Stil.* 1, 188–217.
98. The complex political situation is outlined in Zos. V, 4ff.
99. Isidore of Seville, 15, says he wanted to avenge his lost Gothic troops.
100. Zos. V, 19.
101. Oros. VII, 37.2.
102. Claud., BG, 623–8.
103. CTh 7.20.12, issued to Stilicho at Milan, 30 January 400.
104. Oros. VII, 37.6 and Zos. V, 26.4.
105. Olymp. frag. 9 (Blockley).
106. Zos. V, 27.1.
107. Olymp. frag. 13 (Blockley).
108. Olymp. frag. 7 (2) (Blockey).
109. Zos. V, 29.
110. Wolfram, 1988, 153–4.
111. Oros. VII, 40.4, and Jord. Get. 165.
112. Named Olympius. Zos. V, 34.
113. Zos. V, 34.
114. His death is recounted in Zos. V, 34.
115. Zos. V, 35.
116. Olymp. frag. 7 (Blockley).

Notes

117. Zos. V, 38.
118. Galla Placidia had been brought up in the household of Serena and Stilicho.
119. She was throttled or suffocated. Zos. V, 38.
120. Zos. V, 41.
121. Olymp. frag. 41 (Blockley).
122. Olymp. frag. 13 (1) (Blockley).
123. Zos. V, 50.
124. Zos. V, 50–1.
125. Olymp. frag. 10 (Blockley).
126. He was made emperor a second time by Alaric's successor Athaulf. When he was finally caught, the thumb and forefinger of his right hand were cut off and he was exiled with a small allowance, in 416. Olymp. frag. 14 (Blockley).
127. Olymp. frag. 11 (Blockley).
128. Zos. V, 37.
129. Procop. III, ii, 26.
130. Hyd. Lem. 43.
131. Olymp. frag. 11 (3) (Blockley) and Procop. BG. III, ii, 27.
132. Procop. BG. III, ii, 15–17.
133. Procop. BG. III, ii, 25–6.
134. Oros. VII, 39; also Isidore of Seville, 16 and 17.
135. Hyd. Lem. 45, and Olymp. frag. 11 (4) (Blockley).
136. Jord. Get. 157; Oros. VII, 43.
137. Jord. Get. 158.
138. Wolfram, 1988, 160.
139. Under King Guntiarius.
140. Under King Goar.
141. Olymp. frag. 18 (Blockley).
142. Olymp. frag. 18 (Blockley).
143. Am. Mar. XXXI, ii, 9.
144. Hyd. Lem. 44.
145. Zos. VI, 12.
146. Olymp. frag 24 (Blockley).
147. Olymp. frag. 19 (Blockley).
148. Oros. VII, 43.
149. Olymp. frag. 24 (Blockley).
150. Olymp. frag. 24 (Blockley).
151. Jord. Get. 160.
152. Jord. Get. 158.
153. Hyd. Lem. 57.
154. Oros. VII, 43.1.
155. Olymp. frag. 29 (1) (Blockley).
156. Jord. Get. 163.
157. Olymp. frag. 26 (Blockley).
158. Olymp. frag. 26 (Blockley).
159. Jord. Get. 163.
160. Olymp. frag. 26 (Blockley).
161. Oros. VII, 43.

162. Jord. Get. 164.
163. Isidore of Seville, 21.
164. Jord. Get. 164–5.
165. Olymp. frag. 30 (Blockley) and Jord. Get. 165.
166. Jord. Get. 166–7.
167. Oros. VII, 43; Isidore of Seville, 22.
168. Olymp. frag. 33 (Blockley).
169. Olymp. frag. 23 (Blockley).
170. Olymp. frag. 37 (Blockley).
171. Olymp. frag. 33 (Blockley).
172. The method by which the Empire tended to settle tribal peoples at this point was based on the imperial billetting system (*hospitalitas*). Discussed in Jones, 1966, 98f.
173. This battle is called Châlons in Isidore of Seville, 25, and many later writers have used the name without real basis.
174. These fierce, destructive people were not finally annexed until 585.
175. During the short period in which Theodoric II's son Alaric II ruled, the Visigoths held the huge area from the south bank of the Loire to Gibraltar.
176. These lands were Tarraconensis, Carthaginiensis, Lusitania and Baetica, where they were a small minority, along with Septimania (south-west France from the Pyrenees to the Rhône).
177. Discussed in Thompson, 1969.

Chapter Two

1. Jord. Get. 186, translation from Hodgkin, 1892.
2. Isidore of Seville, 29.
3. The main discussion of the history of the Huns can be found in Thompson, 1995, which is essentially a revision of his earlier book, *The History of Attila and the Huns*, Oxford (1948), with a postscript by Peter Heather. The monumental work by Maenchen-Helfen, 1973, published posthumously, contains material of varying reliability. The best account of the archaeology is to be found in Bona, 1991, though still very useful is Werner, 1956.
4. Am. Mar. XXXI, ii, 6.
5. Isidore of Seville, 29.
6. Claud., *In Ruf.*, i, 329–30.
7. A seventh-century Syrian cleric wrote how they roasted pregnant women, cut out the foetus, put it in a dish, poured water over it and dipped their weapons in the brew, eating the flesh of children and drinking the blood of women. Maenchen-Helfen, 1973, 203.
8. Priscus of Panium is the main source for Attila in everyday life.
9. Jord. Get. 127.
10. Jord. Get. 127.
11. In AD 630 the monk Hsuan-tsang (Tang dynasty) visited north-west India and found 'millions of monasteries' reduced to ruins by the Huns. Distorted skulls are features of the Hsiung-nu nomads who bordered the Chinese empire some six hundred years earlier, for instance. The Hsiung-nu established themselves in the neighbourhood of the Ordos River, and extracted tributes from China. Writing about them, Ssu-ma Ch'ien said they scaled the steepest mountains with amazing speed, swam the deepest rivers

and could withstand rain, hunger and thirst. Their horses were trained to deal with very narrow trails, and the Huns were such good archers they could shoot at a full gallop. Unfortunately for those seeking early Hunnic origins, all nomads would have merited much the same descriptions and the Hsiung-nu were assimilated into China in AD 58, several centuries before the Huns appeared in Europe.

12. Am. Mar. XXXI, ii, 1, and Prisc. frag. 1 (Blockley).
13. Maenchen-Helfen, 1973, chs 8–9, discusses this but comes to no real conclusions. See also Heather, 1996, 98.
14. Jord. Get. 123–6.
15. A Greek playwright of the fifth century BC.
16. They were cast out by a Goth called Filimer during the fifth generation since the exodus from Scandinavia: Jord. Get. 121.
17. Am. Mar. XXXI, ii 13–15.
18. For Huns, Am. Mar. XXXI, ii, 1–10, and for Alans, XXXI, ii, 16ff.
19. Am. Mar. XXXI, ii, 25.
20. Am. Mar. XXXI, ii, 10.
21. A view held by Maenchen-Helfen but not by all later commentators; cf Lindner, 1981, 6, fn.
22. Am. Mar. XXXI, ii, 3–7.
23. Jord. Get. 130.
24. Am. Mar. XXXI, iii, 3.
25. Zos. V, 22.
26. Marcellinus Comes, *Chronicle* says they had been in the area for fifty years in 427.
27. For a summary of the discussion of this date, see Prisc. frag. 11 (Blockley), 386, fn 66.
28. Am. Mar. XXXI, ii, 8–9.
29. Apparently, she and her brother took 'immoderate pleasure' in each other and constantly kissed on the mouth. Various exonerating explanations have been put forward for this statement, ranging from the opinion that it is simply erroneous, to the possibility that it was merely over-enthusiasm by the lonely Honorius who would probably have found his half-sister one of the few people he could feel comfortable with. Olymp. frag. 38 (Blockley).
30. Olymp. frag. 43 (1) (Blockley).
31. J.A. frag. 195.
32. Sid. Ap. *Carm.*, VII, 230, Panegyric on Evitus.
33. Greg. Tours, HF, II (7) 8.
34. J.A. frag. 196.
35. The name may be preserved in Bornholm (Burgundarholm in the Middle Ages).
36. Hyd. Lem. 108.
37. Sid. Ap. *Carm.*, VII, 230.
38. Hyd. Lem. 110.
39. In the *Niebelungenlied*, Kriemhild, a Burgundian princess, is wooed by Siegfried against his parents' advice. A complex story of heroism, courtship, treachery, vengeance and hidden treasure ends with the death of Siegfried. Kriemhild accepts an offer of marriage from Etzel, King of the Huns, so that she may gain vengeance on her brother Gunther and his henchman Hagen. The two are eventually invited to a party and there is a general massacre of the Burgundians, in which the heroine herself wields an axe with fatal results. The whereabouts of Siegfried's treasure is never revealed.

40. Maenchen-Helfen, 1973, discusses this question.
41. Prisc. frag. 2 (Blockley).
42. Prisc. frag. 2 (Blockley).
43. Prisc. frag. 2 (Blockley).
44. Prisc. frag. 2 (Blockley).
45. Prisc. frag. 6 (Blockley).
46. Prisc. frag. 9 (4) (Blockley).
47. Jord. Get. 181.
48. Jord. Get. 181–3, for a description of Attila.
49. Jord. Get. 182.
50. For a discussion of Attila in legend, Hodgkin, 1892.
51. Prisc. frag. 6 (2) (Blockley).
52. Prisc. frag. 9 (3) (Blockley).
53. Prisc. frag. 9 (Blockley).
54. Prisc. frag. 9 (Blockley).
55. Prisc. frag. 11 (1) (Blockley).
56. Prisc. frag. 11 (Blockley).
57. Jord. Get. 182.
58. J.A. frag. 199 (2) and Jord. Get. 224.
59. J.A. frag. 199 (2).
60. Prisc. frag. 38 (Blockley).
61. Jord. Get. 223–4.
62. J.A. frag. 199 (2).
63. Jord. Get. 223–4.
64. Jord. Get. 184.
65. Prisc. frag. 20 (2) (Blockley) and Jord. Get. 184.
66. Jord. Get. 188.
67. Jord. Get. 191.
68. 100 leuva by 70, Jord. Get. 192. One leuva was a Gallic distance approximating to 1,500 Roman paces.
69. Lindner, 1981, 11.
70. The father and two uncles of Theodoric the Great.
71. Jord. Get. 199.
72. Jord. Get. 217.
73. Salin & France-Lanord, 1956, 75.
74. Jord. Get. 215f.
75. Jord. Get. 219f.
76. Jord. Get. 223.
77. Jord. Get. 223–4.
78. Prisc. frag. 24 (1) and frag. 21 (Blockley).
79. Jord. Get. 260f.
80. Jord. Get. 261.
81. Jord. Get. 264.
82. Nickel, 1973.
83. Maenchen-Helfen, 1973, 203.
84. Maenchen-Helfen, 1973, 210. It is found in Scythian graves at Pazyryk.

85. In a Migration Period context at Blucina near Brno, Czechoslovakia, silver mounts for this type of saddle were found in a fifth-century grave, which was not, however, necessarily Hunnic. Maenchen-Helfen, 1973, 208–10.
86. Werner, 1956, and discussion.
87. Nicolle, 1990, 13.
88. Lindner, 1981, 3.
89. Lindner, 1981, 7–9.
90. Oros. VII, 34.
91. Jord. Get. 178–9.
92. Prisc. frag. 11 (2) (Blockley).
93. Prisc. frag. 11 (2) (Blockley).
94. Prisc. frag. 13 (Blockley).
95. Who fought for Galla Placidia.

Chapter Three

1. Jord. Get. 117.
2. For the Ostrogoths, readers should consult the general surveys of the Goths provided by Wolfram, 1988, and Heather, 1996, as well as Heather & Matthews, 1991, and Heather, 1991. In addition, the Ostrogoths are the subject of Burns, 1980 and 1984, and Amory, 1997.
3. Am. Mar. XXXI, iii, 1.
4. Am. Mar. XXXI, iii, 1. See Peter Heather on whether Ermaneric belonged to the Amal family, Heather, 1996, 53–6.
5. Jord. Get. 116.
6. Jord. Get. 120.
7. Heather, 1996, 56, discusses this.
8. Thompson, 1966, 27.
9. Burns 1980, 35f, points out that the story is likely to reflect later attempts to endow his suicide with heroic qualities.
10. Jord. Get. 129.
11. Jord. Get. 130.
12. Am. Mar. XXXI, iii, 2.
13. Am. Mar. XXXI, iii, 3.
14. Am. Mar. XXXI, iii, 3.
15. Jord. Get. 43.
16. Oros. VII, 37.
17. Zos. V, 26.
18. Oros. VII, 37.
19. Oros. VII, 37.
20. Oros. VII, 37.
21. Slaves are discussed in Jones, 1966, 296ff.
22. Jord. Get. 264.
23. Jord. Get. 269–71. Much is known about this man who was very active.
24. Jord. Get. 271.

25. Moss, 1935, 54. He is reputed never to have learned to write, but this may mean that he could not write Latin since he would have been taught Greek, or that he did not obtain the standard of calligraphy expected in imperial circles.
26. Jord. Get. 272ff.
27. Jord. Get. 279.
28. Jord. Get. 282.
29. Jord. Get. 285–6.
30. Jord. Get. 283.
31. Jord. Get. 289.
32. Malchus frag. 18 (in Blockley).
33. Julius Nepos.
34. Maenchen-Helfen rejects this; Thompson, 1982, sees no difficulty, but Moorhead, 1992, 8–9, outlines the view that he was the nephew of the usurper Basiliscus (475–6) and Leo's Empress Verina.
35. Jord. Get. 241–2.
36. Conveniently outlined in Thompson, 1982, 65ff.
37. Bintliff & Hamerow, 1995, 1.
38. Jord. Get. 293–4.
39. J.A. frag. 214a.
40. J.A. frag. 214a.
41. See Heather, 1996, 216f, for one discussion of this period.
42. Jord. Get. 298.
43. Jord. Get, 297ff.
44. Bullough, 1965, 168.
45. Jord. Get. 306.
46. Jord. Get. 307.

Chapter Four

1. Procop. BV. III. viii. 27.
2. There are no general surveys devoted solely to the Vandals in English; the standard reference is Courtois, 1955.
3. Clover, 1993, 2.
4. Jord. Get. 26.
5. Procop. BV. III, iii, 23–4.
6. Originally from near the Elbe, the Sueves were dislodged by Huns. They included Marcommanni, Hermunduri, Semnones and Langobardi.
7. Discussed in Burns, 253ff.
8. The period and Hydatius are conveniently discussed in Thompson, 1982, pp. 137–60.
9. Hyd. Lem. 49.
10. Hyd. Lem. 49.
11. Hyd. Lem. 68.
12. Hyd. Lem. 49.
13. Olymp. frag. 29 (Blockley).
14. Olymp. frag. 29 (Blockley) and fn 62.
15. Hyd. Lem. 71.
16. Thompson, 1969, chs 8 and 9, is convenient for the Sueves in Spain.

17. Olymp. frag. 40 (Blockley).
18. Olymp. frag. 40 (Blockley).
19. Jord. Get. 167.
20. Hyd. Lem. 89.
21. Procop. BV. III, iii, 32.
22. Vict. Vita, II, 14.
23. Vict. Vita, I, 2.
24. Procop. III, v, 18.
25. Jord, Get. 167.
26. Vict. Vita, I, 7.
27. Courtois, 1955, gives an authoritative discussion.
28. Procop. III, iv, 3–11.
29. Hyd. Lem. 115.
30. Salvian, *De Gub.*, VII, 23.
31. Hyd. Lem. 120.
32. Procop. III, iv, 12–14. The treaty he refers to was made after the defeat of Aspar and Bonifacius.
33. Jord. Get. 184.
34. Jord. Get. 184–5 and Prisc. frag. 20 (Blockley).
35. Procop. BV. III, iv, 16ff.
36. J.A. frag. 201 (1) and (2).
37. J.A. frag. 201 (2).
38. J.A frag. 201 (5) and J.A. frag. 201 (4). Aëtius may have had a daughter who was married to Thraustila.
39. Procop. III, iv, 36.
40. Procop. III, iv, 39, and J.A. frag. 201 (6).
41. This was found when the Vandals were overthrown by Belisarius in 533; Procop. IV, ix, 5–6.
42. Plutarch, Publ, 15.
43. Procop. III, v, 3–6.
44. Procop. III, v, 6–7.
45. Procop. III, v, 8–9
46. Hyd. Lem. 162; Procop. III, v, 2–3.
47. Prisc. frag. 38 (Blockley).
48. Sid. Ap. *Carm..*, II, 361–2.
49. Sid. Ap. *Carm.*, II, 367.
50. Avitus died shortly after, in a bishopric.
51. This is denied by Sidonius Apollinaris.
52. Jord. Get. 236.
53. Candidus frag. 2 (Blockley).
54. Procop. III, vi, 14–15.
55. Procop. III, vi, 17–22.
56. Procop. III, vii, 26.
57. Greg. Tours, II, 3.
58. Vict. Vita, II, 9.
59. Vict. Vita, II, 14.
60. Procop. III, v, 13.

61. Procop. III, v, 13–14.
62. Procop. BV., III, v, 17.
63. Courtois, 1955.
64. Vict. Vita, III, 55–60.
65. This period and the subject are conveniently discussed in Clover, 1993, 8–9.
66. Procop. III, xvii, 10.
67. British Museum, acc no. GR 1860. 10–2.
68. Donatism.
69. Vict. Vita, I, 37.
70. Vict. Vita, I, 33.
71. Vict. Vita, I, 39.
72. Vict. Vita, I, 46.
73. Vict. Vita, I, 24–6.
74. This must have happened before the end of 457; Moorhead, 1992, p. xi.
75. Procop. III, viii, 14–28.
76. Procop. BV., III, ix, 8.
77. Procop. BV., III, ix, 10.
78. Jord. Get. 170; Procop. BV., III, xvii, 12.
79. Procop. III, v, 8.

Chapter Five

1. Sid. Ap. *Carm.*, V, 251–2, trs E. James.
2. The most useful recent general surveys of the history of the Franks are to be found in James, 1982 and 1988, and in Geary, 1988. A useful short survey, albeit dated, is provided by Lasko, 1971. For the archaeology (and much else besides) the two-volume collection of studies, edited by von Welck, 1996, is invaluable.
3. Geary, 1988, 78.
4. James, 1988, 35.
5. Fredegar, writing in the seventh century, preferred to give them a Trojan (modern Turkey) origin so that they could be compared with the Romans. Geary, 1988, 77–8.
6. The Alamanni were a loose confederacy of people who settled between the Rivers Rhine and Danube from around AD 300, and saw employment in the Roman army. Julian the Apostate campaigned against them, defeating them near Strasbourg in 357, and in 406–7 they were involved in the invasion of Gaul. Some settled in Alsace and the Pfalz and during the later fifth century raided eastern Gaul, Italy and Noricum. Early in the sixth century they settled in Raetia and by 536 were subject to the Franks, a situation which remained until Charles Martel (*c.* 689–741) absorbed them totally into the Frankish empire.
7. The Emperor Probus restored over sixty (nearly half) the towns in Gaul.
8. Zos. I, 71.
9. Zos. I, 71.
10. Zos. I, 71.
11. Greg. Tours, HF, II (8) 9.
12. Defeated soldiers who were granted land in return for military service.

13. Am. Mar. XVII, viii, 3.
14. As a *laetus*.
15. Zos. II, 53.
16. Am. Mar. XV, v, 33.
17. This story is in Am. Mar. XV, v, 1f.
18. Am. Mar. XV, v, 31.
19. Am. Mar. XXXI, x, 6.
20. Am. Mar. XXX, iii, 3.
21. Am. Mar. XXX, iii, 7.
22. Am. Mar. XXXI, x, 5.
23. He is called both king of the Franks and commander of the household troops in Am. Mar. XXXI, x, 6.
24. Am. Mar. XXXI, x, 6–10.
25. Zos. IV, 33, and Eunap. frag. 53.
26. Eunap. frag. 58 (2) (Blockley). He may not have been his son, however.
27. Eunap. frag. 58 (1) (Blockley).
28. Eunap. frag. 58 (2) (Blockley).
29. Eunap. frag. 58 (2) (Blockley).
30. Eunap. frag. 58 (2) (Blockley).
31. Zos. IV, 54.
32. Oros. VII, 35.
33. Zos. IV, 53–5.
34. Oros. VII, 35.
35. Olymp. frag. 17 (Blockley).
36. Böhme, 1996, distribution maps: figs 68 and 69, tutulus brooches and weapon graves. See also Böhme, 1974, for a general discussion.
37. This question is discussed in detail by Goffart, 1980, whose ideas are controversial.
38. The 'kingdom of Soissons' centred on Soissons often alluded to by modern historians probably did not exist, as James has argued, 1988, 70.
39. It is possible that the Franks, who remained pagan until Clovis, were accepted in Gaul because of a high tolerance of paganism in general. This is discussed in easily understood form in Dill, 1905.
40. Bachrach, 1972, 3.
41. Pilloy, 1895, original publication.
42. Pirling, 1996, gives a useful summary of current work. See Pirling 1966, 1974, 1979, for full reports.
43. Lemant *et al.* 1985.
44. Seillier, 1986.
45. James, 1988, 48.
46. Hawkes & Dunning, 1961, for belt fittings; Evison, 1965, on the Vermand style.
47. Böhme, 1974, pl. 137.
48. Böhme, 1974, 180, and pls 118–19.
49. Sid. Ap. *Ep.*, IV, 20.
50. Hyd. Lem. 98; Jord. Get. 176.
51. Greg. Tours, HF, II, 8 (9).
52. Sid. Ap. *Carm.*, V, 220ff.

53. Prisc. frag. 20 (Blockley).
54. Greg. Tours, HF, II, 11 (12).
55. James, 1988, 64–5, with the problems of this interpretation.
56. James, 1988, 69.
57. Greg. Tours, II, 12.
58. Bachrach, 1972, 4.
59. The most recent appraisals are found in Kazanski & Périn, 1988, and Périn & Kazanski, 1996; English summary in James, 1992.
60. Bachrach, 1972, 8.
61. James, 1982, 28.
62. Périn, 1996.
63. James, 1982, 30.
64. James, 1982, 31.

Chapter Six

1. Sid. Ap. *Ep.*, VIII, vi, 14.
2. Much work has recently been carried out on the north European groups for which Genrich, 1970; Todd, 1994; Groenman van Waateringe, 1983; Wheeler, 1956; and Randsborg, 1991, are recommended for a few aspects.
3. Johnson, 1976; Johnson, 1979, ch. 1.
4. Sid. Ap. *Ep.*, VIII, vi, 13.
5. See particularly Wood, 1992, and Hodges, 1989. For the growth of Kent, Hawkes, 1982.
6. Evison, 1965.
7. Hines, 1984; Hines, 1992.
8. Scull, 1993, 71.
9. Sid. Ap. *Ep.*, VIII, ix, 25.
10. Am. Mar. XXIX, iv, 7.
11. It is unknown whether this 'conspiratio' was planned or fortuitous: Higham, 1992, ch. 3; Frere, 1974, 391.
12. Olymp. frag. 13 (1) (Blockley).
13. Zos. VI, 1–5.
14. As occurred in Dacia, for under the Goths some Roman attributes remained for centuries.
15. For example, Cadbury Castle, Somerset: Alcock, 1995.
16. This date is now suggested to be as early as the mid-420s: discussion in Higham, 1992, 157.
17. Gildas, 26.
18. Kent, 1961; Kent, 1979, 28. New find, Orna-Ornstein, 1998.
19. Frere, 1974, 412–14.
20. Morris, 1975.
21. David Dumville has questioned the value of almost all the sources for the fifth and sixth centuries in Britain (except Gildas and St Patrick), though this is a view now seen to be extreme. John Morris can be argued as doing what Christian Courtois did for Hydatius. Dumville, 1977; but see now Snyder, 1998, 30.

Notes

22. Vortigern was the son of Vitalis and grandson of Vitalinus: Nennius, 49.
23. They are generally accepted now as real people. Chadwick, 1959, 22.
24. The 'Germanic' interpretation of such burials is discussed in Hawkes & Dunning, 1961, but for a more cautious view see Cleary, 1989, 191.
25. Portchester: Cunliffe, 1975, 301; Richborough; Cunliffe, 1968, 250.
26. The development of a more clearly defined hierarchy among the Saxons from the Roman Iron Age onwards (as attested at cemeteries such as that at Federssen Wierde; Haarnagel, 1979), is not apparent in England.
27. Welch, 1992, ch. 7. For the beginnings of state formation, Bassett. (ed.) 1989; Yorke, 1997. For the theories behind state formation in England, see also Arnold, 1987, and Hodges, 1989, especially ch. 2.
28. Alcock, 1987, 301.
29. Todd, 1972, 172–3; Todd, 1975, 191–2.
30. Arnold, 1997, 20. See also discussions by Scull, 1993, 1995; Hamerow, 1994; and Hines, 1990, 1996.
31. Nennius, 37.
32. Cleary, 1989, 151; Brooks, 1988.
33. White, 1988; White, 1990.
34. Nennius, 38.
35. Dark, 1998, 9.
36. Nennius, 46
37. Gildas 19.3.
38. Morris, 1975, 250.
39. Morris, 1975, 251.
40. Morris, 1975, 251.
41. Jord. Get. 327.
42. Gildas, *De Excidio*, 25, 1.
43. Gildas, *De Excidio*, 25, 1.
44. Sid. Ap. *Carm.*, III, ix, 1–2.
45. The evidence is discussed at length in Chadwick, 1969, ch. 6, and Chadwick, 1965.
46. Chadwick, 1965, 268–9.
47. Mackreth, 1978; Laing & Laing, 1990, 87.
48. Laing & Laing, 1990, ch. 4; Dark, 1994, ch. 4; Davis, 1982, for Chilterns region.
49. Kent was, significantly, named after Durovernum Cantiacorum, the Roman regional capital of the Iron Age Celtic tribe, of the Cantiaci.
50. Evans, 1994, 33.
51. Although the earliest existing text of *Beowulf* is much later (*c.* AD 1000), current opinion assigns its composition to East Anglia in the early years of the eighth century, and its oral predecessor to the late seventh. Evans, 1977, 144, gives a summary of the debate. See also Newton, 1992.
52. Chadwick, 1912, 1–3.
53. Newton, 1992.
54. Chadwick, 1912, 3.
55. Chadwick, 1912, 3–4.
56. Quoted in Pollington, 1996, 22.
57. (Lines 2493–6). Evans, 1997, 33.

Chapter Seven

1. Sid. Ap. *Ep.*, I, ii.
2. Cowie & Clarke, 1985, 1–13, on symbols of power.
3. The literature on the sumptuary arts of the barbarians is scattered, and tends to merge with discussions of the art of the Migration Period. On this subject, sources include Haseloff, 1981; Holmqvist, 1955; and, for England, Laing & Laing, 1996 and Speake, 1980.
4. Sid. Ap. *Carm.*, V, 219–29.
5. Sid. Ap. *Ep.*, I, ii, to Agricola.
6. James, 1988, 62, discusses some of the views.
7. Arrhenius, 1985.
8. Todd, 1992, 140, but see Bona 1991.
9. Bona, 1991, pls I–VI, and notes.
10. Odobescu, 1889–1900.
11. Werner, 1956, 57–61; Maenchen-Helfen, 1973, 306–37.
12. Fitzgerald, 1978, 68–71; Watson, 1973, nos 70–82, 85 and 98, gives a variety of types.
13. Randers-Pehrson, 1983, 46; Maenchen-Helfen, 1973, 299–302.
14. Maenchen-Helfen, 1973, 305–6; Randers-Pehrson, 1983, 46.
15. Maenchen-Helfen, 1973, 354.
16. Distribution map of brooches and cauldrons, Dixon, 1976, 14. For a discussion of the type see Leeds, 1951.
17. Hachmann, 1971, pl. 118.
18. Werner, 1956, 19–24; Maenchen-Helfen, 1973, 337–54.
19. Minns, 1945; Rostovtzeff, 1929; Jettmar, 1964, for general discussions of the style.
20. Burns, 1984, 139.
21. Bierbrauer, 1975, 180–8 and 263–72.
22. Von Hessen, Kurze & Mastrelli, 1977, esp. 94–101.
23. Werner, 1949–50, on these helmets generally.
24. Brulet, 1980; Brulet, 1996.
25. Sansterre, 1996.

Chapter Eight

1. Jord. Get. 259.
2. Among the best studies of warrior societies are those that relate to Britain where the evidence is particularly useful, e.g. Evans, 1997; Snyder, 1998; Pollington, 1996. Studies of weapons are scattered, but useful material on swords (not just in England) can be found in Davidson, 1962. Warfare and weaponry can also be found in Hawkes (ed.), 1989.
3. McCauley, 1990, 2.
4. Service, 1968.
5. McCauley, 1990, 10.
6. McCauley, 1990, 11.
7. Ferguson, 1990, 48–9.
8. Evans, 1997, 75.

9. Chadwick, 1912, 5.
10. Chadwick, 1912, 7.
11. Am. Mar. XXXI, ii, 20.
12. Colgrave, 1936, XVII–XIX.
13. Hawkes, 1989, 2.
14. Harke, 1993, 156–7.
15. Harke, 1993, 157.
16. Summarised in Carver, 1998, 110.
17. Carver, 1998, 108–13.
18. Scathach, in the *Tain bo Cuailgne*.
19. Eunap. frag. 79 (Blockley).
20. Jordanes, VII, 49.
21. For a discussion of this and other literary allusions see Pollington, 1996, 69–70.
22. Fell, 1984, 35.
23. Pollington, 1996, 70.
24. Greg. Tours, HF, II, 1 (2).
25. For example, Bury, 1923, I, 105, Appendix on the Numbers of the Barbarians.
26. Goffart, 1980, 233n.
27. Todd, 1972, 122.
28. Alcock, 1987, 232 and 300.
29. Wenham, 1989.
30. Bachrach, 1972, Appendix, discusses all the sources and their divergences for the Franks.
31. Sid. Ap. *Ep.*, iv, 20; *Pan.*, v, 247f.
32. Dierkens & Périn, 1997, 157.
33. Pirling, 1996, with refs.
34. Harke, 1989, 49.
35. Harke, 1989, 51–2.
36. Harke, 1989, 52.
37. Harke, 1989, 55.
38. Hines, 1989, 43.
39. Some statistics are provided by Hines, 1989, 43.
40. Périn, 1996b, summary.
41. James, 1988, 76–7.
42. Périn, 1996b.
43. Davidson, 1962, 212.
44. Davidson, 1962, 217.
45. Bone, 1989, 63.
46. Lang & Ager, 1989, 100–13.
47. Maenchen-Helfen, 1973, 280.
48. Nicolle, 1990, 13.
49. Maenchen-Helfen, 1973, 237.
50. For example, Werner, 1956, pl .49, 8, from Russia.
51. Discussions of pattern-welding include Davidson, 1962, 20–30; Anstee & Biek, 1961; Engstrom *et al.* 1989; Lang & Ager, 1989.
52. Lang & Ager, 1989, 85–122.
53. Newark, 1985, 61.
54. Davidson, 1962, 42–3.

55. Davidson, 1962, 79.
56. Davidson, 1962, 67.
57. Hawkes & Page, 1967.
58. Davidson, 1962, 49.
59. Lethbridge, 1931, 64.
60. Davidson, 1962, 61–2.
61. Davidson, 1962, 58.
62. Hawkes, 1986.
63. The type conforms to the Scandinavian group known as Behmer Type I, which was current in the Scandinavian Iron Age, cf. Behmer, 1939. For discussion of the hilt see Bone, 1989, 64.
64. Behmer, 1939, Type VI.
65. Bone, 1989, 65.
66. Speake, 1980, 51.
67. Evison, 1965; Evison, 1967; for an earlier discussion of ring hilts see Davidson, 1962, 71–7.
68. Bone, 1898, 65.
69. Pirling, 1996, pl. 192.
70. Werner, 1956, 32.
71. Werner, 1956, 31–2.
72. Davidson, 1962, 88–103.
73. Davidson, 1962, 89.
74. Davidson, 1962, 113.
75. Davidson, 1962, 85–8; Evans, 1994, 42–6, for the Sutton Hoo sword and its fittings.
76. Davidson, 1962, 94.
77. *History of the Franks*, x, 21 (trs. Dalton).
78. Nicolle, 1990, 14.
79. Nicolle, 1990, 14.
80. Todd, 1975, 163–4.
81. Gale, 1989; Pollington, 1996, 146–50.
82. Pollington, 1996, 147.
83. Pollington, 1996, 149.
84. Pollington, 1996, 118.
85. Böhme, 1974, fig. 40.
86. Böhme, 1974, pl. 137.
87. Werner, 1968, pl. V: distribution map.
88. Evans, 1994, 42.
89. Bohner, 1968, pl. 1A; Kruger, 1983, fig. 107, shows the sequence of weapon types in Frankish graves around Trier.
90. Salin, 1949–59, I, 356, 377 and 389 for angons; Salin, III, 13ff for spear types.
91. Swanton, 1973a, 3; catalogue of examples, Swanton, 1974.
92. Swanton, 1973, 4.
93. Swanton, 1973, 4.
94. Evans, 1994, 42.
95. Davidson, 1962, 102.
96. Werner, 1956, pl. 11, 1.
97. Maenchen-Helfen, 1973, 239.

98. Todd, 1975, 175.
99. Baldwin Brown, 1915, 231.
100. Oakeshott, 1974, 89.
101. Baldwin Brown, 1915, 234.
102. Pollington, 1996, 127.
103. Evans, 1994, 41.
104. Todd, 1975, 175.
105. Böhme, 1974, pl. 77.
106. Périn, 1996a, pl. 165.
107. Von Freeden, 1996, pl. 255a.
108. Schmidt, 1996, pl. 227.
109. Rausing, 1967.
110. Newark, 1985, 17.
111. Werner, 1932; Werner, 1956, 46–50, pl. 61, distribution pl. 70. For the two bows cited, see Laszlo, 1951.
112. Newark, 1985, 17.
113. Nicolle, 1990, 12.
114. Maenchen-Helfen, 1973, 224–50.
115. Nicolle, 1990, 12.
116. Pollington, 1996, 151.
117. Pollington, 1996, 151.
118. Oakeshott, 1974, 90.
119. Todd, 1975, 175.
120. Oakeshott, 1974, 90.
121. Baldwin Brown, 1915, 242.
122. Evison, 1963, 46n.
123. Maenchen-Helfen, 1973, 249–51.
124. Maenchen-Helfen, 1973, 251.
125. Fitzgerald, 1978, 81.
126. Nicolle, 1990, 12.
127. Evans, 1994, 41.
128. Newark, 1985, 60.
129. Todd, 1972, 110–11.
130. Todd, 1972, 111.
131. Hauser, 1996, gives a recent summary of the burial. For an English account, see Werner, 1964; Dopperfeld & Pirling, 1988.
132. See, for example, James, 1992, 248.
133. Todd, 1972, 109.
134. Evans, 1994, 46–9; Bruce-Mitford, 1974.
135. Bruce-Mitford & Luscombe, 1974.
136. Meadows, 1997, 394–5; Underwood, 1999, 103.
137. Maenchen-Helfen, 1973, 253.
138. Pollington, 1996, 129.
139. Dickinson & Harke, 1993.
140. Pollington, 1996, 134.
141. Evans, 1994, 49.
142. Pollington, 1996, 132.

143. Evison, 1963.
144. Green & Rogerson, 1978.
145. Evans, 1994, 49–55.
146. Claud. *In Ruf.*, ii, 360.
147. Giesler, 1996.

Chapter Nine

1. Chadwick, 1912.
2. The issues are conveniently discussed in Wolfram, 1988.
3. Drew, 1970, 2.
4. Todd, 1975, 19; Capelle, 1928; von See, 1970.
5. For Kossina's methods, see Eggers, 1959; Todd, 1975, 19; Heather, 1996, 13–17.
6. Higham, 1992, 1–2.
7. Drew, 1970; Havinghurst, 1976.
8. Haywood, 1962, 1–2.
9. Haywood, 1962, 2.
10. Brown, 1967.
11. Bintliff & Hamerow, 1995, 1.

Chapter Ten

1. Procop., *BV.*, I, i, 3.
2. Drew, 1949.
3. Drew, 1991.
4. Drew, 1973.
5. Attenborough, 1922.
6. For English place-names, see Wainwright, 1962, Gelling, 1973; Cameron, 1977; for *-inga* names, see Dodgson, 1966.
7. Heather, 1996, 209; Billy, 1992.
8. Amory, 1997, 333.
9. Hedeager, 1992, 287.
10. Green, 1996, 145–6.
11. Green, 1996, 157.
12. Green, 1996, 151.

Bibliography

A. Primary Sources

Ammianus Marcellinus: Works (Loeb edn, trans. Rolfe, J.C., Cambridge, Mass. & London, 1950–2, 3 vols)
Anglo-Saxon Chronicle (trans. Garmonsway, G.N., London, 1953)
Bede: Ecclesiastical History (trans. Plummer, C., Oxford, 1896; reprint, 1966)
Claudian: Poems (Loeb edn, trans. Platnauer M., Cambridge, Mass. & London, 1963, 2 vols)
Eunapius, Olympiodorus, Priscus (trans. Blockley, R.C., in *The Fragmentary Classicising Historians of the Later Roman Empire*, vol. II, Liverpool, 1983)
Gildas: The Ruin of Britain and other Works (trans. Winterbottom, M., Chichester, 1976)
Gregory of Tours: Histories (trans. Thorpe, L., London, 1974)
Hydatius: Chronicle (trans. Burgess, 1933, in English; Tranoy, A. as *Hydace, Chronique*, Paris, 1974)
Isidore of Seville: History of the Goths, Vandals and Suevi (trans. Donni, G. & Ford, G.R., Leiden, 1970)
Jordanes: The Gothic History (trans. Mierow, C.C., Cambridge, 1912, reprint, Cambridge, 1966)
Nennius: British History (trans. Morris, J., Chichester, 1980)
Orosius: Seven Books Against the Pagans (trans. Deferrari, R., Washington, D.C., 1964)
Panegyrici Latini (coll. and trans. Galletier, E., *Panégyriques Latins*, I, Paris, 1949)
Procopius: Works (Loeb edn, trans. Dewing, H.B., London, 1914–40, 7 vols)
Salvian: On the Government of God (trans. Sanford, E.M., New York, 1966)
Sidonius Apollinaris: Poems and Letters (Loeb edn, trans. Anderson, W.B., Cambridge, Mass., 1965, 2 vols)
Victor of Vita: History of the Vandal Persecution (trans. Moorhead, J., Liverpool, 1992)
Zosimus: The New History (trans. Buchanan, J.T. & Davis, H.T., San Antonio, Texas, 1967)

Anthologies of Texts

Age of Attila (coll. and trans. Gordon, C.D., Ann Arbor, 1972)

Secondary Sources

ALCOCK, L. 1971 *Arthur's Britain*, London
ALCOCK, L. 1987 *Economy, Society and Warfare among the Britons and Saxons*, Cardiff
ALCOCK, L. 1995 *Cadbury Castle Somerset, The Early Medieval Archaeology*, Cardiff
ALTHEIM, F. 1959–62 *Geschichte der Hunnen*, 5 vols, Berlin
AMORY, P. 1997 *People and Identity in Ostrogothic Italy, 489–554*, Cambridge
ANSTEE, J.W. & BIEK, L. 1961 'A Study in Pattern-welding', *Medieval Archaeology*, V, 71–93
ARNOLD, C.J. 1997 *An Archaeology of the Early Anglo-Saxon Kingdoms*, 2nd edn, London
ARRHENIUS, B. 1985 *Merovingian Garnet Jewellery: Emergence and Social Implications*, Stockholm
ATTENBOROUGH, F.L. 1922 *The Laws of the Earliest English Kings*, Cambridge
BACHRACH, B.S. 1972 *Merovingian Military Organization, 481–571*, Minneapolis
BASSETT, S. (ed.) 1989 *The Origins of the Anglo-Saxon Kingdoms*, Leicester
BEHMER, E.H. 1939 *Das Zweischeidige Schwert des Germanischen Volkerwanderungszeit*, Stockholm
BIERBRAUER, V. 1975 *Die ostgotischen Grab – und Schatzfunde in Italien*, Biblioteca degli Studi Medievali, no. 7, Spoleto
BILLY, P.-H. 1992 'Souvenirs wisigothiques dans la toponymie de la Gaule méridionale', in Fontaine, J. & Pellistrandi, C. (eds) *L'Europe héritière de l'Espagne wisigothique*, Madrid, 101–23
BINTLIFF, J. & HAMEROW, H. 1995 *Europe Between Late Antiquity and the Middle Ages*, Oxford (= BAR int. ser. 617)
BINTLIFF, J. & HAMEROW, H. 1995 'Europe between late Antiquity and the Middle Ages: recent Archaeological and Historical research in Western and Southern Europe', in Bintliff, J. & Hamerow, H. (eds), 1–7.
BÖHME, H.W. 1974 'Germanische Grabfunde des 4. bis 5. Jahrhunderts zwischen unterer Elbe und Loire. Studien zur Chonologie und Bevölkerungsgeschichte' (*Münchner Beiträge z. Vor- und Frügeschicht*, 19), 2 vols, Munich
BÖHME, H.W. 1986 'Das Ende der Romerherrschaft in Britannien und die angelsachsiche Besiedlung Englands im 5. *Jarhundert*', *Jahrbuch der Romanisches-Germanischen Zentralsmuseums*, 33, 469–574
BÖHME, H.W. 1996 'Soldner und Siedler im spätantiken Nordgallien', in von Welck (ed.), 91–101
BOHNER, K. 1968 'Zur Zeitstellung der beiden fränkischen Graber im Kölner Dom.', *Kölner Jahrbuch. Vor- u. Frügeschicht*, 9 (1967–8), 124f
BONA, I. 1991 *Das Hunnenreich*, Stuttgart
BONE, P. 1989 'The Development of Anglo-Saxon swords from the fifth to the eleventh century', in Hawkes (ed.), 62–70
BROOKS, D.A. 1988 'The case for continuity in fifth-century Canterbury re-examined', *Oxford Journal of Archaeology*, VII, i, 99–114
BROWN, G.B. 1915 *The Arts in Early England, III, Saxon Art and Industry in the Pagan Period*, London

Bibliography

BROWN, P. 1967 *Augustine of Hippo: a Biography*, London
BROWN, P. 1971 *The World of Late Antiquity*, London
BRUCE-MITFORD, R.L.S. 1974 *Aspects of Anglo-Saxon Archaeology*, London
BRUCE-MITFORD, R.L.S. (ed.) 1978 *The Sutton Hoo ship burial, vol. 2. The Arms, armour and regalia*, London
BRUCE-MITFORD, R.L.S. & LUSCOMBE, M.R. 1974 'The Benty Grange helmet', in Bruce-Mitford, 1974, 223–32
BRULET, R. 1980 'Tournai, fouillé d'une nécropole de Bas-Empire', *Archeologia*, 145, 55–9
BRULET, R. 1996 'Tournai und der Bestattungplatz um Saint-Brice', in von Welck (ed.), 163–70
BULLOUGH, D. 1965 'The Ostrogothic and Lombard Kingdoms', in Talbot Rice, D. (ed.) *The Dark Ages*, London, 157–74
BURNS, T.S. 1973 'The Battle of Adrianople', *Historia*, 22, 336–45
BURNS, T.S. 1980 *The Ostrogoths. Kingship and Society*, Wiesbaden
BURNS, T.S. 1984 *A History of the Ostrogoths*, Bloomington
BURNS, T.S. 1994 *Barbarians within the Gates of Rome*, Bloomington
BURY, J.B. 1923 *History of the Later Roman Empire from the Death of Theodosius to the Death of Justinian*, 2 vols, London
CAANDINI, A. 1983 'Pottery and the African economy', in Garnsey, P., Hopkins, K. & Whittaker, C.R. (eds) *Trade in the Ancient Economy*, Berkeley, 145–62
CAMERON, K. 1977 *English Place-names*, rev. edn, London
CAPELLE, W. 1928 *Die Germanen in Frühlicht der Geschichte*, Leipzig
CARVER, M. 1998 *Sutton Hoo, Burial ground of Kings?*, London
CHADWICK, H.M. 1912 *The Heroic Age*, Cambridge
CHADWICK, H.M. 1959 'Vortigern', in Chadwick, H.M. (ed.) *Studies in Early British History*, Cambridge, 21–46
CHADWICK, N.K. 1965 'The Colonization of Britanny from Celtic Britain', *Proc. British Academy*, LI, 235–99
CHADWICK, N.K. 1969 *Early Britanny*, Cardiff
CHARLES-EDWARDS, T. 1989 'Early Medieval Kingships in the British Isles', in Bassett, S. (ed.) *The Origins of Anglo-Saxon Kingdoms*, Leicester, 28–39
CLEARY, J.E. 1989 *The Ending of Roman Britain*, London
CLOVER, F.M. 1993 *The Late Roman West and the Vandals*, Aldershot
COLGRAVE, B. (trans.) 1936 *Felix's Life of St Guthlac*, Cambridge
CONSTANTINESCU, M. et al. (eds) *Relations Between the Autochthonous Population and the Migratory Populations in the Territory of Romania*, Bucharest
COURTOIS, C. 1955 *Les Vandales et l'Afrique*, Paris
COWIE, T. & CLARKE, D. 1985 *Symbols of Power in the Time of Stonehenge*, Edinburgh
CUNLIFFE, B. 1968 *Fifth Report on the Excavations at Richborough, Kent*, London (= Soc. Ant. Res. Rep. XXIII)
CUNLIFFE, B. 1975 *Excavations at Portchester, Hants*, II, Saxon, London (= Soc. Ant. Res. Rep. XXXIII)
CUNLIFFE, B. (ed.) 1994 *Prehistoric Europe: an Ilustrated History*, Oxford
DARK, K.R. 1994 *Civitas to Kingdom: British political continuity, 300–800*, Leicester
DARK, K.R. 1998 'Centuries of Roman Survival in the West', *British Archaeology*, March 1998, 8–9
DAVIDSON, H.R.E. 1962 *The Sword in Anglo-Saxon England: its Archaeology and Literature*, Oxford

DAVIDSON, H.R.E. 1989 'The Training of Warriors', in Hawkes, S.C. (ed.), 11–23
DAVIS, K.R. 1982 *Britons and Saxons: The Chiltern Region 400–700*, Chichester
DICKINSON, T. & HARKE, H. 1993 *Early Anglo-Saxon Shields* (= *Archaeologia*)
DIERKENS, A. & PÉRIN, P. 1997 'Death and burial in Gaul and Germania, 4th–8th century', in Webster, L. (ed.) *Transformation of the Roman World*, London, 79–95
DILL, S. 1905 *Roman Society in the Last Century of the Western Empire*, 2nd edn, London
DIXON, P. 1976 *Barbarian Europe*, Oxford
DODGSON, J. McN. 1966 'The significance of the distribution of place-names in -ingas, -inga in south-east England', *Medieval Archaeology*, X, 1–29
DOPPERFELD O. & PIRLING, R. 1966 *Fränkische Fürsten im Rheinland. Die Graber aus dem Kölner Dom, von Krefeld-Gellep und Morken*, Schr. Rhein. Landesmus. Bonn. 2, Dusseldorf
DREW, K.F. 1949 *The Burgundian Code*, Pennsylvania
DREW, K.F. (ed.) 1970 *The Barbarian Invasions: Catalyst of a New Order*, New York
DREW, K.F. 1973 *The Lombard Laws*, Pennsylvania
DREW, K.F. 1991 *The Laws of the Salian Franks*, Pennsylvania
DRINKWATER, J. & ELTON, J. (eds) 1992 *Fifth-century Gaul: a Crisis of Identity?* Cambridge
DUMVILLE, D.N. 1977 'Sub-Roman Britain: History and Legend', *History*, 62, 173–93
DUNAREANU-VULPE, E. 1967 *Der Schatz von Petrossa*, Bucharest
EGGERS, H.J. 1959 *Einführung in die Vorgeschichte*, Munich
ENGSTROM, R., LANKTON, S.M. & LESHER-ENGSTROM, A. 1989 *A Modern Replication Based on the Pattern-Welded Sword of Sutton Hoo*, Kalamazoo
EVANS, A.C. 1994 *The Sutton Hoo Ship Burial*, rev. edn, London
EVANS, S.S. 1997 *The Lords of Battle. Image and Reality of the Comitatus in Dark Age Britain*, Woodbridge
EVISON, V. 1963 'Sugar loaf shield bosses', *Antiquaries Journal*, XLIII, 38–96
EVISON, V. 1965 *Fifth-Century Invasions South of the Thames*, London
EVISON, V. 1967 'The Dover ring sword and other ring swords and beads,' *Archaeologia*, 101, 63–118
EVISON, V. 1975 'Sword rings and beads', *Archaeologia*, 105, 303–15
FELL, C. 1984 *Women in Anglo-Saxon England*, London
FERGUSON, R.B. 1990 'Explaining War', in Haas, J. (ed.) 1990, 26–55
FITZGERALD, P. 1978 *Ancient China*, Oxford
FRERE, S.S. 1974 *Britannia*, London, rev. edn
GALE, 1989 'The Seax', in Hawkes, S.C. (ed.), ch. 6
GEARY, P.J. 1988 *Before France and Germany. The Creation and Transformation of the Merovingian World*, Oxford
GELLING, M. 1978 *Signposts to the Past*, London
GENRICH, A. 1970 *Liebenau. Ein sachsisches Graberfeld* (Wegweiser z. Vor- und Frühgech. Niedersaachsens, 3), Hildesheim
GIESLER, J. 1996 'Rekonstruktion eines Sattels aus dem fränkischen Gräberfeld von Wesel-Bislich', in von Welck (ed.), 808–11.
GOFFART, W. 1980 *Barbarians and Romans, AD 418–584, The Techniques of Accommodation*, Princeton
GREEN B. & ROGERSON, A. 1978 *The Anglo-Saxon Cemetery at Berg Apton, Norfolk: Catalogue* (= *East Anglian Archaeology* 7) Gressenhall.
GREEN, D.H. 1996 'The Rise of Germania in the Light of Linguistic evidence', in Ausenda, G. *After Empire: Towards an Ethnology of Europe's Barbarians*, San Marino, 143–62

Bibliography

GROENMAN-VAN WAATERINGE, W. 1983 'The disastrous effect of the Roman occupation', in Brandt R.W. & Slofstra, J. (eds), *Roman and Native in the Low Countries: Spheres of Interaction*, Oxford (= BAR Int. Ser. 184), 147–57

HAARNAGEL, W. 1979 *Die Grabungen Federssen Wierde*, 2 vols, Berlin

HAAS, J. (ed.) 1990 *The Anthropology of War*, Cambridge

HACHMANN, R. 1971 *The Germanic Peoples*, Geneva

HALSALL, G. 1992 'The Bacaudae of Fifth-Century Gaul', in Drinkwater & Elton (eds), 208–17

HAMEROW, H. 1994 'Migration theory and the migration period,' in Vyner, B. (ed.) *Building the Past*, London, 164–77

HARKE, H. 1989 'Early Saxon Weapon Burials: frequencies, distributions and weapon combinations', in Hawkes, S.C. (ed.), 49–59

HARKE, H. 1993 'Changing symbols in a changing society; the Anglo-Saxon weapon burial rite in the seventh century', in Carver, M. (ed.), 149–66

HASELOFF, G. 1981 *Die germanische Tierornamentik der Volkerwanderungszeit, Studien zu Salin's Stil I*, 3 vols, Berlin

HAUSER, G. 1996 'Das frankische Graberfeld unter dem Kölner Dom', in von Welck (ed.), 438–47

HAVINGHURST, A.F. (ed.) 1976 *The Pirenne Thesis*, Lexington

HAWKES, S.C. 1982 'Anglo-Saxon Kent c. 425–725', in Leach, P. (ed.) *Archaeology in Kent to AD 1500*, London (= *CBA Res. Rep.* 48), 64–78

HAWKES, S.C. 1986 'The sword from the Feltwell Villa', in Gurney, D. (ed.) *Settlement, Religion and Industry in the Roman Fen Edge, Norfolk* (= *East Anglian Archaeology* 31), 32–7

HAWKES, S.C. (ed.) 1989 *Weapons and Warfare in Anglo-Saxon England*, Oxford (Oxford Univ. Committee for Arch. Monographs 21), esp. 'Weapons and Warfare in Anglo-Saxon England: an Introduction', 1–9

HAWKES, S.C. & DUNNING, G.C. 1961 'Soldiers and Settlers in Britain, fourth to fifth century', *Medieval Archaeology*, V, 1–70

HAWKES, S.C. & PAGE, R. 1967 'Swords and runes in south-east England', *Antiquaries Journal* 47, 1–26

HAYWOOD, R.M. 1962 *The Myth of Rome's Fall*, reprint, New York

HEATHER, P. 1991 *Goths and Romans, 332–489*, Oxford

HEATHER, P. 1996 *The Goths*, Oxford

HEATHER, P. & MATTHEWS, J. 1991 *The Goths in the Fourth Century*, Liverpool

HEDEAGER, L. 1978 'A Quantitative Analysis of Roman Imports in Europe North of the Limes (AD 0–400), and the Question of Roman-Germanic Exchange', in Kristiansen, K. & Paludan-Muller, C. (eds) *New Directions in Scandinavian Archaeology* (Studies in Scandinavian Prehistory and Early History, vol. 1) Copenhagen, 191–223

HEDEAGER, L. 1987 'Empire, Frontier and the Barbarian Hinterland. Rome and Northern Europe from AD 1–400', in Kristiansen K. et al. (eds) *Centre and Periphery in the Ancient World* (Cambridge), 125–40

HEDEAGER, L. 1988 'The evolution of Germanic Society, AD 1–400', in Jones, Dyson, et al. (eds), 129–44

HEDEAGER, L. 1992 'Kingdoms, Ethnicity and Material culture: Denmark in a European perspective', in Carver, M. (ed.), 279–300

HIGHAM, N. 1992 *Rome, Britain and the Anglo-Saxons*, London

HIGHAM, N. 1993 *The Kingdom of Northumbria, AD 350–1000*, Stroud

HINES, J. 1984 *The Scandinavian Character of Anglian England in the pre-Viking Period*, Oxford (= BAR 124)
HINES, J. 1989 'The Military Context of the *adventus Saxonum*: some continental evidence', in Hawkes, S.C. (ed.), 25–48
HINES, J. 1990 'Philology, archaeology and the adventus Saxonum vel Anglorum,' in Bammesberger, A. & Wollmann, A. (eds) *Britain 400–600, language and history*, Heidelberg, 17–36
HINES, J. 1992 'The Scandinavian character of Anglian England: an update', in Carver, M. (ed.), 315–29
HINES, J. 1994 'The becoming of the English: identity, material culture and language in Anglo-Saxon England,' *Anglo-Saxon Studies in Archaeology and History*, 7, 49–59
HINES, J. 1996 'Cultural Change and Social organization in Early Anglo-Saxon England', in Ausenda, G. (ed.) *After Empire, Towards an Ethnology of Europe's Barbarians*, San Marino, 75–88
HODGES, R. 1989 *The Anglo-Saxon Achievement*, London
HODGKIN, T. 1892 *Italy and her Invaders, II, The Hunnish and Vandal Invasions*, London
HOLMQVIST, W. 1955 *Germanic Art*, Stockholm
ILKJAER, J. 1995 'Illerup Ådal (Danemark). Un lieu de sacrifices du IIIe siècle de n.e. en Scandinavie méridionale', in Vallet, F. & Kazanski, M. (eds) *La Noblesse romaine et les Chefs barbares*, Paris, 101–12
ILKJAER, J. & LONSTRUP, J. 1983 'Der Moorfund in Tal der Illerup-A bei Skanderborg im Ostjutland', *Germania*, 61, 95–126
JAMES, E. 1982 *The Origins of France. From Clovis to the Capetians, 500–1000*, London
JAMES, E. 1988 *The Franks*, Oxford
JAMES, E. 1992 'Royal burials among the Franks', in Carver, M. (ed.) *The Age of Sutton Hoo*, Woodbridge, 243–54.
JETTMAR, K. 1964 *Art of the Steppes*, London
JOHNSON, S. 1976 *The Roman Forts of the Saxon Shore*, London
JOHNSON, S. 1979 *Later Roman Britain*, London
JONES, A.H.M. 1966 *The Decline of the Ancient World*, London
JONES, M. 1999 'Rebellion Remains the Decisive Factor', *British Archaeology* 20 (Dec), 8–9
KAZANSKI, M. 1982 'Deux riches tombes de l'époque des Grandes Invasions au nord de la Gaule: Airan et Pouan', *Archéologie Médiévale*, 12, 17–33
KAZANSKI, M. & PÉRIN, P. 1988 'Le mobilier funéraire de la tombe de Childeric Ier; état de la question et perspectives', *Revue Archéologique de Picardie*, 3–4 (= *Actes des VIIIe Journéees internationales d'archéologie mérovingienne de Soissons*), 13–38
KENT, J.P.C. 1961 'From Roman Britain to Saxon England', in Dolley, M. (ed.) *Anglo-Saxon Coins*, London, 1–22
KENT, J.P.C. 1979 'The end of Roman Britain: the literary and numismatic evidence reviewed', in Casey, P.J. (ed.) *The End of Roman Britain*, Oxford, (BAR 71), 15–27
KRUGER, B. (ed.) 1983 *Die Germanen, Geschichte und Kultur der germanischen Stamme in Mitterleuropa, Ein Handbuch*, 2 vols, Berlin, 1983
LAING, L. & LAING, J. 1990 *Celtic Britain and Ireland, AD 200–800*, Dublin
LAING, L. & LAING, J. 1996 *Early English Art and Architecture*, Stroud
LANG, J. & AGER, B. 1989 'Swords of the Anglo-Saxon Periods in the British Museum: a Radiographic Study', in Hawkes, S.C. (ed.), 85–122.
LASKO, P. 1971 *The Kingdom of the Franks*, London

Bibliography

LASZLO, G. 1951 'The Significance of the Hun Golden Bow', *Acta Archaeologica Hungarica* 1, 91–106

LEEDS, E.T. 1951 'Visigoth or Vandal?' *Archaeologia*, XCIV, 195–212

LEMANT, J.-P. et al. 1985 *Le cimetière et la fortification du Bas-Empire de Vireux-Molhain (Ardennes)*, Mainz

LETHBRIDGE, T. 1931 'A sword from the River Lark', *Cambs. Ant. Soc. Proc.* XXXII, 64

LEUBE, A. 1983 'Die Sachsen' in Kruger, B. (ed.) *Die Germanen*, vol. 2, Berlin, 443–85

LINDNER, R.P. 1981 'Nomadism, Horses and Huns, *Past and Present*, XLII, 4–19

McCAULEY, C. 1990 'Conference Overview' in Haas, J. (ed.), 1–25

MACKRETH, D. 1978 'Orton Hall Farm, Peterborough: a Roman and Saxon settlement', in Todd, M. (ed.) *Studies in the Romano-British Villa*, Leicester, 209–28

MAENCHEN-HELFEN, J.O. 1973 *The World of the Huns*, Berkeley

MATHISEN, R.W. 1993 *Roman Aristocrats in Barbarian Gaul*, Austin, Texas

MATTHEWS, J. 1975 *Western Aristocracies and Imperial Court, AD 364–425*, Oxford

MEADOWS, I. 1997 'Wollaston: The "Pioneer" burial', *Current Arch.*, 154, 391–5

MILLARD, A. 1985 *Treasures from Bible Times*, London

MINNS, E. 1945 'The Art of the Northern Nomads', *Proc. British Academy*, 28, 47–99

MOORHEAD, J. 1992 *Theoderic in Italy*, Oxford

MORRIS, J. 1975 *The Age of Arthur*, rev. edn, London

MOSS, H. St L. B. 1935 *The Birth of the Middle Ages, 395–814*, Oxford

MYRES, J.N.L. 1969 *Anglo-Saxon Pottery and the Settlement of England*, Oxford

MYRES, J.N.L. 1986 *The English Settlements*, Oxford

NEWARK, T. 1985 *The Barbarians. Warriors and Wars of the Dark Ages*, Poole

NEWTON, S. 1992 'Beowulf and the East Anglian Royal Pedigree', in Carver, M. (ed.) *The Age of Sutton Hoo*, Woodbridge, 65–74

NICKEL, H. 1973 'About the sword of the Huns and the "Urepos" of the Steppes', *Metropolitan Museum Journal*, XII, 131–42

NICOLLE, D. 1990 *Attila and the Nomad Hordes*, London

OAKESHOTT, W. 1974 *Dark Age Warrior*, Guildford & London

ODOBESCO, A. 1889–1900 *Le Trésor de Petrossa*, Bucharest (reprinted in Obodesco, *Opera*, vol. IV, with update and commentary, Bucharest, 1976)

OOST, S.I. 1968 *Galla Placidia Augusta: a biographical essay*, Chicago

ORNA-ORNSTEIN, J. 1998 'Coin Hoards 1998, 27, Patching, West Sussex', *Numismatic Chronicle*, 158

ORSNES, M. 1963 'The Weapon Find in Ejsbol Mose at Haderslev', *Acta Archaeologica*, 34 (1963), 232–47

PÉRIN, P. 1980 *La Datation des Tombes Mérovingiennes: Historique – Méthodes – Applications*, Geneva

PÉRIN, P. & KAZANSKI, M. 1996a 'Das Grab Childerichs I' in von Welck (ed.), 1996, 173–82

PÉRIN, P. & KAZANSKI, M. 1996b 'Männerkleidung und Bewaffnung im Wandel der Zeit', in von Welck (ed.), 707–11.

PÉRIN, P. 1996c 'Paris, merowingische Metropole', in von Welck (ed.), 121–8

PÉRIN, P. 1996d 'Die archäologischen Zeugnisse der frankischen Expansion in Gallien', in von Welck (ed.), 227–32

PILLOY, J. 1895 *Études sur d'anciens lieux de sépultures dans Aisne*, 2

PIRLING, R. 1966–79 *Das römisch-fränkische Gräberfeld von Krefeld-Gellep*, Berlin (2 vols, 1966; 2 vols, 1974; 2 vols, 1979)

PIRLING, R. 1996 'Krefeld-Gellep im Frümittelalter', in von Welck (ed.), 261–5
POLLINGTON, S. 1996 *The English Warrior from Earliest Times to 1066*, Hockwold
RANDERS-PEHRSON, J. 1983 *Barbarians and Romans, The Birth Struggle of Europe, AD 400–700*, London
RANDSBORG, K. (ed.) 1989 *The Birth of Europe: Archaeology and Social Development in the First Millennium AD*, Rome
RANDSBORG, K. 1991 *The First Millennium in Europe and the Mediterranean*, Cambridge
RANDSBORG, K. 1995 *Hjortspring. Warfare and Sacrifice in Early Europe*, Aarhus
RAUSING, G. 1967 *The Bow*, Lund
ROSTOVTZEFF, M. 1929 *The Animal Style in South Russia and China*, Princeton
SALIN, E. 1949–59 *La Civilization mérovingienne*, 4 vols, Paris
SALIN, E. & FRANCE-LANORD, A. 1956 'Sur le trésor barbare de Pouan', *Gallia*, XIV, 65–75
SANSTERRE, J.-M. 1996 'Die Franken und Byzanz', in von Welck (ed.), 395–400.
SCHMIDT, B. 1996 'Das Königreich der Thüringer und seine Eingliederung in das Frankenreich', in von Welck (ed.), 285–97
SCULL, C. 1993 'Archaeology, early Anglo-Saxon society and the origins of the Anglo-Saxon kingdoms', *Anglo-Saxon Studies in Archaeology and History*, 6, 117–24
SCULL, C. 1995 'Approaches to Material Culture and Social Dynamics of the Migration period in eastern England', in Bintliff, J. & Hamerow, H. (eds) *Europe between Late Antiquity and the Middle Ages*, Oxford (= BAR Int. Ser. 617), 71–83
SEILLIER, C. 1986 'Développement topographique et caractères généraux de la nécropole de Vron (Somme)', *Archéologie Médiévale*, 16, 7–32
SERVICE, E.R. 1968 'War and our Contemporary Ancestors', in Fried, M., Harris, M. Murphy, R. (eds) *War: An Anthropology of Armed Conflict and Aggression*, New York, 160–7
SIMS-WILLIAMS, P. 1983 'The settlement of England in Bede and the *Chronicle*', *Anglo-Saxon England*, 12, 1–41
SNYDER, C.A. 1998 *An Age of Tyrants*, Stroud
SPEAKE, G. 1980 *Anglo-Saxon Animal Art*, Oxford
STEIN, F. 1996 'Die Graber unter dem Kölner Dom im Vergleich zu anderen Grablegen der Merovingerfamilie', in Wolff, A. (ed.) *Studien Kölner Dom 2*, Cologne, 99–
STEUER, H. 1987 Helm and Ringschweert: *Prunkbewaffnung und Rangabzeichen germanischer Krieger. Eine* 6, 189–236
SWANTON, M.J. 1967 'An early Alamannic brooch from Yorkshire', *Antiquaries Journal*, 47, 43–50
SWANTON, M.J. 1973 *The Spearheads of the Anglo-Saxon Settlements*, London (= RAI monograph)
SWANTON, M.J. 1974 *A Corpus of Pagan Anglo-Saxon Spear Types*, Oxford (= BAR Brit. Ser. 7)
THOMPSON, E.A. 1966 *The Visigoths in the time of Ulfila*, Oxford
THOMPSON, E.A. 1969 *The Goths in Spain*, Oxford
THOMPSON, E.A. 1982 *Romans and Barbarians*, London
THOMPSON, E.A. 1995 *The Huns*, Oxford
TODD, M. 1972 *Everyday Life of the Barbarians*, London
TODD, M. 1975 *The Northern Barbarians, 100 BC–AD 300*, London
TODD, M. 1992 *The Early Germans*, Oxford

TODD, M. 1994 'Barbarian Europe, AD 300–700', in Cunliffe, B. (ed.) *Prehistoric Europe, an Illustrated History*, Oxford, 447–82
UNDERWOOD, R. 1999 *Anglo-Saxon Weapons and Warfare*, Stroud
van DAM, R. 1985 *Leadership and Community in Late Antique Gaul*, Berkeley
van ES, W.A. 1967 *Wijster. A Native Village beyond the Roman Frontier*, Groningen
VENTURI, L. 1964 *History of Art Criticism*, New York (rev. edn)
von FREEDEN, U. 1996 'Die Bajuwaren – Nachbarb der Franken', in von Welck (ed.), 308–18
von HESSEN, O., KURZE, W. & MASTRELLI, C.A., 1977 *Il Tesoro di Golognano*, Firenze
von SEE, K. 1970 *Deutsche Germanen-Ideologie*, Frankfurt
von WELCK, K. (ed.) 1996 *Die Franken, Wergbereiter Europas*, 2 vols, Mainz
WAINWRIGHT, F.T. 1962 *Archaeology, Place-names and Society*, London
WALLACE-HADRILL, J.M. 1962a *The Long-Haired Kings and other studies in Frankish history*, London
WALLACE-HADRILL, J.M. 1962b *The Barbarian West*, London
WATSON, W. 1973 *The Genius of China*, London
WELCH, M. 1992 *Anglo-Saxon England*, London
WENHAM, S.J. 1989 'Anatomical Interpretations of Anglo-Saxon Weapon Injuries', in Hawkes, S. (ed.) 123–40.
WERNER, J. 1932 'Bogenfragmente aus Carnuntum und von der unteren Wolga', *Eurasia Septentrionale Antiqua*, 7, 33–58
WERNER, J. 1949–50 'Zur Herkunft der frühmittelalterlichen Spangenhelme', *Prähistorische Zeitschrift*, 34–5, 178–93
WERNER, J. 1956 *Beitrage zur Archaeologie des Attila-Reiches, Vorgetagen am 4. März 1955: Bayerische Akademie der Wissenschaften, Philosophisch-historische Klasse, Abhandlungen n.f. 38 A/B*, Munich
WERNER, J. 1964 'Frankish royal tombs in the cathedrals of Cologne and Saint Denis', *Antiquity*, 38, 201–16
WERNER, J. 1968 'Bewaffnung und Waffenbeigrabe in der Merowingerzeit', *Ordinamenti Militari in Occidente nell 'Alto Medioevo*, XV, I, Spoleto, 95–108
WHEELER, R.E.M. 1956 *Rome Beyond the Imperial Frontiers*, Harmondsworth
WHITE, R. 1988 *Roman and Celtic Objects from Anglo-Saxon Graves*, Oxford (= BAR British Ser)
WHITE, R. 1990 'Scrap or substitute; Roman material in Anglo-Saxon Graves', in Southworth, E. (ed.) *Anglo-Saxon Cemeteries: a Reappraisal*, Stroud, 125–52
WILSON, D.M. (ed.) 1976a *The Archaeology of Anglo-Saxon England*, London
WILSON, D.M. 1976b 'Introduction', in Wilson, D.M. (ed.) 1–22
WILSON, D.M. (ed.) 1980 *The Northern World*, London
WOLFRAM, H. 1988 *The History of the Goths*, Berkeley
WOOD, I. 1992 'Frankish hegemony in England', in Carver, M. (ed.) 235–42
YORKE, B. 1997 *Kings and Kingdoms of Anglo-Saxon England*, 2nd edn, London

Index

Adrianople, 11, 19; battle of, 25–6; 61; siege, 86

Ad Silices, battle of, 24–5

Aetius, Roman general (d. 454), 7, 10, 45, 46, 47; defeated Attila, 51–3; 55, 58, 72, 76; murdered by Valentinian III, 76; 88; relations with Franks, 90; 96, 136

Alamanni, 28, 36, 64, 83, 84, 85, 86, 87, 91, 92, 96, 147, 154, 158, 159, 173

Alans, 17, 21, 26, 32, 34, 36, 38, 42; lifestyle, 42; 43, 52, 55, 57, 60, 61, 70, 71, 73, 74, 92; warrior training, 145; 146

Alaric, Visigothic leader (d. 410), 7, 11, 15, 29, 30–3, 34; sacked Rome, 34–5; 38, 43, 45, 47, 54, 69, 70, 87, 96

Alaric II of the Visigoths (d. 507), 67, 92

Alatheus, Greutungian *leader*, at Adrianople, 25; 61

Alaviv, Gothic leader, 22, 23

Allectus, third-century British usurper, 85, 96

Amalasuintha, 66; regent to Athalaric, 67

Amals, 61, 63, 64, 65, 67

Ammianus Marcellinus, historian (d. 395), 22, 23, 25, 26, 27, 36, 42, 43, 44, 45, 57, 85, 146, 148, 172, 175

Angles, 94, 95, 104, 105, 144

Anglo-Saxon Chronicle, 98, 103, 148

Anglo-Saxons, 94–105; treasures, 140–1

Angon see weapons

Anthemius, Western Emperor (d. 472), 77, 78, 101

Arbogastes, Frankish general in Roman army (d. 394), 29; rise to power 86–7; suicide, 88

Arcadius, Eastern Emperor (d. 408), 29–30, 31, 33, 44, 45, 86

Ardabur, the Alan, 45, 63

Ardaric, king of the Gepids, 55

Armorica see Britanny

Armour see weapons

Arthur, semi-legendary British king, 103

Aspar, the Alan (d. 471), 45; defeated by Gaiseric of the Vandals, 46; negotiated truce with Huns, 48; owner of Zercon, 58; 63, 74, 78

Athalaric, king of the Ostrogoths, 68

Athanaric, pagan Gothic leader; negotiated with Valens, 21–2; fled and died in Constantinople, 28–9

Athaulf, Visigothic leader, 15; pursues Sarus, 34; took up leadership, 36, relationship with Rome, 37; murdered, 38; 71, 72

Attacotti, 96

Attalus, usurper and Gothophile, 8, 34, 37, 66

Attila, Hunnic leader (fl. mid-fifth century AD), 9, 40; secretaries, 41; destroyed Burgundians, 46–7; in folklore and literature, 47; description, 49; murdered Bleda,

48; 49, 50, 51; defeated at Catalaunian
  Plains, 52–5; threatened Rome, 53; death,
  53; 53, 54; description of his home, 58; at
  a feast, 65; 62, 63, 64, 69, 76, 88, 90, 104,
  136, 142, 146
Audefleda, wife of Theodoric the
  Great, 67
Augustine of Canterbury, Saint (d. 604/5),
  106
Augustine of Hippo, Saint (d. 430); writing
  on sack of Rome, 35; 62, 70; died in siege,
  74; 99, 169

Babai, king of the Sarmatians, 64
Baetica, province of Spain, 71
Barritus, battle cry, 20, 97
Basiliscus, Eastern Roman general
  (d. 477), 78
Battles, see Adrianople, Ad Silices,
  Catalaunian Plains, Frigidus, Nedeo,
  Verona, Vouille
Bauto, Frankish general, 86, 87
Belisarius, Byzantine general (d. 565), 55;
  recaptures Italy from Goths, 67–70; 71;
  recovers Africa from Vandals, 82; 176
Bleda, brother of Attila the Hun, 46, 47, 48,
  58, 59
Boats, Goths in Aegean, 21; across Danube,
  23; Gothic, 24; 25; Hunnic, 57; Vandal
  fleet, 73; Vandal sea battle, 78; see also
  ships, keels, Hjortspring, Nydam
Bonifacius, Roman general (d. 432), 45;
  posted to Africa, 46; relationship with
  Vandals 72, 73, 74
Bonitus, Frank in Roman army, 85
Britannia (Roman province), 94–96,
  103, 106
Britanny, 101–2
Burgundians, 36; destroyed by Aetius and
  Attila 46–7; 51, 65, 88

Carausius, British usurper (d. 293), 96
Carthage, 69, 72; description at Vandal capture, 74–6; 70; starving crowd repelled by
  Vandals, 80; 80, 81, 82, 88
Catalaunian Plains (Battle), 39, 52, 55, 70
Cauldrons, Hunnic, 138

Cherchel, North Africa, 74
Childeric, Frankish king (d. c. 481/2), 90–1,
  135, 140, 141, 146, 151, 158, 164
Chlogio, Frankish leader, 90
Christianity, 19–22; 23; as factor in warfare,
  31; during sack of Rome, 35; factor in
  Hunnic reputations, 41; reactions to
  Radagaisus' paganism, 63; 66, 69, 72; 75;
  Vandals, 79; in Africa, 81; Frankish, 88;
  90; Pelagianism, 97; Britain, 105; 166,
  174, 175
Chrysaphius, Eastern Court eunuch, 50–1
Cirta, 74
Claudian, poet (d. c. 404), 24, 29, 30, 32, 57,
  164, 174
Clovis, Frankish king, defeated Visigoths
  (d. 511), 39, 88; his campaigns, 91–6; 136,
  140, 150, 151
Constantine I, the Great (d. 337), 19, 80,
  84, 85
Constantine III, usurper, vi, 36; recognised by
  Honorius, 33; killed, 36; effect on Vandals,
  70; 87, 96
Constantinople, i, 19, 22, 27, 28, 29, 30,
  31, 44, 45, 47, 50, 51, 63, 64, 70, 75,
  78, 175
Constantius I, Chlorus, emperor (d. 306),
  84, 96
Constantius, Roman general (d. 421), 37, 38,
  39, 45, 51, 71, 72, 84, 96, 137
Constantius, secretary to Attila, 47

Dacia, 16, 19, 21, 22, 55, 64, 103
Danes, 94–5, 98
Decius, Emperor (d. 251), 16, 17
Dengizich, son of Attila, 63
Dubius, alleged murderer of Athaulf, 38
Dynamius, 85

Edeco, aide to Attila, 50–1, 65
Epic literature, 144
Ermaneric, Gothic leader (d. between 370 and
  376), 60–1, 63
Estremadura, brooches, 137
Eudocia, daughter of Valentinian III, 75; captured and married to Huniric of Vandals,
  77–8; 82

Eudoxia, Empress of Valentinian III, forcibly married to Petronius Maximus, 76; captured by Vandals, 77; freed, 78
Euerwulf, alleged murderer of Athaulf, 38
Eugenius, emperor (d. 394), 29, 87, 88
Eunapius, historiographer (d. *c.* 420), 20, 21, 146, 172
Euric, Visigothic leader, 39
Eutropius, 30, 31

Fiesole, Gothic defeat, 32, 44, 62–3
Finns, 60, 167
Folklore, Hunnic, 55–6
Franks, 29, 36, 46; at Catalaunian Plains, 55, 69, 70; origins and development, 83–92; graves, 89–91; early kingdoms, 83f; chieftain's burial, 89; 91, 99, 104, 135, 136; Frankish treasures, 140, 144, 147, 149, 150, 153, 154, 155, 156, 157, 158, 159, 161, 162, 164, 169, 173, 174
Fraomarius, Alamannic king in Britain, 96
Frigidus, battle, 29, 30, 87
Frisians, 95, 96
Fritigern, Gothic leader, 22–3; at Adrianople, 25; 28

Gainas, 30, 31, 44
Gaiseric, king of the Vandals (d. 477), defeated Aspar and Bonifacius, 46; made peace with Eastern Empire, 48; 51; rise to power, 70; description, 86; captured Carthage 74; 75; offended Visigoths, 76; captured Rome, 77, 78, 79, 81, 86, 143
Galla Placidia, daughter of Theodosius I, 9, 33; hostage of Visigoths, married Athaulf, 36–7; returned to Honorius, 38–9; opposed Joannes, 45; regent to Valentinian III, 45; 51, 52, 71, 73, 146
Genghis Khan (d. 1227), 40
Gennobaud, Frankish leader, 84
Gepids, 46, 52, 55, 64
Germanus of Auxerre, Saint (d. 448), 145, 175
Gildas, Saint and writer (d. 570), 96, 101, 102, 174
Glycerius, Western Emperor (reigned 473–4), 79
Gothia, 15, 19, 31, 36, 94

Goths, 15–39; *laager*, 24; 27–9, 88
Gratian, Western Emperor (d. 383), involvement in Adrianople, 25–6; 86, 137
Gregory of Tours, Saint and Pope (d. 604), 70, 83, 84, 85, 91, 92, 140, 147, 149, 155, 156, 161, 172, 174
Greutungi, a Gothic people, 15, 17, 19, 21; cross the Danube, 23; at Adrianople, 26; under threat from Huns, 43; early history, 63
Gunderic of the Vandals, 70, 71, 73, 74
Gundobad, king of the Burgundians, 78

Hadrian's Wall, 95, 96, 99
Hengest, Saxon mercenary leader; invited to post-Roman Britannia, 97–101; campaigns, 103; in literature, 105
Hippo Regius, North Africa, 72, 74, 75
Hjortspring boat, 98
Honoria, sister of Valentinian III, daughter of Galla Placidia, 39; political relationship with Attila, 50–1; 76, 90
Honorius, Western Emperor (d. 423), 8, 29; withdrew to Ravenna, 31; summoned Stilicho, 32; 33; negotiates with Goths, 33–4; his pet chicken, 35; relations with Athaulf, 36–8; 39, 44; dies of dropsy, 45; 70, 96, 147
Horreus Margus, Treaty, 47–8
Horsa, Saxon mercenary, 97, 100, 103, 105, 144
Horsemanship: in Clovis' army, 92; of Huns, 40, 41, 44; of Alans, 43; of Vandals, 70
Horses: of Huns, 56–7; of Vandals, 69; 71, 80, 81, 88, 94; in burials, 140, 141, 145, 146; 159, 161, 164; in battle, 164
Huniric, Vandal king, 75, 77, 79, 80, 82
Huns, 7, 11, 17, 19, 21, 22, 27, 30, 32, 34; use of lassoes, 36; 40; reputations of, 41; origins, 42–3; and Alans, 43–4; lifestyle, 43; earliest Huns in Europe, 44–5; warfare techniques, 45; relationship with Aetius, 45–6; destruction of Burgundians, 46; after Rua, 47; Treaty of Horreus Margus, 47; under Attila, 48–54; attacked Greutungi, 60; 61, 63, 74, 76, 79, 83, 91,

94, 98, 105, 137; treasures, 137–8; 146, 148; weapons, 152; swords, 154–6; bow, 159; 174, 176
Hyacinthus, eunuch to Honoria 51, 52

Ildico, last wife of Attila, 54
Injuries from battle, 148–9

Joannes, Roman usurper, 45
Jordanes, sixth-century Gothic writer, 15, 23, 29, 37, 38, 40, 42, 48, 50, 52, 55, 60, 61, 63, 64, 70, 73, 101, 142, 146, 152, 173, 174, 176
Justinian, Eastern Emperor, 68, 82

keels, 97
Krefeld-Gellep, 89, 92, 150, 154, 158
Kreka, wife of Attila, 58

Leo I, Eastern Emperor (d. 474), 63, 64, 77, 78, 140, 161
Leo I, Pope (d. 461), 54
Lifestyles: of Huns, 43; of Alans, 43; Romano-British and Anglo-Saxon, 102; barbarians at leisure, 104f
Lupercinus, Roman commander in Thrace, 22, 23

Macrianus, Alammanic king, 86, 96
Mallobaudes, Frankish king, 85
Marcian, Eastern Emperor (d. 457), 51, 54, 55, 74, 77
Marcianopolis, 19, 23
Marcomeres, Frankish leader, 84
Morris, John, historian, 97

Naissus, 19, 49, 148
Namatius, 94, 95
Nedao, battle of, 55
Nennius, ninth-century historian, 96, 97, 99, 101, 105, 144, 174
Norwegians, 95, 168
Notitia Dignitatum, 88
Nydam boat, 98

Odoacer, barbarian king of Italy, 11, 64, 65–6, 90

Olybrius, Western Emperor (d. 472), 77, 78, 79
Olympiodorus of Egyptian Thebes, Greek historian (fl. fifth century AD), 37, 72, 171, 175
Onegesius, aide to Attila the Hun, 57
Optila, assassin of Valentinian III, 76
Orestes, aide of Attila, father of Romulus Augustulus (d. 476), 50, 65, 66, 67
Orosius, theologian (fl. 414–17), 15, 29, 31, 35, 41, 57, 62, 175
Ostrogoths, 15, 28, 32, 52, 51ff; under Ermaneric, 60–1; flight over Danube, 61; under Theodoric the Great, 64; end of Ostrogothic Italy, 66; 72; treasures, 139

Pelagianism, see Christianity
Penda, pagan king of Mercia (d. 655), 106
Petronius Maximus, Western Emperor, 76, 77, 78
Philippopolis; 16, 17, 19
Picts, 28, 96
Pietroassa Treasure, 137
Placidia, daughter of Valentinian III, 77, 78, 79, 146
Pollentia, battle, 31
Portchester, 98
Priscus of Panium, writer (fl. mid-fifth century), 47, 49, 50, 54, 57, 58, 59, 172
Probus, Western Emperor, 84
Procopius, writer (sixth century), 34, 35, 69, 70, 73, 75, 76, 77, 78, 80, 82, 149, 160, 171, 172, 175

Radagaisus, Gothic leader (d. 406); defeat at Fiesole, 32; 44, 61, 62, 95, 148
Ravenna: court of Western Empire, 31, 33, 35, 45; siege, 65, 66, 67, 148
Richborough, 98
Richomeres, Frankish general in Roman army, 24, 25, 29, 86
Ricimer, Roman general (d. 472), 77, 78–9
Riothamus, Breton king, 101, 102
Roman Britain – see Britannia
Rome; Millennium celebrations, 16; threatened by Radagaisus, 32, 33, 62; besieged

by Alaric, 32–4; sacked by Goths, 34–5; threatened by Attila, 53; 65, 69, 71; Vandal sack, 77
Romulus Augustulus, usurper (fl. late fifth century), 11, 65, 66, 67, 88
Rua, leader of the Huns, 46, 47
Rufinus, regent of Arcadius (d. 395), 29, 30, 31, 174

Salvian, Christian writer, 69, 75, 173, 175
Saphrax, Gothic leader, 25, 61
Saracens, at Constantinople, 27
Sarus, Gothic leader in Roman pay; at Fiesole, 32; murdered Stilicho's Hunnic bodyguard, 33; 34; heroic death, 36; 38, 72
Saxons, 51, 64, 94; appearance, 95; 96, 97, 99, 100, 103, 104, 137, 150, 155, 158, 172, 173, 174
Scots, 96
Sebastianus, Roman general, 24, 25, 26
Serena, wife of Stilicho, niece of Theodosius I, 29, 33
Ships, 18, 32; Visigothic, 35; Byzantine fleet, 77; Vandal sea battle, 78; Belisarius' fleet, 82; Frankish, 84; keels, 97
Sidonius Apollinaris 83, 88, 89, 94, 95, 101, 102, 135–6, 149, 160, 173, 175
Sigeric, Gothic leader, 38
Sigismer, Frankish prince, 89
Sigismund of the Burgundians, 67
Silvanus, Frankish emperor, 85
Stilicho, Vandal general in Roman army (d. 408), 28, 29, 30, 31, 32, 33, 34, 43, 44, 47, 62, 70, 87, 96, 173
Sueves, 39, 55, 63, 70, 71, 72, 95
Sunno, Frankish leader, 84
Sutton Hoo, 98, 104, 136, 140, 145, 146, 153, 155, 156, 157, 158, 160, 161, 163
Szilagysomlyo treasure, 137

Tervingi, 15, 17, 19, 21, 22, 43, 60
Theodahad, king of the Ostrogoths (d. 536), 67
Theodoric I of the Ostrogoths (the Great, d. 526), 60, 63, 64, 65, 66, 67, 70, 91

Theodoric I of the Visigoths (d. 451), 28, 29, 33, 37, 43, 57, 86
Theodoric II of the Visigoths, 39, 52, 53, 75, 135, 136
Theodoric of the Vandals, son of Gaiseric, 81
Theodoric Strabo, son of Triarius, 60
Theodosius I, the Great, emperor (d. 395), 28, 29, 33, 37, 43, 57, 87
Theodosius II, emperor (d. 450), 8, 45, 50, 51, 77, 149
Thiudimir, 63
Thraustila, murderer of Valentinian III, 76
Tiberius, emperor (d. 37), 10
Tipasa, North Africa, 74

Uldin, Hunnic leader, 31–2, 44
Ulfilas, Gothic bishop, 19; Codex Argenteus, 20

Valens, Eastern Emperor, 20–1, 22, 24, 25; death at Adrianople, 26; 26, 27, 86, 137
Valentinian I, emperor (d. 375), 21, 25, 86, 96
Valentinian II, emperor (d. 392), 8, 86
Valentinian III, emperor (d. 455), 39, 45, 46, 50, 51, 55, 71, 72, 75, 76, 88
Vandals, 16, 19, 32, 35, 37, 38, 46, 48, 51, 55, 62, 67, 69–82; early history, 70–1; to Spain, 70; in Africa, 72; as landlords, 79–80; Christianity, 79–80
Verona, battles of, Philip the Arab dies, 16; Gothic battle, 31
Verulamium, 96
Victor of Vita, Christian writer, 73, 78, 79, 81, 175
Visigoths, 15–39, 46, 47, 51, 53, 54, 66, 69, 70, 71, 72, 73, 75, 76, 77, 88, 90, 91, 92, 96, 101, 135, 136, 137, 138, 158, 171, 173, 176
Vortigern, post-Roman British leader, 97, 98, 99, 100, 101
Vouille, battle, 39, 91, 158

Warriors: in literature, 100f; career options, 105; barbarian warriors in Roman army,

96; Frankish, 82f; societies, 111f; training, 145–6

Weapons: Gothic armour, 20; 135, 148, 149; swords 151; sword hilts, 153; ring swords, 154; scabbards, 155; seax, 156; angons and spears, 157; battle axes, 158; bows and arrows, 159; armour, 160; helmets, 161, shields 163

Weddings: Athaulf's, 37; Frankish, 89

Women and girls; in graves, 87; in warfare, 145–7

Wroxeter, 96

Zeno, Eastern Emperor (d. 491), 11, 62, 64, 65, 67, 78

Zercon, dwarf comedian to Bleda and Attila, 58